THE
REEMERGENCE
OF WORLD LITERATURE

THE REEMERGENCE OF WORLD LITERATURE

A Study of Asia and the West

A. Owen Aldridge

NEWARK: UNIVERSITY OF DELAWARE PRESS
LONDON AND TORONTO: ASSOCIATED UNIVERSITY PRESSES

Associated University Presses
440 Forsgate Drive
Cranbury, NJ 08512

Associated University Presses
25 Sicilian Avenue
London WC1A 2QH, England

Associated University Presses
2133 Royal Windsor Drive
Unit 1
Mississauga, Ontario
Canada L5J 1K5

Library of Congress Cataloging in Publication Data

Aldridge, Alfred Owen, 1915–
   The reemergence of world literature.

   Includes bibliographies and index.
   1. Literature, Comparative—Oriental and Occidental.
2. Literature, Comparative—Occidental and Oriental.
I. Title.
PJ312.A42   1986   809   84-40806
ISBN 0-87413-277-0 (alk. paper)

Printed in the United States of America

to Etiemble
scholar
intellectual crusader
dean of East-West comparative studies

Contents

Preface

WHEN GOETHE EARLY IN THE NINETEENTH CENTURY MADE A
stirring call for world literature, at the same time inventing the
expression, he was in large measure responding to the extraordinary increase in trade and communication brought on by the
Industrial Revolution and widespread political reforms on the
European continent. From the time of Goethe until the second
half of the twentieth century, world literature as represented by
printed anthologies and college surveys has consisted almost
exclusively of the masterpieces of the Western world. At the
present time, however, new technological and political developments—particularly jet travel, the media of mass communication and commercial links between Japan, China, and the
West—have stimulated a revived awareness of world literature
and of the need for a new definition, one that recognizes Africa
and Asia as equal partners. In other words, contemporary world
literature has taken on a truly global dimension, no longer
merely reflecting traditional cultural patterns of the West.

The most recent and perhaps most significant step taken in
this direction consists in a movement to discover parallels in
various writings from the Eastern and Western hemispheres.
The academic discipline of comparative literature has come into
being as part of the general recognition of the economic, social,
and technological interconnection of all nations and cultural
groups in the world.

Joining aesthetic criticism with history, the discipline has professed to embrace all literatures in its purview and to apply
universal standards in appraising them. The first generation of
students after World War II accepted these professions enthu-
siastically and unhesitatingly even though in practice some literatures, particularly those from the East and the Third World,

9

failed to receive appropriate attention. Many of the succeeding present generation, however, are disturbed by the Eurocentric character of the study of comparative literature as it is actually carried on in Europe and the United States. They have perceived that European literatures have dominated attention to such a degree that those from other parts of the world are in large measure neglected. Even American literature has been passed over by most comparatists, including those from the United States. As a result, the question has been raised, how can the discipline of comparative literature hope to derive universal standards if it fails to seek and attain universal coverage?

In the minds of many Third World critics, the concentration on European values and texts represents a survival or reflection of a colonialist mentality. Present-day comparative literature curricula and critical doctrines are interpreted as reflecting presumably benevolent colonizers carrying their culture to presumably underprivileged or underdeveloped nations. Even when Eastern masterpieces have been recognized as such, they have often been treated as precursors of later European works, not as models or cultural achievements in their own right. It is now time for the classics of the East to be viewed as the foundations of independent traditions and made available to Western students.

Although there can be no justification of any kind for a colonialist attitude in literary relations, the language barrier does represent a valid excuse for the neglect in the West of Eastern literatures. The number of Western comparatists who know an Eastern language is negligible, and the acquiring of a reading knowledge of languages such as Chinese and Japanese requires years of continuous application. It is precisely because of the language obstacle—which will continue to exist for at least another generation—that East-West literary study must depend upon translations. Within the past twenty years there has been a tremendous surge of activity in the translation of both modern and classical texts from the East, and these translations are waiting to be used by Western students.

Although nearly all American comparatists vociferously oppose in theory the use of translations in comparative studies, in actual practice translations have been permitted in almost all academic programs. At the present time there is scarcely an undergraduate course in any comparative literature department in the United States that does not accept the use of translations for part of its content, particularly when the Greek and Latin classics or the Eastern European languages are involved. Students with strong proficiency in one or two modern European languages are commonly allowed to use translations for the languages that they do not know.

The point of view of the following chapters is that the perspective of comparative literature as an academic discipline should be expanded to include all of the world, not only a favored segment of it, and that whenever necessary translations should be accepted as a tool. This does not mean that translations should be admitted in any context in which *explication de texte* is being attempted. Nor should they be considered as adequate in studies that profess to make original contributions bearing upon linguistic matters. But they are legitimate and indispensable in the area of general culture in which comparisons are made between literary works in a familiar language and those in a language that is completely unknown, that is to say, for the study of literature East-West.

So far, however, no satisfactory methodology for this joint study has been devised. The limited approach in the West has ordinarily been to introduce a few Eastern masterpieces into the hierarchy of what has erroneously been termed world literature. In the East, the most common effort has been to apply Western critical theories to Eastern writings. Unfortunately neither method provides readers of one hemisphere with much feeling for the literary climate of the other. The present book is addressed to the steadily increasing number of Western students and teachers who are faced with the necessity of expanding their own literary awareness to encompass the perspectives of the East. It attempts to provide a framework not only for cross-cultural penetration, but also for illuminating works of one culture by bringing them into contact with those of the other. It was originally published in Japan in a shorter translated version entitled *Hikaku Bungaku—Nihon to Seiyō (Comparative Literature—Japan and the West.)* Although this title resembles that of a valuable work in English, *Japanese and Western Literature, A*

Comparative Study by Armando Martins Janeira, the two books do not by any means cover the same ground. The present book is primarily critical, whereas Janeira's consists for the most part of literary history of the major Japanese genres with reference to similar trends in the West. The methodology of the present book owes a great deal to a stimulating study by the French comparatist Etiemble, *Comment lire un roman japonais,* 1980, a critical exposition of the practice of comparative literature, which is also based entirely on the use of translations.

In both China and Japan, a person's family name is customarily written before his given name, contrary to the Western practice in which the given name comes first. All Japanese and Chinese names in this book are written in the Western fashion except those of famous Chinese personalities such as Li Po or Mao Tse-tung. This is standard procedure in translations from the Japanese and the Chinese. There is even a partial parallel in Western literature. The full name of the author of the *Divine Comedy* is Dante Alighieri, but because of his great fame he is regularly called by his given name alone.

The first of the two following parts is historical and theoretical; the second, pragmatic. The first part traces the history of scholarly efforts to promote East-West literary study, analyzes the major theoretical principles involved, and summarizes the proceedings of international comparative conferences held in Taiwan and Hong Kong. It will be seen that in the East the use of translations is accepted much more widely than in Europe and the United States. The second part proposes practical models or methods for the joint study of Eastern and Western literary works. The first of these models illustrates the influence of the East upon the West, specifically the culture of China upon the thought of the French Enlightenment figure Voltaire; the other two models illustrate analogy rather than influence by indicating affinities or parallels between Western fiction and novels of twentieth-century Japan.

Acknowledgments

I AM DEEPLY INDEBTED TO A LARGE NUMBER OF INDIVIDUALS and institutions for stimulating my interest in East-West relations and for providing opportunities for development of this interest. Toward Claudio Guillén of Harvard University I am grateful for my first contact with comparatists in the East. Through his influence one of his former colleagues, Wai-lim Yip of the University of California, San Diego, to whom I feel equal gratitude, arranged my invitation to the first international conference on comparative literature held in the East, which took place at Tamkang College, now Tamkang University, Taiwan, in 1971. On the way to this conference I received invaluable information concerning the practice of comparative literature in Japan from a former student Shunsuke Kamei, now professor of comparative literature at the University of Tokyo. At the original Tamkang congress as well as at three subsequent ones at four-year intervals, I learned much from other distinguished comparatists, representing Taiwan, Hong Kong, Japan, Korea, and the Philippines. I wish to acknowledge the many kindnesses of Clement C. P. Chang and Limin Chu, president and vice president respectively of Tamkang University. Two scholars from the Chinese University of Hong Kong, Heh hsiang Yuan and John J. Deeney, have also each in his own way greatly helped me obtain increased understanding of some of the unique problems involved in the East-West dimension.

For working contacts with students, I am grateful to Nihon University in Japan, which has twice afforded me the opportunity of lecturing to both graduate and undergraduate students at its Tokyo and Mishima campuses. My closest ties at Nihon were with Masayuki Akiyama, a scholar devoted to interpreting the fiction of Henry James, who accompanied me throughout the pleasant routine of lectures. I shall always remember the many attentions of Professor Akiyama and of Dean Yukinori Iwaki.

The final stages of composition of this book took place during a residency at the Study and Conference Center of the Rockefeller Foundation at the Villa Serbelloni in Bellagio, Italy. Solutions to many of the most difficult problems in arranging and articulating the miscellaneous materials in this book emerged from the intellectual atmosphere of the center. The combination of seclusion during working hours and dialogue with resident scholars in periods of relaxation provided the optimum environment for writing. I am particularly indebted, among the other resident scholars at that time, to C. D. Narasimhaiah, who read the introduction and contributed information on Commonwealth writers, and to Leon Edel, who read the chapter on Henry James, corrected some of its parts, and suggested new perspectives.

My final debt is to Etiemble of the University of Paris, who has served as constant model and source of inspiration and who kindly read and criticized the preliminary draft of the entire book.

The original version of this book was published in Japanese translation in Tokyo. The second chapter has been published in English in the journal *Neo-Helicon,* Hungary, and parts of the second, third, fourth and fifth chapters, also in English, in the *Tamkang Review,* Taipei, Taiwan. The fifth chapter has been translated into Chinese and published in Hong Kong in *Ch'un Wen-hsueh* [*The Pure Literature Monthly*].

THE
REEMERGENCE
OF WORLD LITERATURE

Part I
THEORY

1
Introduction

THIS BOOK IS NOT AND DOES NOT PRETEND TO BE A HISTORY OF the literatures of the Far East in their relations with those of the West. A history on this massive scale, which has indeed never been attempted, would require a cooperative intellectual effort as Herculean in its way as that required of technology when it placed a man on the moon. There still exists no history of European literatures from a comparatist perspective (although a multivolume cooperative project is now being organized and carried out by the International Comparative Literature Association). Even individual histories of either Chinese or Japanese literatures were not undertaken until the last years of the nineteenth century. No serious effort, furthermore, to systematize the study of East-West literary relations was initiated anywhere in the world until the present generation. In keeping with contemporary interest in Asian culture, however, a *History of Japanese Literature* by Katō Shūichi has recently appeared in English, and Donald Keene has published a number of anthologies and works on Japanese literary history.

The main obstacle to the study of East-West literary relations and even to that of intra-Asian relations has been and still remains the multiplicity of languages. In India alone there exist fifteen major languages and two hundred minor ones. At the present time, more people speak each one of these major languages, including Hindi, Bengali, Urdu, Tamil, and Marathi than speak such European ones as Dutch, Polish, Swedish, or Greek; moreover, these Indian languages are as different from each other as are those of Europe. The Chinese language, which is probably used by more people than any other in the world, has two major divisions, Cantonese and Mandarin. Although these linguistic branches utilize the same system of ideograms, they are not much closer to each other than are English and German. Japanese is not only a language completely independent from Chinese, but it possesses a separate ideogrammatic system. A small country such as the Philippines—not much larger than the state of Rhode Island—uses four languages, Chinese, English, Spanish, and the native Tagalog, and its literature is written in the latter three. In India the language issue is "at the center of social conflict and the topic of heated debate. It is complex, tortuous, and wrapped up in sentiment" (Gandhi 1977, 131). English is the medium for commerce, and the Indian government has adopted Hindi as the official national language. Natives of southern and eastern sectors of the country where Hindi is not the regional tongue must learn three languages: the regional, Hindi, and English.

Few Western literary scholars know more than a single Asiatic language (and included among these few are not only comparatists, but area specialists as well). Many Koreans and some Japanese read Chinese, but most Asians are unacquainted with any major Asiatic language other than their own. "At a recent triennial meeting of the Asian Writers' Conference," according to Robert Clements, "the Korean Ko Yo Sup complained that Koreans wishing to translate Asian works must get hold of the English, French, or German versions of such works before turning them into Korean. So complicated are Asian languages even to close neighbors that Ryoto Sato of Tokyo claimed that it takes him an entire year to translate one Chinese novel into Japanese" (Clements 1978, 34). The task of mastering Asian literatures is almost as difficult for Asian comparatists, therefore, as it is for Americans and Europeans.

At first glance the obvious solution would seem to be for scholars in both the West and the East to learn more Asiatic languages. This solution may be a practical one in years to come, but it offers no help to the present academic generation. To be sure, the study of Asiatic languages in American universities has increased dramatically during the last thirty years. Every institution of consequence boasts an Asian studies center and offers a battery of oriental language courses, in contrast to the nineteenth century when programs in Chinese or Japanese were few in number and intended primarily for missionaries. At the same time it must be recognized that most students of Asian languages today are not potential comparatists any more than they are potential missionaries—they are preparing for careers in commerce, government service, economics, history, and linguistics. Their academic efforts, therefore, do very little to promote the study of comparative literature. Also language study as a whole has drastically declined on both the secondary and university levels throughout the United States. The situation in the East is parallel. The major Western languages continue to be taught primarily as an adjunct to commerce and government service, and comparatists learn only a single Western language, ordinarily English. In one of the most solid programs in comparative literature offered anywhere in the Orient, that leading to the Master of Philosophy degree at the Chinese University of Hong Kong, the only languages required are Chinese and English. The major international conferences on comparative literature held in the Chinese-speaking areas of Asia, moreover, have adopted English as the official language for all plenary and most sectional papers. There can be little realistic expectation, therefore, for any appreciable extension of linguistic proficiency in the mutual study of East-West cultures for the rest of the twentieth century.

Yet the study of literary relationships may still be carried on by means of translations. The classics of each culture are readily available in the languages of the other, and in the modern period a wide sampling of the poetry, fiction, drama, and criticism produced in Chinese and Japanese is regularly translated into English. Indeed, as I have already indicated, English maintains a privileged position as the *lingua franca* among comparatists in East Asia. No better illustration of this can be reported than the experience of an American scholar who was taken to dinner in a Hong Kong restaurant by a prominent Chinese comparatist. The latter spoke in Mandarin to the waiter, a recent immigrant from the mainland who spoke only Cantonese. Unable to communicate in either language, these two knowledgeable Chinese switched to English.

By and large, Chinese and Japanese comparatists take a more

liberal view of the legitimacy of translations for scholarly study than does the official report on standards of the American Comparative Literature Association. Paradoxically, many comparative literature departments in the United States emphasize the art of translation, some even awarding Master of Arts degrees in the area, while the American Comparative Literature Association as an official posture continues to reject translations as a valid tool in the discipline.

Only a small minority of those who accept the use of translations in closing the gap between East and West adopt, on the other hand, the extreme view that the English language is a completely adequate vehicle for the study of the literature of all nations. The vice chancellor of the University of Mysore in India has affirmed, however, that "it is easier today to savour the beauty and wisdom of the classics in Latin, Greek and Sanskrit in the English language than to go back to their originals. Omar Khayyam or Dostoevski, Cervantes or Victor Hugo are better known in the world through English than their original forms" (Hedge 1980, 16–17). Such an exaggerated notion of the importance of the English language may be appropriate for an Anglo-Indian university administrator, but it unfortunately reflects the colonialist attitude that has turned many students of the Third World away from comparative literature. If the authors mentioned by the vice chancellor actually have attained maximum circulation in their English dress, all that this really means is that the population of Anglophone nations is greater than that of those using other Western languages. In point of fact, however, there are more editions of Cervantes in Spanish throughout the world than in English translation. It may be that it is easier for most Anglophones to use English translations of classic authors, but the easy way is not necessarily the more rewarding. No comparatist, moreover, would accept the view that any one language—whether English, French, or Chinese—is so important in the contemporary world scheme that it can be made to serve in literature, as in commerce, as a universal instrument of communication. There is a fundamental difference between the assumption of the vice chancellor that English translations are adequate for all purposes today and will continue to be so and the attitude that translations represent a necessary compromise.

In the linguistic conditions prevailing at present, translations are inevitable in the East-West context, but it is to be hoped that large numbers of scholars in future generations in both the East and the West will be able to use at least one major language of the other hemisphere.

To be sure, purists in both the East and the West will continue to find untenable the suggestion that any serious comparative study may be based on the use of translations. A parallel may be drawn, however, with the problem of the legitimacy of generalizing in the writing of history. The choice, according to one prominent scholar, "is not between making proved statements or unproved ones, but between unproved ones or keeping silent" (Aydelotte 1963, 159). At the present stage of linguistic development, the choice in treating East-West relations is between using translations or remaining uninformed.

Much of the argument against the use of translations in literary research resembles the theories of the New Critics that the essence of a creative work cannot be transmitted if it is changed in any way from its pristine form—whether by translation, paraphrase, or any other method. It might be said in rebuttal that some translations are considered to be aesthetically superior to their originals. This is not to say that any translation, whether mediocre, average, or brilliant, communicates the same sensations as the initial text. But it must be kept in mind that no two people reading an original work receive from it the same sensations, and no single reader reacts in exactly the same manner to consecutive exposures to the same text. The translation of a literary work is like the printed reproduction of an oil painting; although not by any means the same as its prototype, the copy, nevertheless, communicates a considerable amount of knowledge concerning the created work. Translations are valid for narrative and expository prose, and they succeed for the most part in conveying ideas and emotions. Obviously there are degrees in the accuracy and aesthetic appeal of various translations. A good case can be made, however, for the reported opinion of one professor from the Chinese mainland that even a bad translation is better than no translation at all. And despite all the arguments of purists concerning the deficiencies and inadequacies of translations as such, they remain the only generally applicable means now available for the transcending of literary exclusiveness, either Western or Eastern.

Western critics who object to the use of translations do not consider that when the Nobel Prize for literature was awarded on two occasions to writers from the East, Tagore of India and Kawabata of Japan, the jury worked entirely from translations. Many people believe that Tagore wrote his poetry originally in English, but this is a misconception. The poet himself translated his work from their original in Bengali. To be sure, some critics may believe that the decisions of the Nobel prize committee do not necessarily represent the informed aesthetic opinion of the world, but it can hardly be denied that its deliberations represent a higher level of critical sophistication than those encountered in an ordinary university course in comparative literature. Those who maintain that serious criticism cannot be based on translated texts should bear in mind not only that Etiemble's *Comment lire un roman japonais* belongs in that category, but also that Marguerite Yourcenar, the first female member of the illustrious French Academy, has written a book-length analysis of the works of the Japanese novelist Mishima, working entirely with translations (*Mishima ou la vision du vide* [Gallimard 1981]). Armando Martins Janeira has pointed out, moreover, that it was on the basis of a translation that "C. G. Jung, although completely ignorant of the Chinese language, wrote the deepest and clearest interpretation of the classic *Secret of the Golden Flower*" (1970, 14). Janeira has also observed that the most profound and far-reaching sociological and philosophical studies of Chinese and Indian religions and religious authors "were written by Max Weber and Karl Jaspers, who did not know Chinese, Sanscrit, Pali, or any other language in which those sacred books are written" (1970, 14–15). The contentions of the purists against translations in East-West relations, if carried to their logical conclusion, would lead to the interdiction of all instruction in the Old and New Testaments in both hemispheres except by clergymen who read the original languages in which these ancient texts were written.

One of the arguments sometimes advanced in favor of translations is that there is greater pleasure and profit to be found in reading outstanding works from other cultures than from inferior works in one's own. According to Etiemble, there is more literary value in reading Saikaku in translation than Péladan in the original French, Ilankovatikal in translation than Françoise Sagan in the original, Hallaj in translation than Géraldy in the original, or Kabir in translation than Anna de Noailles in the original (1974, 27). One may accept these preferences and agree with Etiemble on the value of translations without adopting as a general principle that it is better to read major authors of other cultures in translation than minor ones of our own in the original. The hierarchies of major and minor can never be completely resolved; they are not historical constants. Also, as specialists in the history of ideas maintain, there is sometimes more historical knowledge to be derived from studying minor works than from major ones. Whether to adopt the broad or the narrow perspective is essentially a matter of what one is looking for; the choice is for the individual. It is certainly desirable for comparatists to extend their knowledge beyond America and Europe on one hand or China and Japan on the other, but there is nothing wrong, for those who so choose, in becoming a specialist in one's native literature. Specialists, however, run the risk of becoming narrow and provincial if they devote their attention exclusively to any one literature, no matter how rich it may be.

The philosopher Sartre on a visit to the United States explained the failure of the American authors Henry James and Theodore Dreiser to attain popularity in his country on the grounds that the techniques of psychological literary analysis were created in France and developed there to their greatest heights by Benjamin Constant and Marcel Proust as those of realism were refined by Flaubert, Maupassant, and Zola. The talents of James and Dreiser were, therefore, superfluous for French readers (Sartre 1946, 115–16). These critical observations may be valid, but they still do not justify French indifference to particular American authors. Even less do they justify slighting foreign authors on nationalistic grounds as a general principle. One could argue that a French reader who enjoys the psychological probing and social observation of Flaubert would appreciate the same qualities in Henry James just as an Italian who admires the great historical novel of Manzoni *I promessi sposi* would turn with pleasure to one by Walter Scott. French people reading James, moreover, learn about a society and a way of life different from their own. In addition to undergoing a pleasurable aesthetic experience, they expand their knowledge and enrich their understanding. Intercultural literature may be defended, therefore, on the grounds of cosmopolitanism as well as artistic value. To use Etiemble's dichotomies once more, a Japanese would benefit from reading Péladan, an Iranian from Géraldy, a Pakistani from Anna de Noailles, and a South Indian from Fran-çoise Sagan.

The study of intercultural or transcultural literature provides a means of adjustment to one of the major social tensions brought about by the technology of the twentieth century—that is, the presence of conflicting cultural norms and ideals in nearly all parts of the world. This is, of course, not an entirely new condi-tion and it is not attributable entirely to modern technology. In the age of exploration, European conquerors imposed their way of life upon the Indians of North and South America, and in the succeeding age of colonization, Western concepts of civilization were impressed upon Asia and Africa. The twentieth century has set in motion a certain reversal, however, by means of which large numbers of Africans and Asians have taken up residence in Europe and the Americas. Japanese culture, as well as Japanese automobile and television production, for example, has accom-plished a large-scale invasion of the West. In the nineteenth century, the United States met the problem of multinational im-migration with the concept of the "melting-pot," according to which representatives of alien cultures were expected to con-form to the American way of life by adopting a homogeneous scheme of values and behavior. This conformity can no longer be enforced in the United States or anywhere else. Societies in all parts of the world are now required to cope with the coexistence of more than one set of cultural norms and ideals within their boundaries, a situation described as bicultural or multicultural development. A new discipline has arisen known as "ethnic liter-ature." The problem in both literature and life, according to Lloyd Fernando, is that one searches for unity and homogeneity "while being confronted by the reality of heterogeneity" (1978, 329). Works of imagination cited by this critic that "reveal the complexity of possible responses to the promise, or threat, of a

bicultural universe" include Joseph Conrad's *Heart of Darkness,*
E. M. Forster's *A Passage to India,* William Faulkner's "A Rose
for Emily," and Raja Rao's *The Serpent and the Rope.*

In the twentieth century, the study of the interaction of literature and society is an acknowledged dimension of literary
studies. The comparatist perspective, moreover, transcends in
value that provided by a single national literature. As Fernando
observes,

> scholars have for too long tended to assume that a sufficient
> knowledge of the interaction between literature and society
> and culture may be had from the study of English literature
> alone or combined with some knowledge of the European tra-
> dition. In a bicultural age we need a knowledge of another
> literature from a quite different cultural area, preferably in the
> original, or at least in translation, so that we may prevent the
> study of literature itself from becoming more and more remote
> from present needs, or from becoming unnecessarily paro-
> chial. Western definitions of literary conventions—theatre
> conventions, for example—and of the image of man, the state
> and God are nowhere near self-sufficiency. In the field of cul-
> tures in contact, Asian literatures have as much to teach as
> literatures elsewhere: the entire field offers a unique way of
> considering literature as a whole. (1978, 336).

During the period between the two world wars, many American universities offered an undergraduate course in Western
civilization as the core of a humanities requirement, but as a
result of student turmoil of the 1960s and 1970s this basic course
was generally dropped, along with nearly all other requirements.
As more recent years have witnessed a renewed recognition of
the value of general education, some universities have restored
core courses devoted to the Western heritage. Their prescribed
readings, usually ranging from Plato and the Old Testament to
Marx and Freud, differ very little from those of the older, prewar
courses. Critics of the revamped courses, moreover, have
pointed out that the authors included are almost exclusively
white males and that the contributions of women and minorities
are almost entirely ignored. In regard to the course in Western
culture offered at Stanford University, an undergraduate objected in the school newspaper, "And why, for that matter,

should we decree that the civilization of Aristotle, Moses or Karl Marx is any more important than that of Confucius, Buddha or Lao-tzu. If any requirement is to be imposed, why should it be a Western culture requirement and not a human culture requirement?" (*New York Times*, 26 February 1980). The University of Illinois has subsequently instituted a requirement that all majors in letters and sciences take a course in "non-western cultures and traditions."

So far I have been referring to the literatures of the East and the West with no clear understanding of what nations or precise geographical areas they represent. Those of the West present no difficulty: they consist of all those in Europe and the two Americas. The boundaries of Eastern literatures, however, are somewhat problematical. As George L. Anderson explains:

> The word "Orient" itself is a vague term, of use only for convenience. "East" would not be better: there is an Arab literature in Morocco, which is 1,500 miles west of Athens, and there is a Western literature in Vladivostok, almost a thousand miles east of Peking. "Asiatic"—a term frowned upon by Asians as reflecting nineteenth-century Western attitudes toward the Orient—and "Asian" will not do. The literature of the Arabs has largely been produced in Africa, but for many centuries in Europe the Near East is the "Orient!" [1961, x].

For our purposes, it is necessary to make arbitrary distinctions. Leaving Europe, the Americas, and most of Africa out of consideration, I shall divide the rest of the world into two literary areas—the Far East (East Asia), including Chinese, Japanese, Korean, Philippine and Indonesian literatures—and the expanded Middle East (India, West Asia, and northern Africa), comprising the literatures that stemmed originally from India, Persia, and Egypt. This book is concerned mainly with the relations between literatures of the West and those of the Far East, primarily Chinese and Japanese.

A digression is, nevertheless, called for concerning Third World and Commonwealth literatures, divisions that are generally considered political but that exist in creative writing as well. As a political concept, Third World refers to nations other than the major powers of the USSR and the United States, but in literary terms the Third World is usually considered to comprise writing in English, French, and Spanish originating in the newly independent black nations of Africa and the Caribbean, together with writing in any language emanating from the Moslem countries of Africa and Asia. Commonwealth literature consists exclusively of creative works in the English language produced in countries that are either former British colonies or present partners in the British Commonwealth, that is, Australia, Canada, India, Pakistan, New Zealand, Singapore, the West Indies, and nations of Africa in which English is the major language. Works originating in French Canada are considered separately. Similarly Indian literature in any of the native languages is not classified as Commonwealth, as for example, the novel in Kannada by Kuvempu, *Subbamma, Wife of a Kauru Chieftain (Kanuru Subbamma Heggatathi)*. Indian novels written in or translated into English assume a double identity, Indian and Commonwealth. Some African literatures may be similarly included under the rubrics of both Commonwealth and Third World. As C. D. Narasimhaiah has observed, the attitudes of Commonwealth writers vary between reaffirming British values and asserting their own cultural identity (1976, 1). These writers have taken from Europe the English language and given back original works of the mind and spirit (Narasimhaiah 1976, 6).

The literature of the Third World nations has been compared to that of the United States at the beginning of the nineteenth century and that of Ireland at its end in the sense that these two Western literatures were at that time newly formed and newly emerging. Most Third World nations have little in common, therefore, with the nations of Asia, which draw upon literary traditions, even older than those of classical Greece and Rome from which European literature has descended. Modern Indian Commonwealth literature occupies an anomalous position in deriving both from the ancient traditions of the Orient and the relatively modern conventions of Great Britain.

Literature in general may be said to have three major functions: to convey meaning, to convey emotion, and to convey aesthetic pleasure. Since these functions exist in all periods of time and in all geographical areas, it would be a valid process in the East-West context to show significant parallels in any of these three functions in any literatures. This is a much more simple process of study than that incorporating the traditional critical methods used for Western literatures, the aim of which is to reveal parallels in style, in cultural-intellectual movements, and in genres. The history of the Western nations so closely involves one literature with the other that parallels of the latter kind may be readily perceived, and they represent, moreover, significant relationships. The histories of the nations of the West and those of the East, however, are not homogeneous, nor have they been closely entwined until very recent times. For this reason the study of East-West literary relations does not adapt itself to the quest for parallels in historical development. Basic linguistic differences, moreover, severely limit the possibilities of parallels in the purely aesthetic realm, with the exception of elements that are capable of being transposed through translation. Even with the aid of translation, aesthetic pleasures depending upon sound together with most poetic effects cannot be transmitted. In a large sense, this is true also of parallels among the Western literatures.

One must, nevertheless, not entirely rule out investigations of parallelisms in poetry and other genres stressing aesthetic effects. A large number of Western poets from the middle of the nineteenth century to the present have sought to translate or imitate the poetic masterpieces of China and Japan. Their activities represent a rich field for investigation both from the perspective of cross-cultural influence and of aesthetic analysis. Many scholars are aware of the extensive use of Chinese materials in the works of Voltaire and Pound, but it is not generally known that many other major authors reveal a substantial debt to the East. It may be true that up to the beginning of the nineteenth century "there has hardly been *any* influence of Asian literature on European" (Kunst 1971, 318), but since that time the influence of the East on both Europe and America has been extensive, and it has increased in geometrical progression. The extent to which American authors, including Emerson, Thoreau, Hearn, and lesser writers, became involved with Eastern classics is vividly presented in a brilliant article in the *Dictionary of the History of Ideas* (Jackson 1973, 3:427–39) and in a comprehensive book by Beongcheon Yu, *The Great Circle. Ameri-*

can Writers and the Orient (Wayne State University Press, 1983).

Probably the most widespread writings of an ideological nature in both the East and the West are those associated with religion. Christian thought has been relayed to the East, and Confucian, Taoist, and Buddhist concepts have been transmitted to the West. Apart from lyric poetry, writings in both parts of the world that communicate feeling or emotional attitudes comprise for the most part prose fiction and drama. Many plots and themes in the East resemble those in the West and vice versa. Some works, moreover, convey both meaning and emotion in almost equal amounts, as, for example, the autobiography of Benjamin Franklin, which is today studied as a school text in both Japan and Taiwan and which has much in common with a nineteenth-century autobiography by Yukichi Fukuzawa (Watanabe 1980, 43–47). Concentration upon meaning, plot, and theme, together with the narrative and dramatic devices by which these elements are conveyed, represents the most feasible and useful method of studying East-West relations. Emphasis should be placed, moreover, not on the intricacies of plot, but on the relationship of plot and character to real life. For the proper exercise of this function, the critic must, of course, have some knowledge and understanding of the historical and cultural backgrounds of the works with which he is dealing.

The formal study of comparative literature was not organized in East Asia until after World War II, when the Japanese Comparative Literature Association was established and began publishing its official journal *Hikaku Bungaku (Comparative Literature)*, an annual. There are now two other Japanese publications, *Hikaku Bungaku Kenkyū (Comparative Literature Studies)*, sponsored by the University of Tokyo, and *Hikaku Bungaku Nenshi (Comparative Literature Yearbook)*, sponsored by Waseda University. Impressive academic programs of comparative literature exist at Tokyo, Waseda, and Nihon universities. In Taiwan, the Comparative Literature Association of the Republic of China was organized in 1973. Academic programs in the discipline are now offered at Tamkang University and at National Taiwan University. A Korean Comparative Literature Association was founded in 1959. It holds biannual meetings and

issues *Journal of Comparative Literature and Culture* annually. I
have already alluded to the strong program at the Chinese University of Hong Kong. In India, the *Jadavpur Journal of Comparative Literature* has been published since 1961, and an All
India Comparative Literature Association was organized in
1980. In the following year Peking University organized the Association for the Study of Comparative Literature with professors of both Chinese and Western languages as members. In the
summer of 1983, ten American comparatists, five specializing in
Chinese and five not, met with Chinese counterparts at a sym-
posium in Peking and subsequently with groups in Chengdu and
Shanghai. In the same year, an annual periodical in English,
COWRIE, A Chinese Journal of Comparative Literature, was
launched at Guangxi University. In 1984, the first periodical in
Chinese devoted solely to comparative literature was published
jointly by the Shanghai Foreign Languages Institute and Hua
Dong Teachers' College. It has the title *Comparative Literature
in China,* and all articles have abstracts in English.

The first truly international comparative literature conference
ever held in the East took place in 1971 at Tamkang University,
Taiwan. Its complete proceedings were later printed in *The Tamkang Review: Comparative Studies between Chinese and
Foreign Literatures,* a periodical that began publication in the
previous year. Three other similar conferences were held under
the same auspices at four-year intervals, in each of which over
two hundred comparatists participated from Taiwan, Hong
Kong, Japan, Korea, the Philippines, the United States, and
various European countries. The wide range of topics covered
by these scholars offers convincing proof that the study of parallels between East and West represents a valid and substantial
branch of comparative literature. The first conference treated six
topics: literary relations between China and the West; literary
relations between China and other Asian and Pacific countries;
the application of Western literary theories and methods in the
study of Chinese literature; problems in analogical studies (rapprochement); problems in literary criticism and literary theory,
and problems in translation. The second conference in 1975 had
merely a single announced theme, "Literary Theory and Criticism East and West," to which all plenary papers adhered, but

sectional papers treated specific topics in the areas of theme, genre, and cross-national relations such as love in Chinese and English poetry, the permeation of Croce's aesthetics in Japan, Confucianism in Korean literature, and utopian literature East and West. The official themes of the third conference in 1979 were literature and social milieu, Chinese images in world literature, and intra-Asian comparative literature studies, but nearly half of the papers given, including some plenary ones, treated completely different topics, chiefly literary theory and problems of translation.

In the week following the 1979 meeting, the Chinese University of Hong Kong hosted a conference on East-West Comparative Literature, which was limited to a select group of invited participants and a smaller number of observers. Organized as an experimental effort to appraise the various methods of East-West study, it was sponsored by the Comparative Literature and Translation Center and the Institute of Chinese Studies of the university. Prior to the conference, the same university instituted a new periodical, the *New Asia Academic Bulletin*, the first number of which consisted of a *Special Issue on East-West Comparative Literature*.

In 1983 a fourth conference was held at Tamkang University that emphasized critical theories, translation, and thematology. All of these conferences included sessions devoted to the application of critical methods from the West to Eastern literary texts. Scholars from the East have been particularly zealous in this activity, using critical theories ranging from Aristoteleanism to structuralism. It is my conviction, as I shall indicate in subsequent chapters, that many of these theories have individual values when applied to single works in a particular national literature, but their pertinence is greatly reduced when used across national boundaries. Indeed it is difficult to point to remarkably successful examples of the pragmatic application of critical systems in a comparative context. The various theories cancel each other out, and they can rarely be used conjointly. As new ones come into fashion and then fade away, the votaries of the most recent assume that the newest is necessarily the best and, accordingly, subject the preceding ones to ridicule or condescension. No adherence to special schools or systems of criticism is required, however, for pointing out parallels and resemblances in ideas, plots, and themes or in revealing historical relationships when they exist. The comparative study of texts from East and West is inherently difficult because of fundamental cultural and linguistic differences. The process need not be further complicated by the introduction of esoteric systems of criticism.

CHAPTER 1. REFERENCES

Aydelotte, William O. 1963. In *Generalization in the writing of history,* ed. Louis R. Gottschalk, Chicago: Univ. of Chicago Press.

Anderson, George L. 1961. *Masterpieces of the orient.* New York: W. W. Norton.

Clements, Robert. 1978. *Comparative literature as academic discipline.* New York: Modern Language Association of America.

Etiemble, René. 1974. *Essais de littérature (vraiment) générale.* Paris: Gallimard.

Fernando, Lloyd. 1978. A note from the Third World towards the re-definition of culture. In *Awakened conscience. Studies in Commonwealth literature,* ed. C. D. Narasimhaiah. New Delhi: Sterling Publishers.

Gandhi, Kishore. 1977. *Issues and choices in higher education.* Delhi: B. R. Publishing Co.

Hedge, K. S. 1980. Chief guest's address. *The Literary Criterion* 15:5–21.

Jackson, C. T. 1973. Oriental ideas in American thought. *Dictionary of the history of ideas.* New York: Charles Scribners & Sons.

Janeira, Armando Martins. 1970. *Japanese and Western literature. A comparative study.* Rutland, Vt.: Charles E. Tuttle Co.

Kunst, Arthur. 1971. Literatures of Asia. In *Comparative literature method and perspective,* rev. ed. ed. Newton P. Stallknecht & Horst Frenz. Carbondale: Southern Illinois Univ. Press.

Narasimhaiah, C. D. 1976. *Commonwealth literature: A handbook of select reading lists.* Delhi: Oxford Univ. Press.

Sartre, Jean-Paul. 1946. American novelists in French eyes. *Atlantic Monthly* 178:114–18.

Watanabe, Toshio. 1980. Benjamin Franklin and the younger generation of Japan. *American Studies International* 18:34–49.

2

The Universal in Literature

IN THE YEAR 1863, ACCORDING TO WESTERN CHRONOLOGY, A Chinese observer made the following statement: "For twenty years we have maintained relations with the foreigners. Some of them know our language and are able to write it and also read our classics. Among our mandarins and literate people, however, nobody knows the foreign culture" (Jost 1974, 272). Essentially the same opinion was expressed in the West a century earlier by Voltaire, who despite his belief in the essential unity of mankind, was aware of various physical and cultural differences. "The fact is," he wrote, "nature has from the very beginning placed west of us and east of us multitudes of beings of our species whom we became acquainted with only yesterday. We are on this globe like insects in a garden: those who live on an oak rarely encounter those who pass their short life on an elm" (1836, 29). In contrast to this state of affairs, many Chinese and Japanese at the present time, prominent among them being students of comparative literature, possess a sound knowledge of many aspects of English and American writing; whereas very few Americans or English, including even professors of comparative literature, have anything more than a superficial acquaintance with the literature of the East, even in translation.

The argument has been advanced that every Sinologist is in a sense a comparatist since he has absorbed the culture of his own country in the course of his daily life and his profession consists in studying the culture of China. The same logic has been applied to Chinese and Japanese professors of English. Much as mutual acquaintance and cultural understanding are to be desired and highly prized, however, familiarity with a national culture other

35

than one's own is not what constitutes the academic discipline known as comparative literature. Even Eastern professors of English and American professors of Chinese or Japanese are not comparatists merely because they are experts in an exotic literature. They become comparatists only when they bring their own and a second national literature into contact—when they place examples from each of two literatures side by side in such a manner as to furnish mutual illumination or to make possible an interpretation of a phenomenon in one literature that would not be apparent without reference to the other. It is certainly true that the Sinologist knows the cultures of both East and West, but his professional duties require him to explore that of China alone, not to bring the two cultures together for joint study. A Sinologist, moreover, may live out a distinguished career without referring to a single literary work from a Western country, or indeed without even treating literature at all.

As far as translations are concerned, a scholar in the East who knows thoroughly the history of Chinese drama and who has also studied all of the works of Shakespeare in a Chinese version is better equipped to handle East-West relations than the Sinologist, whether resident in the East or the West, who concerns himself exclusively with Chinese letters. To be sure, the Eastern scholar who knows Shakespeare only through translation is not qualified to teach Shakespeare or English drama but he is in a better position to make comparisons than a colleague who has read nothing but Chinese drama. This may seem equivalent to stating that a person who reads Shakespeare in translation is not a qualified teacher of Shakespeare, but a person who makes comparisons between Chinese works in their original and Shakespeare in translation is indeed a capable Shakespearean. This is not the meaning at all. What is suggested is that the Chinese scholar who has read Shakespeare merely in translation is better equipped to teach Chinese drama than he would be if he knew only Chinese drama and no dramatist from any other culture. If he makes comparisons between Chinese and Western works, however, these comparisons should throw some new light on one of the works compared. Otherwise there is no point whatsoever in demonstrating resemblances or differences.

Before proceeding to discussion of specific techniques and methods of comparative literature, I shall provide a definition of literature itself. In answer to the frequently asked question, "What is literature?" I would reply that literature consists of communication by means of written words or symbols when the purpose of communication involves some degree of emotional or aesthetic response as well as mere transference of information (Aldridge 1977, 2468). Here we are approaching one of the meanings of universal literature, which I shall discuss later. The definition of literature in the most comprehensive sense embraces not only the broad conventional genres such as poetry, fiction, and drama, but also ideological prose such as most works of history and philosophy, together with some textbooks and even some advertising. It may also include nonsense verse. Obviously this definition excludes utilitarian compilations such as telephone directories as well as classified advertising, most textbooks, and dictionaries. It excludes, moreover, two very closely related artistic genres on the grounds that they do not represent the written word; motion pictures and songs and epics in oral form. Once these songs and epics have been written down, however, they become literature.

To go from literature as such to comparative literature is a progress from unity to plurality. It is obvious that comparison requires two or more elements to be analyzed jointly. At the same time it is a reductive process, going from literature in the mass to constituent elements of two separate national literatures. Even if one considers the concept of literature in the broadest sense as comprising all works of verbal expression in existence, this mass of materials must be broken down into parts or units in order for comparisons to take place. Paradoxically in this process of considering units or individual works rather than entire literatures, the comparatist tends to reveal the totality or universality of literature. To adapt an English aesthetic maxim from the eighteenth century, the comparatist does not seek to demonstrate variety in the midst of uniformity, but instead the reverse, to demonstrate uniformity or aesthetic unity in the midst of variety. The indicating of differences is also a legitimate function of the comparatist.

In ordinary usage, the term *comparative literature* refers to relations between two or more national literatures, but it may also be used to indicate the relations between literature and other humanistic areas of study such as art, music, cinema, the social structure, or science: "Briefly defined, comparative literature can be considered the study of any literary phenomenon from the perspective of more than one national literature or in conjunction with another intellectual discipline or even several" (Aldridge 1969, 1).

In a rigorous sense, the term has been historically confined to studies involving at least two different languages as well as separate cultures. The application of Western critical methods to Eastern literatures represents a special problem; in one sense the process seems to represent the interaction of two literatures, but in another it seems to be merely an exercise involving a single literature. The treatment of relations between English and American works or between Spanish and Argentinian ones has not in the past been classified under comparative literature on the grounds that only a single language is involved. By the same token, the perception of relations between works in British literature and those in Indian or other Commonwealth literatures in English has been regarded as comparative culture, but not strictly comparative literature. If the use of translations in studying East-West relations is to be accepted as comparative literature, however, it would seem to be illogical not to accept as well the study of literary relations between two separate cultures that happen to use the same language. Recently an attempt has been made to classify literatures in English other than those of the United States and Great Britain under the rubric of Literature in English or Anglophone literatures. The situation has been succinctly stated by a contemporary Australian poet, A. D. Hope (1980, 165).

What we are faced with today and from now on, when English is a first or second language in more than forty countries, each with its own social background and its own cultural tradition, is actually the end of what used to be called English literature and its replacement by something which we should call Literature in English. Just as in the British Isles themselves, the main writers over the last two hundred years have belonged to the region as a whole and form part of one literature even if their source and character is English, Scottish, or Welsh, while in England, Scotland, Wales and Ireland there is a regional literature specific to that background—so now this pattern is being reproduced on a world scale. Gone is the concept of a tree with minor branches in which the English of England has dominance and priority, except perhaps as an historical image. Each region is independent of the others, free to develop its form of English and its national character as literature yet bound together by a community of language. The major writers in English in Australia, Pakistan, the United States, India, Singapore, Malaysia, Oceania, New Zealand, the West Indies, Canada, South Africa and so on will belong to the whole, will be read all over and exert a literary and cultural influence in all the regions concerned. Within each one, however, there will be a regional or national literature with its roots in native soil and more or less confined to its own borders.

A number of Western writers such as Dryden and Voltaire have been considered pioneer comparatists because of their critical essays treating examples of a specific genre such as drama or the epic in several national literatures. The term *comparative literature,* however, was first used in 1816 in the title of a book in the French language *Cours de littérature comparée* by Jean-François Michel Noël, but its first appearance in anything like the modern sense took place in 1886 when a British professor Hutcheson Macaulay Posnett published a book with the simple title *Comparative Literature,* which established the term throughout the English-speaking world and had repercussions from Japan to the United States. Four years later Professor Shōyō Tsubouchi introduced the book to his students at Waseda University in Japan (Aldridge and Shunsuke Kamei 1972, 149), and in 1911 an American professor, Alastair S. Mackenzie, published a book heavily indebted to Posnett, *The Evolution of Literature.* Posnett believed that the critical method he set forth was already being widely practiced in England, for he rapturously described it as "the peculiar glory of our nineteenth century," much as French philosophers a century earlier had hailed Diderot's *Encyclopédie* as the glory of the Enlightenment. As a matter of fact, prominent aspects of Posnett's system may be traced back to eighteenth-century theories of Hugh Blair in Scotland and Herder in Germany. In essence, Posnett believed that literature was an echo of sociological change, a means of measuring the upward evolutionary process of social organization. Unlike structuralists and formalists of today, who are largely concerned with description of literary artifacts and are indifferent to their origins, Posnett's main concern was to discover the manner in which great works came to be written. Rejecting equally "the theory that literature is the detached lifework of individuals who are to be worshipped like images fallen down from heaven" and the kindred one "that imagination transcends the associations of space and time," Posnett believed that a scientific explanation of literature may be found by studying the orderly changes in history in the relationship between the individual and the group. He traced, therefore, the reflection in literature of "the gradual expansion of social life, from clan to city, from city to nation, [and] both of these to cosmopolitan humanity" (1886, 86).

In keeping with much of the thought of the late nineteenth century and of that of some critics of the twentieth, Posnett believed that the study of literature could be considered a science, and his book was published in an international scientific series immediately following the titles *Anthropoid Apes* and *The Mammalia in their Relation to Primeval Times.* Apart from his fascination with sociological concepts, now considered old-fashioned, Posnett espoused some belletristic ones that are today considered quite modern. For example, he believed that the function of the literary critic is to examine not only the works themselves, but also the cause of the aesthetic pleasure that they arouse in human emotions and intellect. But what is most important in Posnett's book is the cosmopolitan range of his interests and illustrations, which cover the literatures of Asia as well as the West. Today few comparatists discuss more than one Western and one Eastern literature, but Posnett treats extensively the Japanese, Indian, and Chinese, along with the major ones of Europe. His century-old treatise makes a significant contribution to the study of East-West relations, even by today's standards.

Posnett's theories, despite their international success, seemed to have had negligible influence upon British education, perhaps because he published his system while employed as a professor in New Zealand. He called in vain for the establishment of chairs of comparative literature in British universities; indeed, at the present time—almost a century after the publication of his book—only three departments of comparative literature exist in the British Isles.

Posnett clearly reflected the sociological theories of a famous French critic, Hippolyte Taine, who looked at works of artistic creation as reflections of race, environment, and the historical moment. For Taine, as René Wellek has pointed out, literary criticism is "analogous to botany, which studies the orange, the laurel, the pine, and the birch with equal interest," except that literary criticism seeks to reveal how the individual work reflects humanity in general, a particular nation, and a historical age (1973, 1:600).

The scientific or positivistic orientation of Posnett and Taine strongly conditioned the next important stage in the development of comparative literature—that of the first half of the twentieth century—which was dominated by French thought and French scholarship. The University of Paris established its Institute of Comparative Literature early in the century, and the *Revue de littérature comparée* began publishing in 1921. One must observe, however, that this was by no means the first journal devoted entirely to comparative literature or with the term *comparative* in its title. This distinction belongs to the *Acta Comparationis Litterarum Universarum,* published between 1877–88 in Transylvania, the time segment during which Bram Stoker was writing his famous novel *Dracula* concerning this fascinating part of the world. The professors of the Sorbonne during the period between the two world wars specialized in the tracing of literary influences from one nation to another. Unlike Posnett, who had treated the relations between the individual and society in his own culture, the Paris professors concerned themselves with the relations between different cultures. They treated particularly the fortunes of single authors; the impressions that one country made upon the writers of another, or the literary "mirage," as it is called; and the impact of narratives of travel and discovery. Although some critics with strong formalistic proclivities have sought to disparage studies of this kind, their usefulness has been reaffirmed by an official publication of the Australian Comparative Literature Association (Veit 1972).

In the East, the study of comparative literature developed directly under the influence of Western trends. The pioneer Japanese association of comparatists, the Comparative Literature Society of Japan, founded in 1948, originally turned to the principles and methods of the Sorbonne for guidance. According to Professor Saburō Ōta, one of the early members of the society,

> the positive method of France presented difficulties. First there were relatively few cases in which such a method was applicable. There were many areas of investigation that could not be treated. Second, our study had to be limited chiefly to the Meiji Era, that is, 1868–1912, when the introduction of certain foreign authors or books could be traced fairly minutely, because the readers of foreign literature were pretty much limited to a narrow literary circle. But we see a far wider introduction and influence of foreign literatures in the present day. Thus we began to form two groups: one which closely adhered to the French school, and another which was trying to find a new method applicable to present day conditions and which was unwilling to follow blindly the pattern of the Sorbonne. The result was that the spring meeting of the society for 1954 was devoted to the discussion of the character and methodology of Comparative Literature. . . . Five persons expressed their opinion, of whom one followed the French school, keeping to strict positivism. Others insisted that we should devise a number of methods, which could be applied to the literature of different ages.

At about this time, the center of comparatist activity shifted from France to the United States. The Second Congress of the International Comparative Literature Association, which in 1958 met in Chapel Hill, North Carolina, was organized to feature the topics and themes traditionally favored by the University of Paris, but René Wellek in a paper on the crisis in the discipline announced that this emphasis was all wrong and that attention should be shifted from extrinsic to intrinsic matters. The congress occurred at a time when most English departments in American universities were dominated by the so-called new criticism, which was in fact an elaboration of a European movement begun a century before in Italy. For the next dozen or so years, therefore, most American comparatists decried influence studies, inveighed against positivistic aims and methods, and concentrated on the literary work itself. Since it is impossible to be comparative while examining merely a single artifact, the method of confrontation or "rapprochement" was developed.

During this period, the discipline of comparative literature continued to expand in the East, where emphasis was placed upon East-West relations. In the Western world, however, comparatist study and critical theory still concentrated for the most part upon European literatures until the 1970s, when a demand began to be expressed for a truly universal perspective. Sections devoted to East-West relations started to appear in meetings of the American and the International Comparative Literature Associations, in a trend led by scholars such as Etiemble in Europe and Horst Frenz and Earl Miner in the United States.

In one area in the study of comparative literature the discipline may aspire to scientific precision. This is the historical record of the reception of a work or series of related works in one national literature by the reading public of another nation. Such indications as translations, reviews, critical commentaries, and the number of printed editions may be objectively measured and classified. The carrying out of studies of this kind represents a tracing of literary penetration. The study of reception is in a large sense an aspect of sociology; whereas the parallel study of influence concerns artistic creation and is, therefore, more important in the domain of pure literature. Influence is the reflection of the style or thought of one author in the work of a subsequent one. The reflected elements would not have existed in the second author had he or she not read his predecessor and been sufficiently impressed to follow the latter's example. There is also negative influence, the deliberate avoidance by one author of something encountered in a previous writer. Influence is not easy to determine unless authors specifically indicate by references in their works or private letters that they have been inspired by particular predecessors. Sometimes the mere evidence that they have read a previous author is taken as an indication of influence, but this is by no means a certain sign. A man or woman of letters, just like anyone else in the general public, may read a literary work without experiencing any significant intellectual or aesthetic reaction as a result.

A distinction must be made, moreover, between direct and indirect influence. When influence is direct it means that particular authors have borrowed specific elements from the works of their predecessors and that they were conscious of the borrowing when it took place. Indirect influence, on the other hand, means that authors may have borrowed from predecessors without being conscious of doing so or that they may not even have had personal contact with works relevant to their own thought in their printed form, but have learned of their contents through intermediaries. Intermediary sources may consist of other printed materials dealing with the original relevant works or even of oral references to them.

It is even more difficult to demonstrate that writers have not been influenced by a preceding work that is similar to their own than to show that they actually have had some contact with it. Indeed it is impossible to prove the complete absence of influence, granting accessibility and the appropriate chronological relationship. Even though a writer specifically declares that he or she has no knowledge of a particular author, he may not be telling the truth or she may even have completely forgotten all contact with a work that was actually read. Two recent publications by Göran Hermerén (1975) and Ulrich Weisstein (1975) include nearly everything that can be said about influence studies.

The difference between reception and influence may be illustrated in the history of relations between Japan and the West by reference to the American humorist Mark Twain and the French naturalist Emile Zola. Twain is one of the favorite authors of the Japanese public, but he has not been imitated or followed to any great extent by Japanese writers. Zola, however, has been both read and assimilated by Japanese novelists. Twain, therefore, illustrates reception and Zola, influence (Balakian 1963, 148).

The vast majority of studies in comparative literature at the present time are devoted to an exploration and presentation of resemblances in particular works of two or more national literatures. Resemblance studies are completely different from studies of reception. They may include influence, but the majority concern works by authors who have had no direct contact with each other and who may not even have been aware of each other's existence. Parenthetically, influence may be studied under the rubrics of both reception and resemblance. The method of studying resemblance is variously described in Western countries. The most common term is *rapprochement,* which means literally "to come close" or "to bring together." The process consists in pointing out analogies, similarities and differences, or common elements of any kind in two or more literary works selected because in some way or other they are artistically akin. A similar term used by S. S. Prawer is "placing," which refers to putting two or more works figuratively side by side (1973, 143). François Jost describes the process humorously, but no less seriously: "If a critic sights a horse and a bull grazing together in his pasture and supposes that both, rather than either one alone, can help him to understand *his* literary quadrupeds, *his* mammals, and *his* herbivores, he may certainly compare them intellectually without having to prove beforehand that the bull descended from the horse. Relational studies for the comparatist can proceed from an agenetic or a polygenetic method, from one that does or does not refer to cause and effect" [1974, 74]. A superb discussion of all methods of investigation between the two poles of influence studies and rapprochement studies is given by Ulrich Weisstein in the work previously mentioned.

Regardless of the value of reception studies among European literatures, there is no question that they have only a limited application to the relations between East and West. To concentrate briefly upon Japan, no significant literary relations of any kind with the West existed during the first period of contact from the middle of the sixteenth century until the middle of the nineteenth. Even in the subsequent period ending with the Second World War, very few direct exchanges took place. Western writers most affected by Japanese models were Claudel, Lafcadio Hearn, Louis Viaud (Pierre Loti), Ezra Pound, and William Butler Yeats (Miner 1958, 66–76). Perhaps the greatest contribution in the West during this period to the study of resemblances was the translation in 1935 of the *Tale of Genji* by Arthur Waley, which made the great Japanese classic available throughout all Western countries. Waley's edition illustrates the service that translations may perform in the transmission of literature between the two hemispheres. A contemporary German critic, Max Kommerell, perhaps the most eminent of the century from his country, has written a sensitive characterization of the *Tale of Genji,* using the English translation. (Wellek 1975, 487). This is a remarkable example of literary criticism based upon the use of a translated text, perhaps all the more remarkable because it has been highly praised by René Wellek, who is otherwise ranked among the staunch opponents of translations in comparatist study.

Resemblances in literary works may conveniently be divided into three major groups: those of form, those of idea, and those of human relationships.

Form represents the major kinds or types of literature, such as poetry, drama, and fiction. These categories may be broken down into an almost endless variety of subgenres. In poetry, the Japanese form that has had greatest impact upon the West is that of the haiku, practiced in Europe and America so extensively during the last three-quarters of a century that a bibliography of the genre in Western languages has been published in the United States (Brower 1972), to which the eminent French comparatist Etiemble in a superb review has added many missing items (1974b, 1–19). At an international meeting, Professor Yūzō Saitō of Nihon University compared the poetic sensibility of the Japanese poet Bashō to that of the English poet John Keats (1966, 1399–1403). The epic is usually considered in the West to be the highest of poetic forms, and modern critical opinion accepts the Japanese *Tales of the Heike [Heike monogatari]* as appropriate to be compared to the Greek *Iliad* or the French *Chanson de Roland* (Etiemble 1974a, 168). In the realm of drama, moreover, some direct contact may be demonstrated. The Japanese Noh play has inspired several of the dramas of the Irish playwright William Butler Yeats. There is good reason, moreover, for comparatists to look for resemblances in earlier Western dramatists even though no possibility of direct influence exists (Miner 1958, 251–64). Some of the major Western types of prose fiction that undoubtedly have their counterparts in the East are the Bildungsroman or apprenticeship novel, the picaresque, the science fiction tale, the utopia, the mystery story, the epistolary novel, and the historical novel.

Resemblances in ideas are to be found in all literary genres, but most extensively in philosophical and religious treatises, miscellaneous essays, histories, books of travel, and political propaganda. An early American comparatist, Irving Babbitt, for example, has compared the primitivistic notions of the French Enlightenment philosophe, Jean-Jacques Rousseau, with those of Taoist philosophy, and a Japanese scholar has compared these same primitivistic notions with those of a contemporary Japanese thinker, Shōeki Andō (Komiya 1974, 3). Few complete books, however, have been devoted to the subject of intellectual communications between East and West, with the exception of those in the area of comparative religion. A good example of work in the latter discipline is a doctoral dissertation by a Japanese Christian, Jacob Yuroh Teshima, submitted to the Jewish Theological Seminary of America and entitled "Zen Buddhism and Hasidism, a Comparative Study" (*New York Times,* 31 May 1977).

The richest field for comparative investigation is that of human relationships as they are portrayed in all genres, but primarily in narrative poetry, drama, and prose fiction. The complexities of human behavior are depicted, of course, by means of plot, characterization, and theme, the latter of which ordinarily depends upon the first two. In the Japanese novel *The Setting Sun,* by Osamu Dazai, for example, the plot concerns the love of a daughter toward her mother, her ambivalent love-animosity toward her brother, her proposing herself in writing as a mistress to an elderly novelist whom she has not seen for six years, and her eventually becoming pregnant through him. Characterization in this novel reveals the development of bitterness and frustration in her personality as the result of a series of tragic incidents, including divorce from a none-too-happy marriage, the condition of childlessness, the horror of war, and the loss of her family's fortune and status in society. The theme of the novel as symbolized by the title, on one hand, is the decline of the institution of aristocracy and imperial Japan, and, on the other, the disintegration of the maladjusted personality of the protagonist. The comparatist could illustrate the universal application of these elements by presenting parallels in Western literature. Although very few readers in the modern world may have actually experienced the precise trials and conditions of the protagonist of *The Setting Sun,* nearly all will have been witness to situations closely approaching them. One aspect, perhaps, about which the comparatist could do nothing toward revealing or clarifying the artistry of the author is the area of poetic expression, symbol, sound, and metaphor. Drawing upon related considerations, however, the comparatist could explain the relevance of the author's frequent reference to such Western aesthetic materials as the painters Renoir and Monet.

Professor Robert Clements of New York University has isolated three major segments of comparative literature as it is presently practiced in the United States:

> The narrowest dimension is the Western Heritage and its traditional minimal components French-English, German-French, Latin-English, etc. This narrowest dimension, when restricted to only two authors or literatures within the Western Heritage, is to be discouraged at the level of academic discipline. The second dimension is East-West, an area in which some exploration has been undertaken. The third dimension is World Literature, a much abused term in America [1978, 7].

Clements adds that these dimensions "are not static terms, not passively conjoined, but they must as fiefs of comparative literature, follow the methodology of Western Heritage comparative literature," which embodies essentially five approaches: "the study of (1) themes/myths, (2) genres/forms, (3) movements/ eras, (4) interrelations of literature with other arts and disciplines, and (5) the involvement of literature as illustrative of evolving literary theory and criticism" (7).

John J. Deeney of the Chinese University of Hong Kong has objected to Clements' placing of the East-West dimension among the "fiefs of comparative literature," considering this classification as a condescending and patronizing attitude, smacking of Western chauvinism or colonialism. I do not believe for a moment, however, that Clements intended to suggest that the study of East-West relations is in any way inferior or subordinate to the study of the Western heritage. He undoubtedly meant merely that East-West studies should be classified in the academic system among the properties or "fiefs" of comparative literature programs. In this sense I fully agree with him. I part company, however, in regard to the use of the term *world literature* to describe his third and broadest dimension. I would use instead *universal literature* as the most comprehensive term, and instead of treating world literature as a dimension of comparative literature, would consider the latter as a part of universal literature. As generally understood, world literature possesses two almost contrary meanings: (1) the masterpieces of the major literatures of the world, and (2) all of the literatures of the world themselves. Since the term is imprecise (Clements indicates that it is much abused), a distinction must be made between world literature and universal literature, confining the former to masterpieces but according to the latter the fullest and broadest significance. I also believe that it is more fruitful in the East-West context to emphasize form, idea, and human relationships rather than the five approaches enumerated by Clements to illuminate the Western heritage.

The concept of world literature was originally introduced by Goethe, who proclaimed in 1836, "National literature has little meaning today; the time has come for the epoch of world literature to begin, and everyone must now do his share to hasten its realization" (Jost 1974, 16). Goethe was so advanced beyond his times, moreover, that he included Near Eastern and Chinese works among those to be studied. No one will quarrel with Goethe's view that people should not limit their reading to authors of their own country or to those in their own language, but considerable opposition has been raised to the corollary of this opinion that an attempt should be made to select as a nucleus of attention the most valuable works or the world's masterpieces. Recent objections to this theory have come from socialist countries in eastern Europe, who argue that the concept is elitist, linked to bourgeois culture, and a type of intellectual internationalism based on the theory of an absolute idea of the beautiful. The French critic Etiemble agrees with these strictures and observes in addition that the concept has been used by Western critics to overvalue the works of the major European nations and to minimize those of smaller European nations and the nations of the East. The concept, moreover, works against the aspirations of the emerging literatures of our times (1974a, 13–35). Despite these objections to the cultural elitism implicit in attempts to rank the hundred best books of all mankind or to select a list of books for an ideal library, most critics are willing to accept the view that some works which have stood the test of time are worthy to rank as "classics" in their respective literatures and to be treated with appropriate respect. One must still make an effort, as Etiemble warns, to escape the determinism of one's birth. As we are all blessed or afflicted with the language and religion of our parents, we also acquire associated literary prejudices. Only those fortunate enough to possess leisure, industry, economic freedom, and a large degree of intellectual independence are able to transcend these limitations and prejudices.

Among those so emancipated, the term *universal literature* is gradually acquiring popularity, but critics are still arguing about what it signifies. In the broadest sense, the term represents the definition of literature in general given earlier in this chapter, the sum total of all texts and works throughout the world, or the combination of all national literatures. As the concept *universal* represents a broader perspective than *world* in the cosmic sense, so *universal* covers a greater area in the literary one. *Universal* also suggests that the study of comparative literature rests upon the assumption of the fundamental unity of all mankind. As Voltaire observed in the eighteenth century, "men are born everywhere more or less the same . . . it is government which changes manners, which elevates or debases nations" (Voltaire 1953, 8133). Taoist philosophy also supports the view that "men under all skies regardless of the structure of their language are able to develop the same thoughts, the same philosophical systems" (Etiemble 1980, lxxix). Even allowing for political and cultural differences, the basic human relationships described in all literatures, ancient and modern, are fundamentally identical.

In recent years, however, the concept of universality has encountered opposition or competition from various sources, particularly from ethnic, nationalistic, and special-interest groups.

Feminists, homosexuals, Freudians, and Marxists, for example, subject literary works to interpretive schemes reflecting their particular ideology, while others insist on isolating literatures written by and about blacks, Chicanos, Puerto Ricans, or Cajuns. On the surface this literary splintering seems to suggest that the notion of universality is an illusion or an impractical ideal.

The claims of various national literatures for preferential treatment, moreover, are just as confusing, and they have been in existence for a much longer period of time. Some critics in the eighteenth century, for example, maintained that French letters were of such paramount importance that they should serve as the model for the rest of the world. Naturally these critics belonged to the French nation. One of them, a professor at the Parisian school that Voltaire attended, proposed as a subject for public discussion "whether the French could properly claim the glory of outweighing the other nations of Europe in that which concerns literary works" (Riesz 1975, 227). Another French professor early in the nineteenth century affirmed that it would be easier in London or in Paris than in Canton itself to prepare a Chinese dictionary or to acquire a profound knowledge of the Chinese language in its historical and literary relations (Abel-Rémusat 1829, 1:333). These are extreme examples of the kind of nationalistic pride that still finds expression in the opinion that European literatures are supreme above those in other parts of the world. The French claims of superiority in the eighteenth century were hotly disputed by critics of the other European nations, and eventually the literatures of all of them were admitted on a more or less equal basis. European literature came to mean universal literature. Various nations occasionally attempted to place themselves in the dominating position, but by the end of the nineteenth century general opinion had conceded that no single European literature was superior to the others.

A contemporary Rumanian critic, Adrian Marino, has formulated a conception of universal literature according to which it represents "the *sum* or *totality* of the literatures of the world without any discrimination" (Marino 1975, 79). According to this conception, individual works are not considered to be of a privi-

leged caste merely because they belong to a national literature
that has glorious historical antecedents. Competition exists
among individual writers of all cultures, but they are judged
entirely on the merits of their own productions, not on the basis
of the national literature to which they belong. The concept of
universal literature does not represent a homogenizing process
in which all forms of literary expression, any more than all peoples, gradually adopt a greater uniformity than they have had in
the past. Nor does it represent the use of modern technology,
including mass media, to produce a supranational literature comparable to supranational industrial conglomerates (Marino 1975,
70, 74). Rather, it is an outgrowth of the cosmopolitanism concept of the eighteenth century, of an indivisible "republic of
letters," the recognition of common elements in the human race
to which all literatures conform. In this perspective, historical
chronology is considered irrelevant and all works are regarded
as contemporary in the sense of existing today and being judged
by the needs of modern society. The Irish playwright William
Butler Yeats, for example, affirmed that the men who devised
the Japanese Noh drama had more in common with modern
Europeans and Americans than with the ancient Greeks or
Shakespeare and Corneille (Miner 1958, 268). One of the most
eminent contemporary novelists of Africa, the Guinean Camara
Laye, unlike many nationalists of that continent, strongly expresses in his work the themes of cultural syncretism and ethnic
reciprocity. In an interview he described "the cultures of the
world as all participating in one dance, each with its own special
movement, contributing something significant to the total world
rhythm. Any attempt to suppress one of them takes away an
essential unit or beat from the cohesion of the whole" (Larson
1980, 3, 18). This does not imply, however, that a single system
of music or rhythm exists for all peoples. The "high-floating"
sound of Bach, Brahms, and Mozart may be suitable for the
verse of Yeats, Pound, and Williams, but may have nothing in
common with poetry in other parts of the world (Narasimhaiah
1976, 8).

The concept of the universal in literature corresponds to that
of universality in the plastic arts, which was expressed early in

the twentieth century by Ernest F. Fenollosa, the art critic who in large measure introduced Ezra Pound to the culture of the East. According to Fenollosa,

> we are approaching the time when the art work of all the world of man may be looked upon as one, as infinite variations in a single kind of mental and social effort. . . . Oriental Art has been excluded from most serious art history because of the supposition that its law and form were incommensurate with established European classes. But if we come to see that classification is only a convenience . . . and that the real variations are as infinite as the human spirit, though educed by social and spiritual changes, we come to grasp the real and larger unity of effort that underlies the vast number of technical varieties. A universal scheme or logic of art unfolds, which as easily subsumes all forms of Asiatic and of savage art and the efforts of children as it does accepted European schools (1913, xxiv).

The conception of the universality of literature may seem to be based primarily on a quantitative perspective, but universality may also be viewed in a qualitative sense. Even before Goethe propounded his notion of world literature, his countryman Friedrich Schlegel pointed toward a *Universalpoesie,* by which he meant a synthesis of both prose and poetry, artistic and popular, comprising essentially everything that exists from the largest to the smallest literary system or artistic manifestation (Aldridge 1969, 2). By this he meant that the subject matter of literature must be comprehensive, embracing every possible facet of human experience. After Schlegel, the term *universal* in a qualitative sense has acquired still further meanings. From the perspective of content, *universal literature* may refer to any work that reflects attitudes, situations, or experiences that are felt or understood by human beings in all cultures, as, for example, respect for parents or revolt from them, and success or failure in a career. From the perspective of the reader's reaction, universal literature refers to any work that contains elements broad enough to appeal to the average person in any literate culture. Response to these elements is highly subjective, and it is, of course, frequently impossible to state objectively exactly which characteristics of an artistic work are responsible for its broad appeal. Here reader response is far more important than subject matter, although subject matter is much easier for the critic to analyze.

In recent years considerable attention has been devoted to the concept of reader response on both the individual and the group level. Various theories concerning psychological reactions have been proposed under the heading of reception aesthetics, and sociologists have studied and quantified the reading habits of various classes in society. The latter studies have provided a basis for the principle that the test of a great book consists in its being widely read with approval by a public different from that for which it was originally intended. Obviously popularity, not intrinsic value, is being measured here, but no valid criteria for the latter have ever been devised. It seems reasonable, therefore, to accept this sociological-aesthetic principle as an important contribution to the concept of universal literature, particularly for the appraisal of writings in the East-West context.

At first glance it would seem that readers would ordinarily identify themselves with the protagonist of a literary text and that they would respond most readily to the works that portray situations and feelings they have encountered themselves. Brief reflection will indicate that this is not at all true. To cite one of the most popular works of Western literature, *Hamlet,* almost none of its readers is likely to be a young prince required by circumstances to avenge his father's death at the hands of an uncle living in incestuous relations with his mother. Nor are many of the admirers of the Japanese novel *The Temple of the Golden Pavilion* young priests whose psychological quirks lead them to burn down the temple in which they worship. It is not that readers see themselves in these works, but that they find something in the plot or presentation that gives them aesthetic pleasure. In this sense, therefore, universal literature is the concrete manifestation of "the universality of taste," a concept that the Japanese author Sōseki, among others, has proclaimed (Tsukamoto 1969, xiv). The literary critic may affirm with slight risk of contradiction that such works as *Hamlet* and *The Temple of the Golden Pavilion* belong to universal literature, but students of comparative literature must do more than make declarations. They must reveal parallels or relationships with similar works in other literatures.

The method of comparative literature, moreover, resolves a giant paradox existing in the concept of universal literature, no matter in which of the several senses it is understood. The paradox consists in the fact that universal is an international concept growing in importance at a time when nationalism is becoming increasingly more vociferous, illustrated, for example, by the demands for attention by "emerging" literatures, including some in the Far East. The techniques of comparative literature succeed in relaxing the tension between nationalism and internationalism by recognizing cultural differences as a basic premise, but at the same time calling attention to similarities that reflect the universality of psychological and aesthetic reactions. The problem for Japanese writers, according to Armando Martins Janeira, "is to become universal without dissolving into a vacuous cosmopolitanism." Janeira cites André Gide as the final authority on the question: "It is by becoming national that a literature takes its place in humanity. . . . Is there anything more Spanish than Cervantes, more French than Voltaire, than Descartes, or Pascal, more Russian than Dostoevski; and more universally human than each one of them?" (142). The comparatist is always aware of the national or ethnic character of literary works while perceiving them from the universal perspective.

For clarity and precision, I shall review the various definitions so far introduced.

Literature as such consists of communication by written words or symbols when the purpose of communication involves emotional or aesthetic response in addition to mere transference of information.

Comparative literature can be considered the study of any literary phenomenon from the perspective of more than one national literature or in conjunction with another intellectual discipline or even several.

World literature may be said to comprise the great works or classics of all times selected from all of the various national literatures.

Universal literature in the broadest sense represents the sum total of all texts and works throughout the world, or the combination of all national literatures.

In a restricted and more practical sense, universal literature comprises all works that contain elements cosmopolitan enough to appeal to the average person in any literate culture.

The study of literature East-West in particular consists in revealing connections between one or more works from one hemisphere with one or more from the other.

CHAPTER 2. REFERENCES

Abel-Rémusat, Jean-Pierre. 1829. *Nouveaux mélanges asiatiques.* Paris: Schubart et Heideloff.

Aldridge, A. Owen. 1969. *Comparative literature: Matter and method.* Urbana: Univ. of Illinois Press.

———. 1977. Literature (field of study). *International encyclopedia of higher education.* San Francisco: Jossey-Bass Publishers.

Aldridge, A. Owen, and Shunsuke Kamei. 1972. Problems and vistas of comparative literature in Japan and the United States: A dialogue. *Mosaic* 5:149–63.

Balakian, Anna. 1963. The concept of influence in comparative literature. *Comparative Literature Studies,* Special Advance Number: 146–49.

Brower, G. L., and D. W. Foster. 1972. *Haiku in Western languages: An annotated bibliography.* Metuchen, N.J.: Scarecrow Press.

Clements, Robert. 1978. *Comparative literature as academic discipline.* New York: Modern Language Association of America.

Deeney, John J. 1980. Comparative literature for scholars and administrators. *Tamkang Review* 11:79–106.

Etiemble, René. 1974a. *Essais de littérature (vraiment) générale.* Paris: Gallimard.

———. 1974b. Review of Brower and Foster, *Haiku in Western languages. Comparative Literature Studies* 11:1–19.

———, ed. 1980. *Philosophes taoïstes.* Paris: Gallimard.

Fenollosa, Ernest. 1913. *Epochs of Chinese and Japanese Art.* New York. W. Heineman.

Hermerén, Göran. 1975. *Influence in art and literature.* Princeton, N.J.: Princeton Univ. Press.

Hope, A. D. 1980. Teaching Australian literature. *The Literary Criterion* 15:157–65.

Janeira, Armando Martins. 1970. *Japanese and Western Literature. A comparative study.* Rutland, Vt.: Charles E. Tuttle Co.

Jost, François. 1974. *Introduction to comparative literature.* Indianapolis, Ind.: Bobbs-Merrill Co.

Komiya, Akira. 1974. Andō Shōeki et Jean-Jacques Rousseau. *Hikaku Bungaku Kenkyū. Etudes de Littératures Comparées* No. 26:3 [abstract].

Larson, Charles R. 1980. Master of the Word. *New York Times Book Review,* 16 March:3, 18.

Marino, Adrian. 1975. Où situer la 'littérature universelle'? *Cahiers roumains d'études littéraires 3/1975:64–81.*

Miner, Earl. 1958. The Japanese tradition in British and American literature. Princeton, N.J.: Princeton Univ. Press.

Narasimhaiah, C. D. 1976. *Commonwealth literature. A handbook of select reading lists.* Delhi: Oxford Univ. Press.

Posnett, Hutcheson Macaulay. 1886. *Comparative literature.* New York: D. Appleton Co.

Prawer, S. S. 1973. *Comparative literature studies: An introduction.* New York: Barnes and Noble.

Riesz, Janos. 1975. Eine Metzer Edition . . . von Beat Ludwig von Muralt. In *Teilnahme und Spiegelung,* ed. B. Alleman & E. Koppen. Berlin: Walter D. Gruyter.

Saitō, Yūzō. 1966. The sensibility of Bashō and Keats. In *Proceedings of the IVth congress of the international comparative literature association,* ed. François Jost. The Hague: Mouton.

Tsukamoto, Toshiaki. 1969. Problems of Sōseki's Bungaku-Hyōron. *Hikaku Bungaku. Journal of Comparative Literature* 12:xiv (abstract).

Veit, Walter, ed. 1972. *Captain James Cook: Image and impact.* Melbourne: Hawthorne Press.

Voltaire. 1836. Fragments sur l'histoire. *Oeuvres complètes.* Paris: Furne Librairie-Editeur.

———. 1953–65. *Correspondence.* Ed. Theodore Besterman. Geneva: Musée Voltaire. (Letters are identified by number, not volume and page.)

Weisstein, Ulrich. 1975. Influences and parallels—The place and function of analogy studies in comparative literature. In *Teilnahme und Spiegelung. See* Riesz 1975.

Wellek, René. 1973. Literary criticism. In *Dictionary of the History of Ideas,* ed. Philip R. Wiener. New York: Charles Scribner's Sons.

———. 1975. Max Kommerell as critic of literature. In *Teilnahme und Spiegelung. See* Riesz 1975.

3

Cultural Pluralism and Criticism

ONE OF THE EARLIEST EUROPEAN MINDS TO RECOGNIZE THE importance of Eastern culture was the renowned German philosopher Leibniz. In the formative years of the Enlightenment, he proposed that Chinese missionaries be sent to Europe to teach the use and practice of natural religion *(theologia naturalis),* just as the Europeans would send their missionaries to China to teach revealed religion (Leibniz 1957, preface). Leibniz does not specify whether he was referring to the Taoist or the Confucian tradition, but his references to natural religion undoubtedly suggest Neo-Confucianism. The Jesuits who carried on missionary work in China certainly found the teachings of Confucius more to their liking than those of the Taoists. They attempted to show their own compatibility and pliability by wearing Chinese garb in the East, while incorporating in their European publication of translations from Confucius a portrait of the Chinese sage attired in the Jesuit habit.

Contemporary Chinese comparatists who advocate the use of Western critical concepts in the study of Eastern literatures have given new life to the process advocated by Leibniz. In a sense, they have imitated the practice of the Jesuits by attempting to clothe Eastern literature in Western habiliments. Like the German philosopher, however, they may have failed to give sufficient attention to the ideological disparities in the alien culture. During much of the present century, critics in the Western world have been separated into major camps—variously labeled as formal and historical, synchronic and diachronic, or structural and hermeneutic. The antagonisms between structuralists and traditionalists in the West are as profound as those between Confucians and Taoists in China or the Confucianists and anti-Confucianists in eighteenth-century Japan. The words of the ancient philosopher, Chuang-tzu, in reference to the metaphysical divisions in Chinese culture, are equally applicable to the critical ones in the West: "Each one of these two schools affirms what the other denies, and denies what the other affirms." (Yip 1978, 31). Paradoxically this common ideological belligerence may in itself be an indication of the psycho-social similarity between the two cultures and a demonstration of the eighteenth-century adage that men are fundamentally the same all over the world. At the same time it may serve as a caution for each of the respective cultures against adopting an intellectual system of the other without rigorous discrimination of the applicable from the irrelevant. Literary criticism in general has been compared to seeking nourishment by having some one else eat a dinner and then reciting the menu. When criteria from one culture are applied to creative work from another the process might be compared to reciting the menu in a foreign tongue.

A slight nuance separates the editorial policies of two major journals in Asia, the *Tamkang Review,* published in Taiwan, and the *New Asia Academic Bulletin,* published in Hong Kong. Originally the *Tamkang Review* featured articles on Chinese literature from the point of view of "western critical methods," but it now stresses "the context of world literature." The *New Asia Academic Bulletin* welcomes studies relating Chinese literature to Western or other Eastern literatures and those "applying Western critical theories to Chinese literature" in the effort to elucidate a "common poetics." In practice, many of the articles published in both journals lean heavily on Western methodology, primarily the schemes of New Criticism and structuralism.

Comparative literature implies by definition the treatment of works from at least two national traditions, but it has been said in defense of the application of Western methods to single eastern texts that the process literally "involves a comparative dimension" (Liu 1975, 28). It has also been argued that the process is "in principle, no more inappropriate than the classical scholar's use of modern techniques and methods for his study of

ancient materials" (Yu 1974, 50). It should be remembered, however, that the latter process is always considered to be the study
of Greek and Roman literature, never comparative literature.
The argument for adopting Western criticism rests, moreover, on
the unproved assumptions that "modern" techniques are necessarily superior to traditional ones and that Western methods are
monolithic or unified. In practice, techniques as diverse as Aristoteleanism and structuralism have been applied to Chinese
works, some with great success and some with very little. Also
underlying the application of Western critical methods are the
further assumptions "that comparable features and qualities
exist between Chinese and Western literatures and that comparable standards are applicable to both" (Liu 1975, 28). It is probably true that contemporary Eastern and Western literatures
have more in common than have those of ancient Greece and
contemporary Europe, but identical criteria are not usually applied to the two latter groups. If it does not make sense to judge
modern drama by the Aristotelean unities, it is no more rational
to apply them to Eastern drama of any historical period.

It must be stressed, moreover, that not all Chinese scholars—
even many with a rich background in Western literature—are
enthusiastic about the wholesale adoption of Western criticism.
Chung-shu Ch'ien, for example, in his highly successful novel of
manners, *Fortress Besieged,* ironically portrays the tendency to
overevaluate Western academic culture:

> It may sound a bit absurd for someone majoring in Chinese to
> go abroad for advanced study. In fact, however, it is only for
> those studying Chinese literature that it is absolutely neces-
> sary to study abroad, since all other subjects such as mathe-
> matics, physics, philosophy, psychology, economics, and law,
> which have been imported from abroad, have already been
> Westernized. Chinese literature, the only native product, is
> still in need of a foreign trade-mark before it can hold its own"
> (1979, 11).

We are reminded in addition of the ironical explanation given by
Etiemble of the sudden vogue for Western literature in the East.
"After the Opium War and the Boxer Rebellion, China and Japan
learned that the only way of ridding themselves of the white race

was to adopt their techniques and their weapons; all of a sudden, the philosophies and the literatures of France, England or Germany participated in the respect accorded to their gunners: they began to be translated" (1974, 131).

Much depends on what one calls Western methods. Apparently the first Chinese history of Chinese literature was not published until 1909, eight years subsequently to one in English (Wong 1978, 54), and the pioneer history of Japanese literature in Japanese appeared in 1890, followed by one in English in 1899. I am indebted to Professor Yukinori Iwaki of Nihon University for the latter information. If one considers the writing of literary history per se a Western method, there can be no argument about the need to follow the West. But if one takes a more precise view and considers particular techniques such as applying Aristotelean standards or computer analysis, then many legitimate doubts arise. Hutcheson Macaulay Posnett observed nearly a century ago that literary art consists in something better than an imitation of models and that models are admittedly out of place "when carried into social conditions markedly different from those under which they were produced." Unless we limit the range of our criticism. Posnett warned, "we may find ourselves applying the standards of the Athenian to the Japanese drama, or those of the Greek lyric to the *Shih King* [*Shih Ching*] of ancient China" (1886, 12).

There are essentially two developments in the modern world that have allowed the study of East-West relations to expand beyond the stage where Posnett left it. Neither of these is literary—the invention of jet travel and the discovery of inexpensive methods of printing. Before these mechanical innovations, most people in the West had only the vaguest notions of China and Japan, and these consisted more of fantasy than reality. Jet travel and mass printing methods, however, have brought the two cultures together more rapidly than centuries of patient literary scholarship could have done by itself.

By and large, literary study in both East and West is divided into two main overlapping categories, one synthetic, the other analytical. In essence, literary history records what books have actually been published and circulated; literary criticism makes aesthetic judgments about these books. The basis of literary history is periodization—dividing literary production into time segments that are presumably unified by stylistic and ideological characteristics. It is extremely difficult to divide Chinese literature into periods that have any significance other than purely chronological (Wong 1978, 45–68) and it is impossible to coordinate the more than thirty centuries of Eastern literature with the briefer span of Western except in the relatively short modern period. Little intellectual contact existed for most of these thirty centuries, and there were almost no coinciding "golden" ages or "dark" ages, and few parallel developments in genres and themes. Etiemble has shown, however, that some very ancient commercial relations developed along the overland silk road well before the Christian era, that contacts by sea took place during the Roman Empire, and that communication by both land and sea existed during the Mongolian dynasty (1959, 36).

Since literary history (except for the period from the seventeenth century to the present) offers little scope for drawing Eastern and Western literatures together, attention has been diverted to criticism. Not only have many Eastern scholars advocated the almost wholesale importation of Western methods, but they have enunciated a "common poetics" and assumed as a goal of comparative studies the synthesizing of Eastern and Western aesthetic standards.

One may doubt first of all the possibility of harmonizing the diverse, mutually contradictory, and incommensurable concepts that comprise Western criticism alone at the present time. Bringing these concepts together would not result in a synthesis, but in a clash of conflicting ideologies (Lefevere 1978, 12–13). One may also raise the question of whether comparative literature depends on synthesis at all and argue that common poetics in literature are no more necessary than a common system of worship in religion. In other words, significant conclusions in comparative literature may be reached in the future, as in the present, by the use of a plurality of critical methods. Despite the antagonism between Taoism and Confucianism, the East has already set an example in rational eclecticism in regard to the diversity of religion. The Chinese and the Japanese are apparently able to accept two or three religious faiths equally and concurrently, if not completely. This is in contrast to the notion of toleration in the West, according to which most people believe that their particular single religion is the only true one, while extending to other people the right to have the same attitude toward some other theology. If it is possible to attain eclecticism in religion, why should a similar pluralism in critical theory not be accepted or even welcomed? To accept pluralism, however, is not the same thing as to assume that all schools of criticism have equal validity, but rather that some methods are efficacious for certain problems and irrelevant to others.

One of the great advantages of pluralism is that it rejects the notion that has existed in the West in some form or another for over a hundred years that the study of literature can and should approach scientific exactitude. There are, of course, many significations attached to the notion of science. I am using the term in the broad sense of a discipline professing to comprise knowledge that is precise and undeviating. In the nineteenth century, German universities established a mode of literary research that, its exponents felt, embodied the methodology of science. This mode consisted, according to an eminent French critic, in all types of detail, including "meticulous erudition, narrow philology, dry monographs, statistics and mechanical scrutinies, painstaking collation of manuscripts, [and] positive investigation of sources" (Lanson 1912, 162). The critic whom I am quoting is Gustave Lanson. The term *positive* which he uses, has since acquired derogatory connotations, and it is sometimes applied to Lanson himself. In France, the term *Lansonism* is used as the equivalent of positivism, the terms being considered equally disparaging by some exponents of later critical methods.

Part of the reason for the disrepute into which positivism has fallen among comparatists is the unfortunate decision of some of its advocates to disregard aesthetic considerations entirely in their concern for historical substance and accuracy. This attitude is bluntly stated by Paul Van Tieghem in a manual entitled *La littérature comparée* published in 1931. According to this author, "the character of genuine comparative literature like that of all historical science is to embrace the largest possible number of facts of different origin in order best to explain each one of them; to enlarge the basis of knowledge in order to discover the causes of the greatest possible number of effects. In short, the word 'comparative' must be drained of all esthetic value and receive a scientific value" (1931, 21).

Lanson, however, never rejected aesthetic considerations, and he particularly denied the existence of a universal scientific method, admitting merely a universal scientific attitude. The literary historian, he explained, cannot experiment, but merely observe, and the facts that he observes cannot be measured or weighed—and they do not repeat themselves (1925, 25–27). Science, moreover, according to Lanson, concerns itself with the general and excludes from consideration everything that is "particular, individual, and consequently the concrete, the sensitive, in short, vitality" (1965, 102). In specific reference to French literature, Lanson summarized as follows his notions of literary history: "Our principal operations consist in understanding literary texts, in comparing them in order to distinguish the individual from the collective and the original from the traditional, in grouping them by genres, schools and movements, in determining finally the relationship of these groups with the intellectual, moral and social life of our country as well as with the development of European literature and civilization" (1965, 43). Although Lanson has recently been accused of ontological confusion between literary works as dead historical things or objects and as vital organisms that are still living and giving pleasure (Kushner 1978, 38), he particularly affirmed that "each generation reads its thought or its ideal in the masterpieces of literature, each century remakes them into its own image; and none of these interpretations has the right of excluding the others" (1925, 41–42, 47). Lanson's method was obviously oriented particularly toward French literature, but its basic features could be expanded to encompass East-West relations without encountering the barrier of periodization or the alleged narrowness of positivism.

Other groups of critics use the language of science without making it clear, as Lanson has done, that literature cannot be subsumed under the disciplines that affirm unchanging and undeviating principles, illusory as some of the alleged certainty in some of the laboratory disciplines has been shown to be. Some of the critics who use scientific vocabulary admit the presence of the aesthetic element in style and form, but suggest that this aesthetic element can be measured objectively or explained mechanically. As far back as the eighteenth century the twin theories were enunciated that literary works bear the imprint of the soil upon which they were produced (in Latin America called the telluric influence) and that literary works are the expression of the society and social conditions from which they emerged. The most famous exponent of the social evolutionary theory is Taine, but the pioneer critic in comparative literature with this orientation is Posnett. Although embracing the concept of science as his guiding principle, Posnett nevertheless declared himself firmly opposed to the notion that there exists "some universal human nature which unaffected by differences of language, social organization, sex, climate, and similar causes, has been at all times and in all places the keystone of literary architecture" (1886, 21). It seems to be merely by chance that Posnett chose to speak of "literary architecture" rather than using the more modern term *structure*. Posnett also categorically denied the existence of literary models, beyond those of actual texts. He would not admit others as residing "innate in the human heart or intellect as a kind of literary conscience" (1886, 43). While denying that science itself consists of a body of universal truths, Posnett declared that literature may be understood as a collection of limited truths, some of which are static influences such as the climate, the soil, the animal and plant life of various countries, and others are dynamic forces causing social evolution from communal to individual life (1886, 20). He set out, therefore, to show the "effects of social evolution on literature" (1886, 82). The precise evolution in literature that Posnett attempted to trace in both Eastern and Western cultures consisted of a development in spirit, portraying originally the clan, next the city commonwealth, and finally the individual. This concept of stages is an early and drastic type of literary periodization. In defending his hypothesis, Posnett collected a significant body of documents, his achievement flawed only by the determinism of the evolutionary hypothesis from which he worked. Although rejecting this abstract determinism, I am obviously not objecting to the related concept of social influences upon literature, particularly after my previous reference to the instrumentality of jet travel and mass reproductions.

Theories similar to Posnett's were propounded soon after the publication of his book by a professor at the University of Kentucky, Alastair S. MacKenzie, who, although holding the title of head of the department of English and comparative literature as early as 1911, has been completely ignored by historians of the latter discipline. MacKenzie describes his 1911 book, *The Evolution of Literature,* as an anthropological study designed to elucidate "the organic unity of literary evolution" (vii). In his terminology, MacKenzie makes a basic distinction between the historical method and the comparative method. According to his dichotomy, the investigation of similar ethnic facts not related by continuity or contact represents the comparative method, and the quest for causes of ethnic facts by showing their relation to anterior facts is the historical method. This is an early version of the distinction between synchronic and diachronic criticism, which has become an obsession in much contemporary writing. MacKenzie's stages in literary evolution are essentially the same as Posnett's, except that he divides the clan into a primitive period in which man hunts for his sustenance and a barbaric one in which he domesticates and cultivates. MacKenzie draws his examples not only from China, India, and the West, but also from Africa and Oceana (New Zealand and Australia). In his conclusion, MacKenzie derives three provisional laws of literary evolution, which he casts in the shape of formulae, as he says, to make them "more luminous to some readers" (415). In one of these, which he calls "the law of progress," A equals average literary advance, S equals self-consciousness, and W equals world consciousness. The formula, therefore, reads $A = S + W$. To those who find this formulation absurd, I suggest that a similar reaction might be appropriate to many of the graphs and protomathematical formulae that have proliferated in recent Western criticism. In regard to both nineteenth- and twentieth-century systems, the warning of Lanson is pertinent: science tends constantly to reduce itself to mathematics, to the abstract, and the general; but art and literature concern themselves with the individual qualities of things and being (1965, 102).

Posnett and MacKenzie stress the importance of the individual in both social change and the development of literature, particularly in the most advanced stages. MacKenzie, indeed, accepts the role of genius in literary creativity, explaining it as an indication of superior inventiveness or imagination (404). This humanistic theory goes completely contrary to historical "vulgar" Marxism, which believes in the all-embracing dominance of social-economic forces over the individual. A militant anti-humanism is to be found also in many structuralists of both Marxist and anti-Marxist persuasions, who deny "that man (or human consciousness) is an intelligible entity or field of study in himself" (Jameson 1972, 139–40).

A later group of critics has sought to demonstrate scientific objectivity by concentrating on the literary text—viewing it as an object in itself. Contrary to the emphasis of Posnett on the relativity of literature, these critics assume that the text has an absolute existence or that it may be hypostatized into a distinct reality. One of the most important sectors of this group is the American New Critics, whose influence has been felt in both the East and the West. Until very recently English departments of most American universities emphasized the intrinsic over the extrinsic approach, bowed down to the "verbal icon," warned against the intentional and the affective fallacies, and affirmed the possibility of substituting for "romantic impressionism" a type of criticism that is truly impersonal and objective. Although they did not use the word *scientific,* these critics made strong pretensions of approaching the essence of literature and discerning universal standards.

The trouble with the theory that a poem may be analyzed in itself as something with an independent existence is that no literary work can properly be said to exist in itself. The work in itself is nothing but a manually inscribed or printed series of marks on paper. To have any meaning whatsoever, these marks must be interpreted as symbols by a reader, who adds his own previous experience and knowledge to the aesthetic and intellectual sensation communicated by what he sees. The text itself possesses the qualities attributed to it only as they are perceived by the reader, and each reader has his own individual response. That there can be no single valid interpretation for any literary work is demonstrated by the truism that interpretations of masterpieces change from century to century. As has frequently been remarked, "there are as many *Divine Comedies* as there are readers." The New Critics are far more susceptible than traditional historical criticism to the charge of treating literary works as museum pieces; whereas these works are in actuality still living, still developing, and still giving pleasure.

The advocates of the historical method have always resisted or remained lukewarm in their acceptance of New Criticism, and in recent years its privileged status has been withdrawn in American universities. This type of analysis has been replaced by new techniques that for the most part treat the complexities of literature as mechanical in nature. Not without reason they have been labeled the technocracies of literature (Mounin 1978). The new fashions are commonly subsumed under the rubric of structuralism—although the term in its general application is almost impossible to define. Narrowly the term applies only to analyses of a text in which elements of the vocabulary are given such labels as signifiers and signifieds or in which precise patterns of metaphor/metonymy and other binary relations are noted. In a much broader sense, structures have been perceived in theme and ideology, and in psychological and sociological overtones. Although the exponents of the various structuralist methods do not specifically claim, or admit, that they are, like the New Critics, hypostatizing the works that they treat, the question has been asked "whether structures are perennially present in a Platonic sort of sense, and impose themselves to the creator and through the work of art to the historian; or whether in a manner more consonant with nominalism they are forms imposed by the beholder upon reality as he perceives it" (Kushner 1978, 48). If like Platonic essences structures are considered as inherent in the text, the structural method is subject to the objection that a literary work cannot have independent existence but depends on the mediation of the reader or series of readers; if structures are interpreted in the nominalist sense as based on the perception of the individual beholder, all pretensions by the method to scientific precision are rendered invalid.

To label a word a "sign" or a group of words an "aesthetic sign" does little to explain the meaning of the words or their effect upon a readership. Semiotic interpretations are perhaps valid in showing how a square of paper bearing the number ten that is affixed to an apple is related to the sentence "An apple costs ten cents." But they are unable on their own terms to do more with such semantically rich affirmations as "the wages of sin is death" than with "an apple costs ten cents." Linguistics and literature are fundamentally separate disciplines—literature comprises idea, emotion, and aesthetic pleasure; linguistics consists of the mechanism by which these qualities are conveyed.

Another form of literary study depending on mechanical assistance and, therefore, presumably carrying scientific overtones is that of computerized statistical analysis. This method may have limited value, for example, in the study of the utilization of particular words or ideas in a particular author. One must keep in mind, however, that something that is done by a machine is not necessarily any more scientific than the same process done by hand. Computer analysis, together with any of the forms of structuralism, remains a process that is dependent upon the subjective choice of the analyzer.

A final fashionable method is that of submitting a questionnaire on a text to a group of readers to obtain an opinion sampling, a method claimed to be "the single objective indication" of the aesthetic functioning of the text. It is hard to see how a series of individual subjective responses can add up to a single objective indication. Indeed, all that this kind of sampling does is to provide information about the group of readers involved in the sampling, not about the inherent elements of the text or about its aesthetic appeal to all potential readers.

The fact that certain critical methods hold objectivity in esteem or adopt the vocabulary of science should not necessarily be held against these methods. Most procedures that seek primarily to measure and analyze, however, almost inevitably concentrate upon single texts and are, therefore, irrelevant to comparative studies, which by definition require at least two works in separate literatures for consideration. Studies of structural elements, moreover, whether syntactical, phonic or semantic, cannot be accepted as paradigms for all potential readers or even for the best-informed and aesthetically acute ones, no matter how much satisfaction these studies afford to those who carry them out. There is much to be said for the advice of a European comparatist who advises literary scholars in general to take gastronomy rather than chemistry as a model—to enjoy and savour literature rather than to analyze or dissect it (Stegman 1973, 285). Another European, Hans Robert Jauss, the leader of a new school of reception aesthetics, speaks of *Genuss* or the pure enjoyment of reading (1977, 33).

Jauss and others have recognized that the understanding of literature requires an appreciation of the reader's reaction to a text as well as of the inherent nature of that text. They have developed a set of elements, therefore, to coexist with the classic triad associated with the study of sources and influence, that of Emitter, Intermediary, and Receiver, enshrined in the monumental bibliography of Baldensperger and Friederich. The new triad, which concerns itself with individual texts, consists of Author, Text, and Reader, or, as it has otherwise been expressed, Emitter, Aesthetic Function, and Receiver (Mounin 1978, 154). When one deals with East-West relations and must rely on translations, another element is added to this process: there is now Author, Text (comprising the setting and general context), Translation (comprising the inevitable interpretive process), and Reader. Critics who are aware of the importance of reader reaction in the interpretation of the work are fully cognizant that interpretation is a continuous process—that the meaning and significance of a work change from generation to generation or from century to century. Recognition of this principle gives support and validity to East-West studies.

Some scholars have objected that readers in one hemisphere are unable fully to understand intellectually or appreciate aesthetically works from the other hemisphere because of radical differences in culture and, consequently, aesthetic concepts. The obstacles are, of course, increased if the works are read in translation rather than in the original language. To this one may reply that the variations in perception caused by cultural differences are probably no greater than those caused by chronological gaps between two widely separated periods in the cultures of either East or West.

The preceding views concerning reader response bear close resemblance to what is called reader criticism or transactional theory, the latter concept stemming ultimately from the American philosopher John Dewey. In an epistemological sense, a transaction is a single event comparable to an ecological process in which organism and environment engage in mutual interaction (Rosenblatt 1978, 15–17). The literary work may be compared to an element in a business transaction, consisting of a buyer, a seller, and a commodity. The text is the commodity mediating between the author and the reader. A considerable body of European and American criticism is now stressing this point of view. It is fitting to indicate once more that Posnett observed a century ago that "when men first began to ask themselves why it was that the poet's works pleased them, they sought to find the cause not in human senses, emotions, intellect, but in analyses of the works themselves" and that Posnett approved of investigation of human reactions rather than the contrary process (1886, 10).

When scholars choose a particular method of investigation, they are selecting for attention certain elements in the text or texts they are dealing with. Before proceeding they should ask why they have selected these particular elements for analysis, what the elements are likely to contribute to the understanding or the enjoyment of the text, and, if the investigators are concerned with East-West relations, how the elements reveal parallels between writings in various cultures.

One of the oldest forms of Western criticism is that known as the "beauties and faults" method. Derived from Longinus and practiced extensively in the eighteenth century by Addison in England and Diderot in France, it consists primarily in pointing out passages that give particular pleasure, making personal observations about them, and backing up these observations by rules or authorities to make them appear to be the reflection of common sense or general opinion. Matthew Arnold in the nineteenth century devised a variant of the method by selecting a group of lines of "high poetic quality" from various authors and presenting them as "touchstones" of poetic excellence. W. L. Wong in a recent article has shown parallels between Arnold's method and that of Chinese poetry—talk criticism, which, like the Western "beauties and faults" criticism, selects passages for their intrinsic attractiveness (1978, 33–34). Wong's exposition not only indicates certain aspects of impressionistic criticism, but also provides a basis by which a reader unfamiliar with Chinese prosody may understand other Chinese poems as well as those treated in the article itself. Although intuitions and impressions are inimical to formal scientific method, they still have a place in the process of intercultural awareness. The method of selecting passages of aesthetic appeal as "touchstones" resembles, although it is by no means identical with, late-twentieth-century Western notions of isolating "invariants," "typological analogies," or "convergences of the same nature among literatures of different people who are not in direct contact one with the other" (Marino 1979, 160).

Seeking of parallels between East and West does not depend upon the existence of a common poetics, but upon the notion of a universal literature—not to be confused with the concept of absolutes. I have already suggested that universal literature should be understood in the broadest sense as the sum total of all texts and works throughout the world, or a combination of all national literatures. John Deeney in calling for a "Chinese" school of comparative literature similarly suggests that Chinese scholars should progress "from *national* self-identification, to a broader *regional* cultural awareness, to a '*Third World*' association with neglected or emerging literatures, to a *world-wide* comprehensiveness in scope and, finally—however idealistically—to a *universal* integration of all literatures in their complex relationships" (1977, 233). The literatures of the East and the West do not need in any way to abandon their autonomy or independence in order to be studied in this universal context.

Several advantages may be noticed: (1) In the purely quantitative sense, since universal literature comprises all the works that exist in the world, no single literature, whether French in the West or Chinese in the East, can be considered as superior to the others. (2) In a narrower, qualitative sense, universal literature may be considered equivalent to Schlegel's notion of *Universalpoesie*—that is, as a synthesis of both prose and poetry, artistic and popular, embracing every possible facet of human experience. (3) From the perspective of content, universal literature may refer to any work that reflects attitudes, situations, or experiences that are felt or understood by human beings in all cultures. (4) From the perspective of the reader's response, universal literature may include any work that contains elements broad enough to appeal to the average person in any literate culture. Universal literature, yes; common poetics, no.

A superior work of art does not hold its privileged position because it contains some quintessential element within it, but because it succeeds in arousing a favorable response in a reader or a series of readers. In my opinion, the only universally valid criterion for artistic worth is still the *consensus gentium* or "the general and perpetual voice of men," whether measured by the endurance of a text over a wide period of time or by the number of its editions or copies in circulation. In the areas of East-West relations, a major consideration is the capacity of a work to transcend cultural differences. I have already cited the conclusion of sociologists that the test of a great book is its being read with approval by a public different from that for which it was originally intended. This standard is particularly relevant to the East-West process. As critics we may evaluate texts from any set of criteria or standards we find compatible, but the only certain method of avoiding critical anarchy is to rely on the quality of universal appeal. We may seek the universal without assuming aesthetic absolutes. We may also study subject matter of universal interest, as for example, hunger, sex, crime, parental relations, or love and marriage, and even draw literary conclusions from texts that are not outstanding in literary merit. I am referring here in part to what is known in German as *Trivialliteratur,* but which in English encompasses not really the trivial, but merely that which is not recognized by the Establishment— including such works as *Dracula, Jeeves,* and *Papillon.* In the United States, works of this kind are often studied under the rubric of popular culture.

In summary, a variety of approaches to the study of East-West relations may be taken conjointly without falling into the trap of pseudoscientism. It is also possible to be eclectic without being torn asunder by a battle between conflicting ideologies. To paraphrase one of the sayings of Mao Tse-tung, "let the ancient blend with the modern, and the alien serve China and Japan."

James J. Y. Liu, in commenting on an earlier appearance of part of this chapter in article form, indicates that in favoring a "synthesis of Chinese and Western theories of literature" he does not "mean a grand synthesis of *all* Chinese and Western themes, but only one of *some* elements of certain Chinese themes and *some* elements of certain Western ones" (Liu 1982, 105–6). This is an eminently reasonable position. He argues against critical pluralism, however, on the grounds that "one cannot, for instance, be a structuralist one moment and a phenomenologist the next." Here I am not entirely in agreement. A single musician may play both the piano and the violin, without attempting to perform on the two instruments simultaneously. Although it may not be consistent to combine disparate critical approaches in a single judgment, there is nothing wrong in applying different methods to different texts. Indeed this is absolutely essential. Failure to separate critical approaches would lead to absurdities such as Posnett's examples of "applying the standards of the Athenian to the Japanese drama, or those of the Greek lyric to the *Shih King* of ancient China."

Liu also maintains that "pluralism should not be equated with the abandonment of all standards and the misguided application of the principle of democracy to intellectual endeavors, to the effect that all theories of literature and all critical approaches are created equal." I am in complete agreement, as I have made clear in the preceding pages. Advocating the use of a variety of critical methods is not the same as advocating all or of considering all of equal value. Nor is it equivalent to abdicating standards. It may seem paradoxical, however, to accept Etiemble's "invariables littéraires," as I do, while rejecting a common poetics. My answer is that common poetics is not common standards. There obviously exist common areas in Eastern and Western writing, and we may legitimately seek for the principles or invariables that join them together. But one is not justified in applying the standards of one culture to those of another. Critical rules of judgment are one thing; principles of appreciation are another.

In a sense the dispute over synthesis, shared poetics, or common poetics is a logomachy like much of contemporary critical controversy. James Liu has another phrase that could replace "common poetics" and be generally accepted. This is "comparative poetics." I wholeheartedly join James Liu in his "wish to search for artistic and aesthetic qualities that transcend linguistic, cultural, and historical barriers." This is another way of defining universal literature.

CHAPTER 3. REFERENCES

Ch'ien, Chung-shu. 1979. *Fortress besieged.* Translated by Jeanne Kelly and Nathan K. Mao. Bloomington: Indiana Univ. Press.

Deeney, John J. 1977. New orientations for comparative literature. *Tamkang Review* 8:232–35.

Etiemble, René. 1959. *L'Orient philosophique: Sinophiles et sinophobes.* Paris: C.D.U.

———. 1974. *Essais de littérature (vraiment) générale.* Paris: Gallimard.

Jameson, Frederic. 1972. *Prison house of language.* Princeton, N.J.: Princeton Univ. Press.

Jauss, Hans Robert. 1977. *Aesthetische Erfahrung und literarische Hermeneutik, Band I: Versuche im Feld der aesthetischen Erfahrung.* Munich: W. Fink.

Kushner, Eva. 1978. Diachrony and structure: Thoughts on renewals in the theory of literary history. *Synthesis* 5:21–40.

Lanson, Gustave. 1912. *Trois mois d'enseignement aux Etats-unis.* Paris: Hachette.

———. 1925. *Méthodes de l'histoire littéraire.* Paris: Société des professeurs français en Amérique.

———. 1965. *Essais de méthode, de critique, et d'histoire littéraire.* Ed. Henri Peyre. Paris: Hachette.

Lefevre, André. 1978. Some tactical steps toward a common poetics. *New Asia Academic Bulletin* 1:9–16.

Leibniz, Gottfried W. von [1697] 1957. *The preface to Leibniz' "Novissima Sinica"; Commentary, translation, text.* Honolulu: Univ. of Hawaii Press.

Liu, James J. Y. 1975. The study of Chinese literature in the West: Recent developments, current trends, future prospects. *Journal of Asian Studies* 35:21–30.

———. 1982. *The interlingual critic: Interpreting Chinese poetry.* Bloomington: Indiana Univ. Press.

Mackenzie, Alastair S. 1911. *The evolution of literature.* New York: T. Y. Crowell.

Marino, Adrian. 1979. Etiemble, les "invariants," et la littérature comparée. In *Le Myth d'Etiemble.* Etudes de Littérature Etrangère et Comparée, no. 77. Paris: Didier.

Mounin, Georges. 1978. *La Littérature et ses technocraties.* Paris: Casterman.

Posnett, Hutcheson Macaulay. 1886. *Comparative literature.* New York: D. Appleton Co.

Rosenblatt, Louise M. 1978. *The reader, the text, the poem.* Carbondale, Ill.: Univ. of Southern Illinois Press.

Stegman, André. 1973. Problèmes méthodologiques et terminologiques pour une périodisation en littérature. *Neohelicon* 1:274–85.

Wong, Tak-wai. 1978. Period style and periodization: A survey of theory and practice in the histories of Chinese and European literature. *New Asia Academic Bulletin* 1:45–68.

Wong, W. L. 1978. Selection of lines in Chinese poetry-talk criticism—With a comparison between the selected couplets and Matthew Arnold's "Touchstones." *New Asia Academic Bulletin* 1:33–44.

Yip, Wai-lim. 1978. The Taoist aesthetic: *Wu-yen tu-hua,* the unspeaking, self-generating, self-conditioning, self-transforming, self-complete nature. *New Asia Academic Bulletin* 1:17–32.

Van Tieghem, Paul. 1931. *La Littérature comparée.* Paris: A. Colin.

Yu, Anthony C. 1974. Problems and perspectives in Chinese-Western literary relations. *Yearbook of comparative and general literature* 23:47–53.

4

The Taiwan–Hong Kong Axis

WHEN THE CULTURE OF THE FAR EAST FIRST BECAME KNOWN IN
Europe, it was China that exerted the major influence upon
Western authors; whereas Japan remained practically unknown
until almost modern times. Paradoxically, however, it is Japan,
"a relative newcomer in the family of Oriental cultures," that has
made the dominant impression upon the literature of the United
States (Miner 1958, 269). In so far as this situation is not to be
attributed to a gratuitous accident of history, it seems, according
to Earl Miner,

> most explicable upon the grounds of the needs of Western
> artists in modern times. While some periods, like the middle
> ages, seem to desire new ideas and imaginative materials to fit
> into accepted forms of thought and expression, our modern
> literary artists have sought rather to find new forms with
> which to refresh the tradition and to treat the literary concerns
> of our times. Because our age has been an experimental and
> formalistic era in literature, the search for new forms of ex-
> pression would seem to be the explanation of the modern
> interest in a Japan which our writers have found fertile in its
> literary forms (269).

Today Japan seems to play the role of an intermediary between the East and the West, its high degree of civilization and
technical modernization serving to bring the two cultures closer
together. According to Professor Miner, "some Westerners and
some Japanese have felt that the cultural character or destiny of
Japan has not been to create ideas or philosophies as China and
India have created them, but to re-create through transmission
and refinement what the older Oriental cultures have had to

offer" (270). No matter to what degree this generalization is true, one cannot help noticing a parallel with Japanese industrial achievement, particularly in the development of the automobile, the transistor, and nylon fibers; the latter products are the results of scientific ideas from the outside, like those in the realm of culture, which Japanese ingenuity has modified, improved, and impressed upon the rest of the world. In a broad sense the literature of the United States stands in the same relationship to that of Europe which the literature of Japan bears to that of China. In the two major families of literature, that of the East and that of the West, Japan and the United States may be considered as younger brothers or sisters, even though the disparity in ages is considerable.

Next to the publication of books and periodicals devoted to the study of comparative literature, the best method of promoting the discipline is through meetings and congresses, both on a national and, far more important, international level. Indiana University in the United States has since 1954 organized and hosted quadrennial conferences on oriental-western literary relations, and proceedings of the 1962 and 1966 meetings have been published in the *Yearbook of Comparative and General Literature.* The only truly international comparative literature meetings held in the East have so far not taken place in Japan, despite its historical role as intermediary, but in areas of Chinese culture, specifically Taiwan and Hong Kong. Since close collaboration exists between these two centers and many of the same scholars have attended meetings at Tamkang University in Taiwan and the Chinese University of Hong Kong, I refer to these institutions jointly as the Taiwan–Hong Kong axis. The following account of these meetings is offered primarily as a historical record, to show the nature of research already undertaken and to indicate possible future directions.

The first conference devoted entirely to comparative literature held in the East and attended by scholars from both hemispheres took place at Tamkang University in the summer of 1971. In the opening address the president of the institution, Clement C. P. Chang, observed the advantage for both sides in inspecting the achievements of the other and in looking at one's own literature from drastically dissimilar perspectives and by so doing discerning "qualities which a native viewpoint would never dream of finding."

The keynote of the conference was struck by the late Professor Shih-hsiang Chen in a stimulating portrayal of the orthodox view that lyricism is typical of the literature surrounding China in contrast with the epic and dramatic traditions that dominate the Occident. In the ensuing discussion Claudio Guillén took issue with the European phase of this dichotomy, pointing to the richness of European lyrical poetry in the Renaissance, the Romantic Period, and the Symbolist movement. The Western tradition, Guillén properly insisted, is multiform and manifold, not monolithic. I would add that the American poet Edgar Allan Poe in his essay on the poetic principle argued that all true poetry is short poetry and claimed for the Western lyric essentially the same qualities that Professor Chen attributed to the Chinese. A defender of Professor Chen argued, however, that this eminent scholar did not intend to deny the lyrical accomplishment of the West, but rather to point out that criticism in the East has emphasized the lyric nature of poetry, whereas that of the West has been primarily occupied with the problem of epic and dramatic verse. Strangely enough none of the participants introduced the topic of the epic in Japan and the possibilities of indicating resemblances in this tradition to Western poetic narratives.

Because of the emphasis on lyricism it was quite appropriate that a paper should have been devoted to a consideration of a volume of English translations of contemporary Chinese poets of Taiwan. The editor of the volume, Wai-lim Yip, can be himself considered a symbol of the coalescence of the literatures of the East and West. A native Chinese, he has taught at the University of California, San Diego; the National Taiwan University; and the Chinese University of Hong Kong. The poets in his anthology, as Irving Yucheng Lo revealed, combine the influence of classical models and philosophy with modern themes and techniques. Wai-lim Yip himself participated in the congress by analyzing the "esthetic of pure experience" in the work of a classic eighth-century Chinese poet, Wang Wei, translating many passages into English and citing several parallels in the work of modern American and German poets.

In pure literary criticism, the major contribution of the week was Claudio Guillén's percipient application of the linguistic theories of Roman Jakobson to the Chinese tradition, particularly the principle of the "bipolar structure of language" as related to poetic expression in parallel verse. Guillén's interpretation of ancient Chinese texts by means of twentieth-century techniques led Charles Witke in a subsequent session to refer to a great American scholar of Chinese linguistics by posing the question, will Edward Schoeffer and Roman Jakobson ever meet? Guillén and Witke suggested not only the bringing together of the two great streams of literature in the world, but also the mutual application of critical and linguistic techniques. Unfortunately their prescriptions have remained in the area of the abstract rather than the practical.

The topic of literary criticism and that of the application of Western literary theory and methods to the study of Chinese literature seemed to merge or at least to overlap in several papers dealing with one or the other of these topics. Several excellent critical expositions belong to this joint category. Father Fernando Mateos, in treating the linguistic and conceptual structure of the Chinese proverb, not only analyzed these elements but translated many proverbs and supplied similar parallels from the West. Dean Kao Ming presented an analysis of the relations between Chinese languages and literature somewhat in the manner of Herder's treatment of the German national character as reflected in folklore and legend. John Y. H. Hu analyzed the fourteenth-century *Lute Song* of Kao Ming in the light of Aristotle's definition of tragedy in order to demonstrate the existence in the classical Chinese theater of tragic drama corresponding to the ancient Greek conception. Lily C. Winters applied the techniques of psychoanalytical criticism to conclude that a famous poem *Li Sao* by Ch'u Yuan resembles in its emotional tensions much of the poetry of English romanticism. We shall see below that this classic Chinese text of the fourth-century B.C. has been compared to various other Western works.

The topic of translation was the most popular and perhaps least rewarding of those treated in the conference. Translation has been the theme of innumerable congresses, including those of the International Federation for Modern Languages and Literature and the International Comparative Literature Association, and in English alone the bibliography concerning the theory of translation is staggering. By and large the papers of the Taiwan conference completely ignored previous publications and offered little on theory or general problems of translation that had not already been covered by previous authors. Most speakers were concerned with the translation of Chinese poetry into English and thus based their remarks exclusively on anthologies of actual translations or on their own experience. The primary value of these studies consisted in their pragmatism and references to specific texts. Tsu-wen Chen in particular offered useful illustrations of key passages in English translations of Chinese poetry, and Anacleta M. Encarnación provided an example of parallel Spanish and Tagalog translations of an English original. Obviously there exist special problems in the translation of an oriental language based on symbolic characters into an occidental one using an alphabet, or the reverse, but these special problems were not at all singled out or developed by the papers. Very useful for bibliographical reasons, however, was Roy E. Teele's exposition entitled "Trends in Translation of Chinese Poetry, 1950–70," a critical commentary on the major publications during this period.

A Japanese scholar, Saburō Ōta, considered literary translations from a sociological perspective. In summarizing a survey of the reading habits of seven thousand employees of a Tokyo factory, he revealed that of the 80 percent who showed any interest in literature at all, eight out of ten workers preferred Western writers in translation to native authors. The common reader in Japan at that time seemed to enjoy Western novels that could be characterized as traditional or classical. In the year just before the congress, according to Saburō Ōta, the French *nouveau roman* and American novels of the beat generation had been introduced to Japan, but only the critics paid any attention to them. This circumstance paralleled the situation in France reported by Robert Escarpit at the 1970 meeting of the International Comparative Literature Association. In France only professional critics were impressed by such esoteric authors as Robbe-Grillet, and publishers had difficulty in selling an edition of a few thousand copies; whereas *Papillon,* a type of rogue autobiography scorned by the critics, sold millions of copies.

Both in the East and the West, students of comparative literature need to ponder the question raised by Escarpit: are literary critics making a mistake by devoting most of their talents and energies to works that fail to demonstrate any kind of universal appeal?

Throughout the conference opinion was sharply divided concerning the role that the reading of translations should play in the formal study of comparative literature. The majority, however, felt that translations were indispensable for any realistic crossing of the literary barriers between East and West. A convincing practical example of the possibility of drawing valid aesthetic conclusions from translated texts alone was provided in the section of Claudio Guillén's paper dealing with Chinese poetry. Charles Witke and Father Miguel A. Bernad tended to hold firm, however, to the requirement that all comparative study be based upon texts in the original language. Witke drew a parallel between Chinese in the East and Greek and Latin in the West as the languages of tradition and urged that academic programs in comparative literature be based upon them. A member of the audience, however, objected that these three languages were not really parallel, since Chinese is both a traditional and a modern tongue in use today in contrast to classical Greek and Latin, which are considered dead languages.

Several excellent studies were based on the method of rapprochement or the revealing of analogies without direct contact. A paper by Hen-hsiung Jeng traced the theme of metamorphosis through representative myths in Greek and Bunun, an aboriginal language of Taiwan. As indicated previously, Lily Winters discerned psychological links between *Li Sao* and English Romanticism. Another speaker, Ching-hsien Wang, linked *Li Sao* with Spenser's Renaissance philosophical epic, *The Faerie Queene.* By drawing attention to "formative tropes," Wang succeeded in placing the two poems in a common literary category—that of the allegorical quest. This designation of *Li Sao,* together with the author's elaboration of sartorial emblems, would seem to provide a notable exception to Professor Chen's principle of lyricism as a dominant and prevailing characteristic of Chinese poetry. In the genre of drama, Josephine Huang Hung pointed out resemblances between *The Riverside Pavilion,* a thirteenth-century play by Kuan Han-ch'ing, and G. B. Shaw's nineteenth-century *Candida*. Here the resemblances are based upon character portrayal and the reflection of life. In the related area of pedagogy, Father Bernad embarked upon a novel theme, the techniques of explaining difficult passages in Shakespeare to Chinese university students.

Relatively few papers treated the topic of the relations between China and other Asian and Pacific countries and only three broached that of relations between China and the West. Especially revealing to Western comparatists was Kōki Satō's exposition, "The Role of Classical Chinese in the Introduction of Western Civilization to Japan, Mainly in the First Half of the Meiji Era." According to Satō, Chinese characters or calligraphy were instrumental in the penetration of Western literature into the island empire since the Japanese had access to English works only through Chinese and Dutch editions. Dutch was the only Western language allowed to be studied in Japan during the first half of the nineteenth century and at that only for medical and military purposes. In conventional terms the West served as emitter, Japan was the receiver, and China acted as an intermediary. Japanese editors used Chinese characters for the introducing of Western literature primarily because of the great prestige enjoyed by the Chinese language among the Japanese upper class, a circumstance parallel to the vogue of French at the court of Frederick the Great of Prussia during the eighteenth century.

Satō's exposition of the dependence of nineteenth-century Japan upon China for the dissemination of Western literature gives rise to several intriguing questions. Does this mean that until recent times Japanese should be considered a minor literature and Chinese a major one? Has the West now completely superseded China as the primary source of literary inspiration for Japan? Has Japanese tradition in the past been as much committed to the lyric as has Chinese? If so, do the recent Japanese achievements in fiction represent the breaking away from tradition? Or do they represent the development of new trends based entirely upon Western rather than oriental models? No answers were given in Motoi Oda's paper "A Comparison in Literary Expression Between the Chinese and the Japanese," which revealed linguistic connections but did not concern itself with literary history.

A study of the influence of Chinese tradition over Korean literature revealed that Chinese models affected the myths and legends of Korea, at least in their written form, and that most early Korean novels were imitations of the Chinese. Another paper on Korea by Masaie Matsumura treated in depth the relationship between a classic seventeenth-century novel, *The Cloud Dream of the Nine,* and its major Chinese source *Hsi-Yu Chi, The Journey to the West,* by Wu Ch'eng-en. Matsumura also traced the adaptation of the Korean work by a Japanese author, Tenko Komiyama, a novel called *Mugen* published in the last decade of the nineteenth century.

Elmer A. Ordoñez presented a historical survey of the penetration of Chinese culture in the Philippines from the sixteenth century to the present. His treatment of linguistic assimilation, folklore, mercantile relations, academic curricula, periodical publications, and selected poetry revealed that close historical ties with Asian countries had not been entirely broken down by the subsequent association of Filipinos with Spanish and American literatures. Cirilo F. Bautista, in studying the writing of poetry in English by natives of the Philippines, exposed what he considered a "dichotomous personality" in that poetry. Contrary to the situation in many Commonwealth areas, the use of English apparently represented a disturbing current without direction rather than a positive force. The native Tagalog language, the Spanish of earlier generations, and the English imposed by the American occupation vie with each other for the attention of writers and readers, and this competition—instead of making a better product as in modern commerce—leads to a climate of tentativeness and indecision. According to Bautista, much of the best contemporary writing in the Philippines is *engagé* or committed to social reform, and its exponents waver between Tagalog and English, neither of which is the ideal medium.

The topic of literary relations between China and the West produced only two studies devoted to historical contacts or direct source-influence relationship. Rikutarō Fukuda in "Ezra Pound and the Orient" supplied new and fascinating biographical information concerning Pound's admiration of Tagore, his relations with Japanese intellectuals, his visits to Japan, his interest in Japanese Noh plays, and his correspondence with a Japanese poet, Katsue Kitazono.

I presented the paper entitled "Voltaire and the Cult of China," which is printed in the second section of the present book, but apart from this paper the conference produced no studies of what Jean-Marie Carré has called "mirage," the illusion that one national culture assumes in the literature of another nation. The image of China has figured largely as symbol and source in nearly all Western literatures from the seventeenth century to the present and has been widely analyzed in French and American scholarship. So far as I know, however, no scholar in the West has yet studied in detail the impressions recorded in seventeenth-, eighteenth- or nineteenth-century Chinese letters of the Western missionaries, travelers, diplomats, and adventurers who forced their way into the Middle Kingdom. A Japanese-born scholar teaching in the United States, Chieko Mulhern, however, has published an extensive article showing that the Jesuits introduced the Italian Cinderella cycle into a Japanese genre of *otogizōshi* tales (a dominant genre originating in the medieval period) (*Monumenta Nipponica,* Tokyo, 1979). The stepdaughter theme itself, however, is anterior not only to the Jesuits, but also to the famous *Tale of Genji*. It is to be found in a tenth-century precursor, *Tale of the Lady Ochikubo*.

The reason for the scant coverage in the conference of the impact of the East upon Western nations is obvious. People who belong to a culture affected by some exterior force are the ones who ordinarily discuss that influence. Chinese and Japanese scholars, therefore, both in the conference and elsewhere, have been impelled to study the impact of European or American writers upon their own Eastern literature. It is Westerners who are most likely to treat the influence of oriental literatures upon Europe or America, and in this conference as in later ones Westerners were in the minority. Of those Westerners who presented papers, two chose theoretical subjects, four discussed literary genres or translations, two did not treat East-West relations at all, and only one treated the influence of China on the West.

Although excelling in studies of themes and in parallels between ancient Chinese texts and modern Western ones, the conference was disappointing in the area of literary history. One would have liked to be told more concerning the earliest introduction of oriental literatures to the West and to have had occasional references to periods of Western literature before the twentieth century. A paper by Toshio Hatakenaka, however, analyzed an eighteenth-century Vietnamese narrative, *Kim Van Kieû,* concerning the misfortunes of a young girl, whose sufferings seem almost as extreme as those of another eighteenth-century victim of circumstance, the Marquis de Sade's Justine. It has been known for some time that the source of this Vietnamese poem is a Chinese novel in prose, and Professor Hatakenaka compared this source-influence relationship to Corneille's indebtedness for *Le Cid* to the Spanish *El Cid* of Guillén de Castro.

Rikutarō Fukuda in his paper on Ezra Pound alluded in passing to Tagore and another Bengali author, but otherwise no speaker referred to the rich literature of India, in earlier periods an important intermediary between China and the West. The emphasis in nearly every paper was either on two or three Eastern literatures or on English or American literature combined with a single Eastern literature. It is true, as I have already indicated, that one cannot expect even a superior scholar to have a command of several languages of both the West and the East. At the same time one must make a distinction between what an individual is capable of doing and what a collective body should be able to do. Despite its announced dedication to the literatures of the West as well as the East, the conference unquestionably slighted the literatures of the European continent. The explanation for the virtual monopoly of English is, of course, both political and sociological. Since the English language has been adopted almost uniformly throughout the East as the instrument of business and technology, literary scholars tend to assume that the language should have the same priority when considered as a cultural instrument. There is no reason to question the importance of English literature except to recognize that it is only one force among several equal or nearly equal forces, and not by any means a giant among a tribe of quaint dwarfs.

Sociological overtones kept obtruding into the conference in seminar discussions, particularly in reference to translations and to the simplification of Eastern languages, which was then gradually taking place. Many observers were convinced that the younger generation in the Eastern countries was resentful of many previously sacred literary and linguistic traditions, if not in open revolt against them. Young people in this part of the world no longer implicitly accepted the prestige assigned to the classics any more than they uniformly accepted conventional oriental social patterns, considered as great virtues by some Western participants, particularly a tightly knit family structure and respect for old age. For the younger generation, the West is indubitably the symbol of the modern era. None of the participants of the congress lost sight of the relationship between literature and life, despite the abstract tone and theoretical perspective that pervaded many of the sessions.

It is difficult to draw conclusions based on a theme as vast as East-West relations and the six aspects covered by this congress. A good beginning would be to quote Claudio Guillén's warning that "one tends to believe that to identify a problem is to be well on the way toward its solution." Since the conference was a pioneer effort, there was an overabundance of well-intentioned theory and generalizing and a corresponding shortage of the concrete—whether in literary history or in concentration on specific literary texts. The documentation of some papers was sparse—occasionally nonexistent—and the serious auditor could not help wondering on what authority some of the sweeping generalizations were made.

A second conference held at Tamkang University four years later (August 1975) again offered a preponderance of theory, primarily because of the announced theme of the conference, "Literary Theory and Criticism East and West." It is also true that this is an area in which scholars from East and West can communicate without knowing much or even anything at all about the actual literatures of the other culture. One may argue, however, as I have done in previous chapters, that art is universal and, therefore, common elements may be ascertained in any of the literatures of the world. One may also observe that actual physical contacts between the two cultures have taken place historically and that specifically because of this contact the development of particular phenomena in each culture, including literary ones, has been affected. This principle is not only valid, but capable of producing significant literary knowledge and understanding.

Professor Limin Chu formally introduced the proposal that comparative study in the East be organized on the principle of applying Western methods of literary criticism to the study of both classical and modern Chinese and Japanese literature, and this principle turned into the unofficial theme of the conference. Other speakers, both Eastern and Western, tended to doubt the value and practicality of this suggestion. In defense of his position Professor Chu observed that the Chinese scholar in approaching his own literature is unable to fathom the Chinese mind and that he is helped to do so by enlisting Western methods of criticism. This is one of the most valid arguments in favor of the comparative method, particularly if the principle is not confined to the application of critical methods that are narrow or transitory. A similar intellectual myopia is likely to affect Americans who study the literature of the United States exclusively, even though they possess the presumed advantage of Western critical methods.

The strongest and most precise statement of misgivings concerning the general application of the principle of applying Western criticism to Eastern literature came from David Malone. He pointed out that some linguists and anthropologists have maintained that language itself raises almost impenetrable barriers to the perception and cognition of other cultures. Even more serious, the axioms of Western literature and Western culture have themselves come under attack in the West. The cultural assumptions of occidental literary criticism reflect a social structure badly in need of reform, and the very values embodied in Western culture are in many ways questionable. Some of these "self-conscious" and "self-justifying" values that, according to Professor Malone, may not be relevant to the products of other cultures are the glorification of the individual, the wholesale acceptance of Freudian psychological theories, and the segregation of the poet or literary creator from society. Historically, moreover, the Western nations have "dealt with the rest of the world in an essentially imperialistic manner."

This arrogant pattern of imperialism, Harry Levin pointed

out, has its roots in the culture of the ancient Greeks, who considered everyone else in the world barbarians. The paradox in the concept of empire, either political or cultural, is that its proponents attempt to be both nationalistic and universal—nationalistic by maintaining their own superiority and universal by attempting to enforce their own pattern of behavior upon the rest of the world. Levin treated the parallel phenomenon in literature. He indicated the existence since the time of Goethe of a general yearning for a world culture and a world literature, despite the warning of critics like André Gide that every great writer must first of all "find himself" by immersion in his own nationality. Levin also cited the protest of Alexander Pope that applying the theories of Aristotle to Shakespeare is like judging a citizen by the laws of a country other than his own. Once again the parallel with East-West relations is obvious. Indicating points of similarity between two literatures does not in itself infringe upon the individual character of either one, but a pattern of judging Eastern works by the standards of Western criticism would almost certainly tend to diminish Eastern national identities. When the editors of the *Tamkang Review* drew up their statement of principles, it is perhaps more important that they affirmed the right of expressing "a Chinese point of view, especially toward Chinese literature," than that they guarded themselves against the implication of being nationalistic or parochial in their perspective.

It is, therefore, appropriate that another major theme of the second Tamkang conference should have been the metaphysical basis of Chinese calligraphy and poetic expression. Gunther Debon of the University of Heidelberg based an explanation of the Chinese lyric upon an interpretation of its ontological *situs*. In regard to the absence of the personal pronoun in Chinese diction, he pointed out that the subject observing and the object being observed are not clearly separated as they are in Western language and culture. "Indeed, an identification of the artist with the object he is depicting was elevated to the status of an ideal, particularly under the influence of Taoist mysticism." In further developing this principle, Debon revealed that frequently there exists in addition an emotional identification between the poet and the natural object. "One piece of evidence for this is the word *ch'ing* which describes not only the feelings, but the emotional condition of the person, but also the emotional situation of the object in nature." This seems to be essentially the same condition that John Ruskin condemned as the "pathetic fallacy." This expression is still quite prevalent in modern English criticism, and as a result of Ruskin's derogatory reference, the imparting of feelings to objects in nature is now generally considered a blemish in English poetry. Presumably Chinese poetry would not gain very much by the application of this particular element of Western critical theory. A passage quoted by Wai-lim Yip concerning Jean Dubuffet's portrayal of Western culture may explain why Ruskin, unlike Chinese poets, prefers the stones of architecture to animate nature; the occidental mind conceives of the nature of man as "very different from the nature of other beings in the world. . . . The Western man has, at least, a great contempt for trees and rivers, and hates to be like them. . . . the so-called primitive man loves and admires trees and rivers. . . . He has a very strong sense of continuity of all things." Debon presented an extended parallelism between the lyric of Europe and that of China based upon characteristics developed by Emile Steiger, but he also offered a superb simile of his own concerning the differences between the two: "Whereas the Latin sentences correspond to a piece of constructed masonry, the Chinese words glide like pearls on a tray touching each other only slightly," if at all.

The inherent ambiguity of Chinese diction was stressed by Tse-tsung Chow in his discussion of the sense beyond words, revealing a radical difference between the epistemological function of the poetry of China and that of European cultures. He revealed that the thrust of Chinese lyric poetry points to something called *yi,* which "inhabits" the poem as a result of the words in the poem but is "beyond" the words. This seems to be a blend of ambiguity with intuition, but Chow made clear that the experience conveyed or created in a Chinese lyric poem is not a "moral," still less a message, not even an intuition—but a sense. This suggests both perception before conceptualization and understanding before analysis, of what a phenomenon or reality is.

The ontological basis of Chinese poetry was further utilized by

Hugh Kenner in a treatment of the development of Symbolist doctrine in both France and the United States. I cannot hope to digest in two or three sentences Kenner's concept of translingual poetics, a subject that he indicated deserves at the very least an entire book. His thesis, however, is clear; that certain nineteenth-century Western scholars misinterpreted Chinese poetry by reading into it moral elevation or solemnity, and that certain Symbolists also misconstrued Chinese poetry, but in a contrary direction, by exaggerating the pictorial nature of the ideograph. Pound and others conceived of Chinese poetry as representing an ontologically independent world and then used the notion as the basis of a theory in which "the organic poem's molecules could be words in a comparably organic language." Kenner argued that as an interpretation of Chinese calligraphy this is an erroneous theory, but as an explanation of the poetic process per se it is a close approximation to truth. In his words, the "poem should seem not to have come from an author but from the secret forces of language."

Douwe W. Fokkema studied the same problem of linguistic transference, but shifted the focus of attention from Symbolism to Expressionism. At the same time he widened the area of discussion to embrace not only the relation between the word and the object in regard to the nature of reality, but also the meaning of human experience in phenomenological terms in regard to the threefold nature of truth, that is, "material," "logical," and "poetical." He isolated dichotomies between the word and the world, or the symbol and the meaning, in both Western and Eastern languages, but observed in addition that the understanding of literature requires more than the deciphering of symbols or iconic relations. Even "the focus on the message for its own sake" implies and requires the consideration of the social and literary background against which a given text is interpreted. Fokkema then illustrated his principle that "we cannot abstract literary texts from the context in which they function" by citing the history of the development of Expressionism in West-European literature and its reception in China. In so doing, he outlined a system to obviate one of the main difficulties in treating the comparative history of literature, that of periodization, or the existence of phenomena in one literature that are not to be discovered in another literature in the same segment of time, but in a later one. The system described by Fokkema consists in the construction of a "code" or a series of information signs representing basic features of the texts under consideration. The code of one particular literary period or movement may come into contact with those of other periods or movements in roughly the same cultural region or area. Fokkema expressed doubts, however, about the possibility of transplanting codes used for European phenomena to Asia literature without appropriate revision or redefinition.

The freedom of Chinese calligraphy from the personal identification represented by pronouns in Western languages, together with its apparent ontological independence, may be related to what has been called "the loss of self" in modern literature and art of the West. Wai-lim Yip attempted to explain the link between language and the world by a theory of models in mental constructions—that is, by an interpretation of the thinking process. In contrast to the theories of "monoculture-oriented critics and scholars," he argued that people have different perceptions of reality according to the culture in which they live and that these differences are reflected not only in their responses to linguistic symbols, but also in the nature of linguistic symbols themselves. The two major systems of this kind are, of course, the Western alphabets and the Chinese ideograms, and each functions in a different way. The use of words or "alphabet thinking tends toward elaboration of abstract ideas, analytical discursiveness and syllogistic progression"; whereas the use of ideograms permits the thinker "to perceive concretely in images and objects, to arrest things in their simultaneous multiple spatial relationships, and to suggest and represent an abstract idea by keeping close to the total environment captured in a composite image." Yip treated this difference not only as a problem to be faced in the translation of literary works from one language to another, but equally a problem in the comparative study of Eastern and Western literatures. He asked how a common ground may be reached between the two systems or "models"—whether the notion of universality proclaimed by Plato and Aristotle may be pragmatically realized in literary understanding. Rejecting both the rational approach of Greek-based philosophy and the positive-negative binary system of Lévi-Strauss, Yip doubted the possibility of constructing an artificial language mediating between Eastern and Western systems. As a solution, he proposed to discard the attempt to create a single or uniform "model," but to begin simultaneously with two or three "models," shading into each other, and making full use of comparison and contrast. The area of overlapping, he maintained, represents the arena in which East-West comparatists may work with a reasonable chance of success. Yip also suggested that his method of overlapping models may help to reconcile or minimize the well-publicized differences between the French and the American schools of comparative literature.

An original solution to the problems represented by the three types of truth—material, logical, and poetical—was offered by Vincent Shih under the designation of "The Second Harmony." He suggested that a state of mind may be reached in life in which the world of truth and the world of the senses coalesce; in other words, that noumenal and phenomenal perception may occur simultaneously. This condition of feeling an identity with nature beyond logical verification may also be attained by the poet through the exercise of his functions. Shih gave two examples of this state of mind, one from the New Testament and the other from a statement by a Chan master. The first text is the parable of the Prodigal Son, who after leaving home returns chastened by experience and is joyously received by his father, for he "was dead and is alive again; and was lost and is found." In the second text, the Chan master affirms, "Thirty years ago before I was initiated into Chanism, the mountains I saw were mountains and the rivers I saw were rivers. Then I was initiated into Chanism: mountains were no longer mountains and rivers no longer rivers. Now that I have penetrated into the mystery, mountains are just mountains and rivers rivers."

The common element in these narratives is a kind of mystical epistemology or a metaphysical return to nature. Both the prodigal son and the Chan master have learned through experience with the problems of life—moral for one, intellectual for the other—that naive perception in a condition of innocence provides the deepest internal satisfaction and access to reality. Shih provided a number of texts from Chinese poetry to illustrate this

second harmony, which is attained through a return to the state
of innocence beyond the ken of logical reasoning and linguistic
expression. Several of these texts such as the following one
come from Lao-tzu:

> Leave not the eternal virtue,
> Return to the state of a babe.

Shih's opening parallel with the New Testament could be extended by referring to the theme of childhood as it is portrayed in
various sayings of Christ, the best-known of which is the exhortation in Matthew 18: "Except ye be converted, and become as
little children, ye shall not enter into the kingdom of heaven."
Shih's exposition of the significance of the second harmony
could be utilized almost without change in a sermon on this New
Testament text. I intend the parallel, however, as purely literary,
not theological.

So far in this survey of Chinese metaphysics, I have discussed
papers that share certain premises about the essential nature of
Chinese poetry, particularly that it is impersonal and unemo-
tional, that it utilizes symbol and metaphor to a very high degree, and that this vast body of ancient and modern texts is
relatively uniform and static. These papers have suggested, to
use a Western form of reference, that Chinese poetry has more
in common with the aesthetic theories of Ezra Pound and T. S.
Eliot than with those of Wordsworth. Quite the contrary perspective was presented by Chu-Whan Cha in his exposition of
the theories of a fifth-century critic Chung Hung concerning the
ideal characteristics of poetry. Far from rejecting intense feeling,
this ancient critic considered it to be the primary requisite for
poetic creation. Cha specifically cited Wordsworth and paraphrased his famous dictum in informing us of the oriental critic's
parallel requirement of "the spontaneous expression of natural
emotion." Cha also quoted T. S. Eliot's no less famous definition
of the "objective correlative" and his praise of "emotion which
has its life in the poem and not in the history of the poet." But
instead of indicating agreement with this perspective, Cha cited
approvingly an opposing attitude in the thought of the ancient
critic. The latter says nothing about controlling emotion and

"seems to believe that personal experience of the poet is a potent factor of bringing significant emotion in the poetry." In regard to figures of speech, the ancient critic warned against excessive application of a single mode, either metaphor or description. Cha, in this connection, made an adverse comment concerning Western immoderate indulgence in symbolism, which in his words may be counted as a "self-glorifying agent of metaphor."

Needless to say, Cha and Kenner reveal completely different aesthetic values concerning this point; yet both believe that their standards of excellence are consistent with, if not directly derived from, Chinese traditions. The logical conclusion must be that Chinese poetry is not quite so monolithic as suggested by the majority of the papers presented. It seems to me that Cha's exposition could serve as a model for a type of East-West literary criticism, but of a somewhat different type from that advocated by Limin Chu. Instead of taking Western criticism as a standard of authority and applying it to Chinese literary works, one might also, and perhaps even more profitably, take Chinese literary criticism and Western literary criticism, both ancient and modern, and compare them one to the other.

Saburō Ōta, in treating Chinese tradition as reflected in modern Japanese writers, gave two examples of applying oriental standards to Western literature—one that he considered successful, the other, unsuccessful. One of the Japanese writers he treated had used Chinese critical vocabulary to interpret a poem by Wordsworth, and the technique had worked—perhaps because the poem was heavily laden with metaphysics and the concept of transcendentalism. The second notable example concerned the analysis of the character of Lady Macbeth from the perspective of Confucian ethics, a technique that Ōta branded as a failure.

The impression that Chinese poetry from ancient times to modern has followed a single tradition with essentially no variation was completely shattered by Ch'ing-ping Yeh in his treatment of conservatism and originality in Chinese literature. He indicated that the dominant conservatism of Chinese culture may give the impression of a cyclical pattern of literary history rather than one of continuous progress, but that various creative and original voices have continually pressed for reform so that a pattern of development may be discerned in which "Chinese literature seems to step two paces forward and one pace backward." In reaching this conclusion, Professor Yeh sketched a critical debate closely resembling that in Western literature known as the Quarrel of Ancients and Moderns, a polemic that raged furiously among European critics in the sixteenth, seventeenth, and eighteenth centuries and is still in a sense going on. The Moderns in the West particularly sought to discredit Aristotle, just as the Chinese creative critics cited by Yeh attempted to combat the weight of tradition.

The themes of the Third Tamkang conference in 1979 were considerably broader, comprising literature and social milieu, Chinese images in world literature, and intra-Asian comparative studies. Horst Frenz, in the keynote address on Eugene O'Neill and China, appropriately touched upon the first two of these themes. Pointing out that O'Neill not only visited China but read widely in oriental thought and religion, Frenz argued that one of his most successfully plays, *Marco Millions,* may be interpreted as a symbolic juxtaposition of Western materialism with the subtle quietude of the Orient. In other words, O'Neill's indirect espousal of the ancient philosophy of China may be seen as his reaction to the frustrations inherent in modern American society. Frenz suggested, moreover, that on a more subtle level, Polo symbolizes the typical Western mind as incapable of understanding the mystical wisdom of the East. In one direction Chinese religion and philosophy acted as a catalyst upon O'Neill's creative processes, and in the other O'Neill's innovations in dramaturgy inspired Chinese playwrights to adopt various modern methods of staging, as Frenz revealed in a number of examples of transformation or assimilation.

Another American even more extensively indebted to Asia was a fellow Nobel prize winner, Pearl S. Buck, whose career was briefly sketched by Yuh-chao Yü. The daughter of missionaries, Buck spent her childhood in China, learning to speak Chinese before English, and during her first years of marriage taught English at the University of Nanking. In analyzing her literary works, Yü revealed that her Asian novels, which contain many parallels to the conventions of Chinese narrative, enjoyed greater success than her American ones. The influence of Asia was so important to Buck's life and literary art, according to Yü, that she may be described as a "highly Chinese American writer."

A distinct philosophical approach characterized several of the papers concerning literature and milieu. Perceiving that literary history and literary criticism are frequently products of social change, Wai-lim Yip isolated some of the basic ideological problems that underlie scholarly studies of modern Chinese literature. According to his analysis, all literary history is inevitably partial and selective; even that which appears to be the most objective is based upon the dominant climate of opinion or the milieu. Paradoxically, even though a complete or entire historical perspective is impossible to attain, the awareness of the need for the encompassing of totality is, nevertheless, indispensable. Applying these theoretical considerations to the investigation of Chinese literature subsequent to the period of the May 4th Movement in 1919, in which the impulse toward Westernization established itself upon the Chinese consciousness, Yip argued that standards and goals of one culture (the Western) are not necessarily applicable to conditions in another (the Chinese). The transplantation of Euro-American ideologies and literary theories, a process motivated by a sincere desire to expedite institutional and social reforms, led in China to confusion and even threatened loss of national cultural identity. This is the root of the "love-hate" relationship in which modern Chinese intellectuals confront the antagonisms between traditional and Western cultural modes. Yip took issue with literary historians and critics who select and emphasize only certain aspects of this highly complex social process, questioning, for example, the assumption that what is true of Western literary masterpieces must also be true of native Chinese works. He also provided a number of illustrations of the manner in which literary historians may be led astray by superficial and inconsequential resemblances between Chinese and Western texts—incidentally revealing how comparatist methodology is susceptible to exaggeration or misapplication. In a searching analysis of Western Romanticism, Yip demonstrated that Chinese critics have been even more confused than Western ones in interpreting the movement. Finally, Yip inculcated the principles that both in social reform and in literary criticism, conflicting ideologies cannot be simultaneously absorbed, that Chinese intellectuals must examine each Western ideology individually on its own merits, and that only those which stand the test of scrutiny should be, in Yip's language, appropriated—that is, adapted to native conditions.

In a complementary investigation of modern Chinese literature, Leo Ou-fan Lee adopted a somewhat more pragmatic approach, treating actual history rather than historiography. In a sense, providing concrete examples to illustrate Yip's generalizations, Lee quoted from the prospectus of a poetry journal of the 1950s that advocated "horizontal transplantation" from the West rather than "vertical inheritance" from native roots. In a useful attempt to eliminate some of the ambiguities inherent in the terms *modernism* and *modern,* Lee distinguished first of all in the Western context the distinction between modernity as a stage in civilization characterized by science, technology, and capitalism, and modernism as an aesthetic system that fostered currents such as Symbolism, Cubism, and Surrealism and represented, for the most part, a reaction against bourgeois complacence and material values associated with the industrial age. In China, however, the original stages of modernism that grew out of the May 4th manifestations did not embody this dichotomy, but instead combined wholesale acceptance of Western notions of material progress with a demand for realism or the reflection of authentic life in literature. In Taiwan after World War II, dedication to the material values of the West continued or even increased in society as a whole, and many writers turned to the West in addition for new literary models. Although one manifesto proclaimed a dedication to "all new schools of Western poetry since Baudelaire," the authors subscribing to this manifesto passed over the late-nineteenth-century currents that Lee had previously defined as modernism in favor of twentieth-century writers ranging from Joyce to Sartre. After this second round of Euro-American influence, however, writers in Taiwan began to develop neorealism, turning away from metaphysical poetry, reaffirming vernacular idioms, and striving for "an honest, true-to-life provincialism" that reflected a deep attachment to the land and to its people.

The contrasting aesthetic values of an ancient Chinese treatise and those of Russian and Anglo-American formalists were brought into sharp relief by Ch'iu-liang Chi, who only partly disguised his preference for the Chinese tradition. The treatise that he discussed, *The Literary Mind and the Carving of Dragons,* was written in the fifth century by Liu Hsieh, who like Aristotle in the West represents the fountainhead of his literary tradition. In his exposition, Chi concentrated on the concept of novelty or in formalist terms, defamiliarization. He revealed that in the Chinese tradition naturalness and truthfulness hold priority over novelty and that neither the author of *The Literary Mind* nor he himself adheres to defamiliarization or the exalting of deviations from existing conventions.

The title of a related paper by Donald Wesling, "Methodological Implications of the Philosophy of Jacques Derrida for Comparative Literature: The Opposition East-West and Several Other Oppositions," seemed to recommend the adoption in the East of one of the latest fashions in Western criticism, but in actuality the author exposed the weaknesses of this particular form of poststructuralism. According to Wesling, "Derrida does not just complicate, enormously, the relation between language and the practical world of things and actions, he writes as if there is no relation whatsoever." In reference to East-West comparative literature, Westling subjected some of the articles in the *New Asia Academic Bulletin* to Derrida's method of deconstruction and granted to the method a degree of validity in exposing methodological inconsistencies, even though the same common-sense approach that Wesling used in his own analysis would bring these same logical deficiencies to light. Wesling also revealed the fallacies in Derrida's theories concerning the supposed antilogocentrism of Chinese written characters. He granted that prevalent attitudes which perceive a basic philosophical East-West opposition need to be destroyed, but concluded that the "undoing will not be accomplished merely by bringing French fashions to the Far East."

An even less sympathetic attitude toward poststructuralism surfaced in Charles Witke's comment that "the metaphysical acrobats of many literature departments in universities in America and Europe may think these days that error is more worthy of study than truth." Objecting to Andrew H. Plaks's theory that organizing principles of "complementary bipolarity" and "multiple periodicity" exist in Chinese literary compositions but not in European, Witke produced a number of convincing examples from Western classical antiquity of these presumably significant touchstones, his examples ranging from passages of Platonic philosophy to a hedonistic ode by Horace. Witke agreed that the comparative method may be used for the purpose of "illuminating a complex and monumental work like the *Dream of the Red Chamber* with an awareness of Western allegory" (Plaks's stated objective), but warned that "an understanding of the symbolic processes of literature in any language and the mythic dimensions of human life in any culture must be superordinate to the formulation of anything so broad as a given culture's literary aesthetics." One might add that in literary criticism as in life much is in the eye of the beholder, including monistic, dualistic, and multifarious theories. Even in the post-classical period, which Witke did not discuss, the broad cultural and theological complex of Christianity could be interpreted as unitarian, dualistic, trinitarian, or polytarian.

Some of the techniques of Russian formalism and French structuralism were applied by David Jason Liu to the *Dream of the Red Chamber,* thereby offering a supplement to a famous eighteenth-century commentary, the *Chih-yen-chai,* which although random, impressionistic, and unsystematic, was nevertheless considered by Liu as still valuable in modern times. Subsequently Liu applied to one chapter of the Chinese classic some general principles of Benjamin Hrushovski concerning the manner in which a narrative text gradually develops or unfolds itself.

To return to the theme of literature and milieu, Ying-hsiung Chou in a combination of political and literary history explored the relations between literature and society in the remote past, uncovering ancient Chinese antecedents of public opinion polls and the use of literature as a weapon of political propaganda. In a straightforward historical delineation unhampered by methodological restraints, Chou depicted a partnership between poetry and politics that existed in China for at least two thousand years; that is, the use of folksongs, both written and oral, to serve the political needs of the regime in power. In the archetypal forms of these songs, the king visits the common people in disguise in order to discern their needs and probe their loyalty. In more sophisticated forms the songs vindicate the upper levels of the political hierarchy and press the power of religion into service to provide a theological justification for the status quo. While some emperors sought to suppress literature, others more astute sought to use it in their own interest. The concept of the head of state attempting to counterbalance the power of an entrenched bureaucracy by appealing directly to the common people for suggestions and support is by no means an unfamiliar political phenomenon in the West.

Daniel L. H. Lin approached social problems by analyzing the examination syndrome—that is, the psychological and social effects of formal inquiries into a person's intellectual achievement in which his future status in life depends upon the results of these inquiries. Lin concentrated on an early-nineteenth-century novel, *Flowers in the Mirror,* in describing the phenomenon in the Chinese civil service system, and here again there are undoubtedly parallels in the West. This novel by Li Ju-chen is sometimes called the Chinese *Gulliver's Travels.* The examination syndrome was touched upon also in John Y. H. Hu's structural interpretation of the drama *The Peony Pavilion.*

At first glance, Chou's reconstruction of ancient Chinese history would seem to have little in common with a treatment by John McCormick of Walt Whitman's relationship to his social milieu, but the two papers actually illustrate the same principle—that poetry may be deliberately used to inculcate a particular form of political philosophy. While Chou explained how poetry was enlisted in the service of various types of Chinese imperial government, McCormick revealed how it was used as an instrument for the glorification of peculiarly late-eighteenth- and early-nineteenth-century notions of American democracy. From the period of the Revolution until the Civil War, opinion was unanimous in America (and still exists in certain quarters) that its political system is unique, divinely inspired, and morally superior to anything in the rest of the world. This is the message proclaimed by Whitman in terms, according to McCormick, which have almost nothing in common with philosophies of the East, either Indian or Chinese, even though some American commentators have erroneously sought to discern Eastern parallels in Whitman's brash manner of expression and in his ideological linking of national manifest destiny and the individual ego.

Three separate methods of approaching the theme of the image of China in world literature were presented in a humorous vein by André Lefevre. The first method was to show that some Western author had made a sincere effort to portray China or the Chinese in an authentic manner, but then to complain that his achievement was inadequate. The second was to use the author as a soundingboard by which the critic expounded his own notions of literature, whether Marxist, structuralist, or poststructuralist, and intruded his personal ideology by arguing that the author in question failed to perceive the appropriate alternatives available to him. The third method, the valid one, was to take an eclectic approach, described by Lefevre as polysystematic. The author he used to illustrate the approved method was an early-twentieth-century Dutch writer, Slauerhoff, who portrayed the ninth-century poet Po Chu-i as the protagonist of four novels and three poems. Slauerhoff, whose own conception of poetry was that of the establishment of his time, exploited the persona of the Chinese poet to embody notions of his own, chiefly clichés associated with the Romantic movement.

This writer's utilization of an actual Chinese poet to elaborate his own aesthetic point of view resembles the common eighteenth-century device of inventing various mythical Chinese, Persians, and even Peruvian visitors to Europe as a means of criticizing the writer's own society. Lefevre described the foreign protagonist device as creating an alibi, and Paul F. Hsai in another paper provided an inventory of eighteenth-century mythical travelers from the Orient under the rubric of Chinese secret agents. Two of the most influential of these letter collections attributed to fictional travelers (by the Marquis D'Argens and Oliver Goldsmith) were explored in depth by David Dai. His paper, rich in bibliography, revealed significant parallels in these collections with the *Analects* of Confucius.

A penetrating treatment of the manner in which literature or history may be used (or abused) to portray a writer's personal ideology was given by William Tay in an analysis of Ezra Pound's handling (or mishandling) of Chinese history. Tay's ex-

position drew upon Western critical methods in a unique manner—that is, by turning to theories of historiography rather than
those of literary criticism, and citing philosophers of history
such as Sidney Hook and Hannah Arendt rather than theorists of
literature such as René Wellek or Jacques Derrida. Tay first of all
followed another historian, Bernard Lewis, in specifying three
major types of history: (1) remembered history; that is, records
of past events, their commemorations, and various cultural traditions, or the collective memory of society, which is in large
measure legendary or fragmentary and, therefore, unreliable;
(2) recovered or critical history, which subjects surviving records to critical analysis, attempts to fill in gaps and to correct
errors, and represents as close an approximation to objective
reality as may be obtained; (3) invented history, which recreates,
embellishes, or revises any part of the record of the past that
society or an individual historian finds distasteful or objectionable. These three types of history bear a close analogy in structure, if not in meaning, to three modes of thought isolated by
Pound: "In the first the mind flits aimlessly about the object
[remembered history], in the second it circles about it in a
methodical manner [documented history], in the third it is
unified with the object [invented history]." Briefly pursuing a
theme upon which Wai-lim Yip had organized his discussion of
modern Chinese literature, that of the need for attaining a perspective of totality in history, Tay cited Carl Becker's principle
that different historians may make varying affirmations about a
particular event, and that these varying affirmations may all be
true while containing different degrees of factual information
concerning the total event. In regard to Pound's treatment of
Chinese tradition, Tay argued that all of his sources reproduced
in *The Cantos,* including the Confucian classics, must be
classified as remembered history and that none can lay claim to
objectivity or accuracy. One can understand Tay's reasons for
challenging the authenticity of the Confucian documents, but
one might also observe that the Christian Old and New Testaments are open to precisely the same objections and yet are
widely accepted as valid cultural documents, if not as accurate
historical records.

Tay also explained Pound's occasional synchronic treatment

of history—that is, interpreting all ages as contemporaneous with the present—just as some comparatists treat all literary texts as existing for the present moment. In other passages Pound does not treat historical statements as living thoughts, but as dead ones. Of special interest to the conference, Tay cited Pound's call for the development of a discipline of " 'comparative literature' . . . with a considered conscious method." Although the principal contribution in Tay's paper may consist in its explication of difficult passages—and almost nothing in Pound is noted for simplicity—Tay's illustrations were intended to trace the manner in which Pound used or perverted Chinese history in order to expound a reactionary system of political organization. Pound seems to have been an ardent Confucianist as much in order to justify his Fascist inclinations as to express his admiration for Oriental religion and culture. Tay's conclusion that Pound is not a trustworthy historian was not, therefore, entirely unexpected.

Donald Wesling, in commenting on Tay's paper, made Pound's use of history seem even more careless and unscrupulous. After complimenting Tay for his scholarly and courteous attitude toward Pound's aesthetic and political judgments, which uniformly portray him in an unfavorable light, Wesling affirmed that the solid and incontrovertible conclusions derived from Tay's ideological approach reveal that formalistic criticism is incapable of confronting the will-to-act inherent in the *Cantos*. According to Wesling, the case of Pound challenges the limits of traditional criticism and brings to the forefront the necessity of making a distinction between aesthetic and ideological judgments, particularly when disagreeable opinions assert themselves in the midst of successful poetical evocations.

Dominic Cheung brought to light another American poet who has paid tribute to the ancient traditions and theories of China. Although primarily concerned with establishing a contrast between Eastern and Western attitudes toward the poetic process, Cheung quoted the acknowledgment of a Western poet, Archibald MacLeish, of indebtedness to an Eastern model, the poetics of Lu Chi. "My own guide," wrote MacLeish, "for some ten years past has been a Chinese poet and general who was executed in the year 303 of our era for the mistake of losing a battle, but who found time, prior to that definitive event, to write a Fu, a sort of extended prose poem, on literature and especially on the poet's art." Although Lu Chi lived in a historical period corresponding to that of classical Rome, MacLeish believed that he speaks "to our condition as contemporary men." In his words, "Observations which appear at first glance to be no more than clichés of Chinese rhetoric turn out on reflection to convey timely bits of intelligence from beyond the mountains which the pursuit of poetry must cross."

A contemporary citizen of the United States with a political and social ideological commitment almost contrary to Pound's is Gary Snyder. Like Pound, Snyder drew inspiration from Chinese traditions, but instead of following Confucius as a model, he found Zen Buddhism much more compatible. His principal Chinese source was Han Shan or Cold Mountain, whose lifestyle and literary productions are said to resemble those of the hippies of the 1960s or heroes of the Beat Generation. Snyder's indebtedness to Cold Mountain has been thoroughly treated in the *New Asia Academic Bulletin,* but quite different materials were introduced in the 1979 conference by Dan McLeod, who even detected a Confucian side to Snyder's character. Likening Snyder to Emerson, Thoreau, and Pound, among others, McLeod quoted the poet's supposition that "the whole Western Tradition . . . [might be] off the track" and that many people might profit by the study of "other major civilizations—India and China—to see what they could learn."

McLeod treated in some detail one of Snyder's early works, a long poem-sequence entitled *Myths and Texts,* which contains more allusions to Chinese culture than any of his later books. He also mentioned various translations of Chinese poets and affirmed that Chinese landscape painting has had the longest continuous influence on Snyder's poetry, a plausible opinion in the light of Snyder's translations from the poet-painter Wang Wei. In general terms, McLeod concluded that the image of Asia in American poetry "contributes significantly to those qualities that distinguish American poetry from that written in England or Continental Europe."

Evidence that Chinese poetry exerted extensive influence upon the French Symbolist movement, however, was offered in a paper of Adriana Aldridge concerning a pattern of translations from the Chinese to the French and subsequently from the French to the Spanish. At about the same time that Pound was translating Chinese poetry into English, a major Mexican poet, José Juan Tablada, was translating various Chinese lyrics into Spanish. Aldridge discussed this relationship, together with a somewhat later wave of Chinese influence upon Latin-American writers. There is no evidence that the first of these Spanish-American translators was even aware of Pound, and all were inspired by French translations of Chinese works that they re-translated into Spanish, paraphrased, or utilized as source material for original compositions. None of them read Chinese. According to Aldridge, Tablada quoted a sonnet by the French Symbolist poet Mallarmé, incorporating the injunction to "imitate the Chinese," but Tablada gave no indication of the French sources for his own volume of poems entitled *Li Po,* which combines biographical references to the Chinese master with imitations and translations, all conveyed in the form of shaped verse designed to suggest the pictorial richness of the Chinese ideogram. Aldridge also described a second wave of Chinese influence, consisting of three separate translations in Mexico, Colombia, and Brazil of an early-twentieth-century French anthology of classic Chinese lyrics entitled *The Flute of Jade.* According to Aldridge, the original French version reached 131 separate editions by 1958. This astronomical number of editions would seem to offer impressive evidence that a fair sampling of Chinese classical writing has been available to European readers throughout most of the twentieth century.

A related study of the fortunes of French Symbolism in China and Japan by Kuo-ch'ing Tu revealed that literary movements may travel from one culture to another without carrying with them a real understanding of the fundamental nature of the movements themselves. There is considerable evidence to indicate that Symbolism in France derived at least partly from Chinese models. Mallarmé's sonnet recommending that his fellow poets imitate the Chinese strongly suggests that the oriental ideogram inspired in some measure the Symbolist notion of pure poetry. Tu in his paper indicated that one of the Japanese to introduce Symbolism to his country Bin Ueda, recognized the affiliation, affirming in 1905 that "the use of symbols in poetry is not necessarily a new idea in modern times; it is probably as old as mountains in this world." Tu quoted a passage from another Japanese poet-critic, Ariake Kambara, moreover, which could well have been written by Baudelaire in reference to "correspondances" or by Mallarmé in reference to pure poetry: "Sight and hearing become interwoven with each other, mixed with modern human sentiments, thereupon a sound of silver light exists, thereupon a color of sonorous sound exists. While it is called the mind's eye, the mind's ear, we can use the senses of smell and taste to perceive the fragrant savor of the mind." Although scholars have indicated that Kambara himself associated these techniques with traditional Japanese poetry rather than with Baudelaire, Bin Ueda seems to have been alone among Japanese or Chinese critics in recognizing ancient Eastern elements in the French poetry that they were advocating as a completely new departure. Tu revealed, moreover, that other Oriental critics failed completely to understand the nature of Symbolism, describing it variously as fantastic impressionism or the product of a nervous temperament. The techniques of comparative literature, however, have helped to reveal that the Eastern mode of poetry reached its full circle. After circulating in Europe and America under the banner of Symbolism, it returned to China and Japan under the same standard. We may say with Etiemble that Symbolism represents the first and until now the only instance in the history of universal literature of a literary school propagating its influence over the entire planet (1974, 141). And we may add that this school or movement had its origins in the East.

Andrew H. Plaks in a treatment of the full-length Hsiao-shuo traced the roots of the Chinese novel to historical fiction and to the prose essay in contrast to the Western novel, which represents the continuation of a single narrative tradition originating in epic poetry. Valuable for the direction of future research was his conclusion that the most striking parallels between the conventions of Chinese and European fiction are found in the relation between the novel and intellectual history. Plaks also joined the question of elitist versus popular literature (high or low styles, in Auerbach's terms) with one of the major problems of the study of periods and genres, whether one may correctly ascribe to individual works, particularly major ones, the characteristics assumed to belong to a certain span of time or type of literature. Plaks observed that both in the Western and Eastern traditions the imitation of the rhetoric of the masses or of picaresque types is a deliberate aesthetic choice with no suggestion that the author is attempting to cultivate a popular audience. He also indicated that his conclusions were derived from the great Chinese novels—in conformity to his opinion that all genre study must ultimately base itself upon the major works. These conclusions, bearing on fundamental parallels between the rise and development of the novel in the West and lengthy fiction in China, are of great interest to comparatists. In both cultures, according to Plaks, the rise of the novel coincided with extensive social and economic activity, it focused on mimetic representation while recognizing the limitations of human character (as seen in ambiguous or flawed protagonists), and it developed an ironic perspective, reflecting not only upon the internal events and figures of the narrative but also upon the broad intellectual foundations of each of the respective traditions. Plaks constantly affirmed that there existed no major contact between China and the West that could explain why similar themes and structures should have emerged from parallel historical and social conditions, and he specifically declared himself sceptical of formulae such as "an inevitable function of human culture" or "an inevitable phenomenon of human creativity." He did not justify his doubts, although the tone of his article in general suggests a basic distrust of all theories of historical determinism. Plaks further maintained that an ancient and extensive epic tradition exists in Japan in contrast to China, but he can hardly be justified in discerning epic style in the *Tale of Genji,* which in fact has more resemblance to discursive narratives such as the novels of Proust. Indeed a considerable scholarship has already been devoted to the parallelism Murasaki-Proust. The disparate development of narrative modes in the cultures of China and Japan would seem in itself to disprove theories relating these particular literary manifestations to economic or social causes.

Although no parallels to the Western epic may be found in Chinese literature, Ch'ing-che Lo explained that the closest approximation to it consists of the *fu,* a genre invented during the Han Dynasty. According to Lo's interpretation, the *fu* possesses some narrative elements, but these are submerged by a superabundance of parallelism, antithesis, natural history, classical mythology, and other ornamental devices together with a technique, labeled by Lo as "rhetorical action," which consists in turning everything in a story into still life and then trying to reanimate what may be called a painted story. Lo compared Han *fu* style to that of a narrative prose work in the English Elizabethan period, *Euphues and His England* by John Lyly, which embodies precisely the same elements attributed by Lo to the Han *fu.* In both Euphues and a *fu* by Ssu-ma Hsiang-ju that Lo chose for analysis, the narrative element is so slight that the description overwhelms the action.

Comparative literature scholars and folklorists, according to Patricia Haseltine, have not so far collaborated or shared the results of their researches to any significant degree. As an example of a valid manner in which a combination of literary and folkloristic methodologies may be applied to narrative materials, Haseltine described some European and Asiatic versions of a folktale type, the magic mill, the elements of which are known in the West through one of the Grimms' fairy tales: the protagonist receives a magic vessel that fills itself with some substance, and only the protagonist has the power to make the replenishing come to a halt on command; when the vessel is used by someone other than the owner, it keeps on producing the substance, usually with disastrous effects. Haseltine described various published Chinese versions of the type as well as further ones derived from an oral source in Taiwan.

Another popular tale that has circulated since ancient times throughout Europe and Asia was traced by Mowry Hua-yuan Li. In China the tale is associated with its best-known version, which appeared in the Ming period as the "Story of the Wolf of Chung-shan." A wounded or incapacitated animal persuades a man to carry him in a bag to some other place in order to rescue him from imminent danger. When the animal is released, he turns on his benefactor, and the man and the animal appeal to an arbiter—or to a series of three arbiters—to decide whether the animal's behavior is justified. After the third person says that he

cannot make a decision without a reconstruction of the events
leading to the situation, the animal returns to the bag and is
killed. According to Li's presentation, scholarly opinion is divided over whether the tale originated in Greece or India. Early
versions may be traced in India, Persia, and medieval Europe
prior to a more elaborate statement in China of the Ming period.
In China, the tale was also expanded into a four-act play with
satirical overtones. Li concluded by affirming that since considerable attention has already been paid to Indian influences
upon traditional Chinese fiction and drama, similar scholarly
efforts should be devoted to fables and folktales. Another example of a folklore theme adopted by both Eastern and Western
literature is indicated in chapter 6 of this book.

Only one other paper treated Indian influences of any kind,
that concerning the twentieth-century poet-philosopher Tagore,
who was, like O'Neill and Buck, a Nobel prize winner. In his
opening remarks, Gaylord Kai-Loh Leung compared Tagore's
short verse with the Japanese *haiku* as parallel models for an
ephemeral Little Verse Movement that took place in China during the 1920s. Paradoxically the movement itself began to decline just before Tagore visited China in person, and his presence
did little to revive it. The Chinese attitude, even among Tagore's
former disciples, was at best lukewarm toward his panegyrics on
the value and significance of Eastern (meaning Indian) civilization, which the Chinese disparaged as the "philosophy of the
people whose country has lost its sovereignty." This was precisely the period in the midtwenties when O'Neill also visited
China and, according to Frenz, reflected a somewhat more favorable impression of the mystical wisdom of the East. Although
Leung attributed the source of Tagore's vogue in China to the
genre of short verse, the preponderance of Leung's evidence
concerning Tagore's influence—especially upon a single poet,
Hsü Chi-mo—consisted of ideological echoes.

Two papers concerned relations between China and Japan.
Tokyo Yoshida discussed the theme of loneliness in two poets
associated with mountains, a Japanese Buddhist monk of the
twelfth century, Saigyō, and his Chinese predecessor Han Shan,
who has apparently always enjoyed a greater vogue in Japan
than in his native land. Yoshida explained that the symbolic

values attributed to mountains differed in the two poets, but both sought eternal security of mind.

In a more modern context, James O'Brien spoke about a novel, *Parting Regrets,* by the famous Japanese writer Osamu Dazai based upon the residence in Japan of a celebrated Chinese author of short stories, Lu Hsun, who is often compared to Maxim Gorky. As a young man, Lu Hsun studied medicine in Japan, and his experiences there form the subject of Dazai's work. Since the novel was commissioned by a patriotic society during World War II, O'Brien made some comments concerning literature as propaganda, but otherwise presented the novel by means of extensive quotation. An interesting genre study could perhaps be undertaken by comparing the Dutch fictional portrayal of Po Chu-i, which was described in André Lefevre's paper, with the depiction of Lu Hsun by Dazai.

The reverse situation, that of a Chinese novelist describing another cultural milieu, was treated by Yoon-wah Wong in connection with Lao She's novel *Little P'o's Birthday*. Like *Le petit prince* of Saint Exupéry, the novel has children as its main characters, but it does not belong in the category of children's literature. As interpreted by Wong, the novel could represent an allegory concerning modern Singapore, incorporating the traditional symbol of the garden and portraying the city island as an ideal multiracial society.

The theme of multiracialism was approached from a linguistic perspective by Seng Tong Wong in summarizing the development of Chinese literature in Malaysia during the twentieth century. Among the various ethnic groups in the country, including Malay, Chinese, Tamil, and English, a considerable amount of the total body of writing produced is in Chinese. Stressing sociological and linguistic aspects, Wong traced the efforts made to reduce illiteracy among the Chinese population both through the improving of economic conditions and through reforming the traditional Chinese script to shape it into a valid instrument for the vernacular language. Wong also sketched the efforts of ethnic Chinese in the area to establish a literary milieu during and after World War II.

Among the papers not devoted to one of the official themes, three on the topic of translation aroused most discussion. These papers are difficult to summarize because, in the words of J. I. Crump, the author of one of them, a writer on the art of translation "must either make generalized statements (which I find mostly boring and in the end unhelpful) or involve specific translations of his own and compare them with others." Although of the two methods, Crump expressed a preference for the second, he also elucidated two general principles of special relevance to the translating of Chinese poetry into English—that the translator should utilize the nature and genius of his own language in making equations with the literature of a second language, not the other way around, and that in translating works from a period in the remote past the diction should be neither noticeably modern nor consciously archaic.

Joseph S. M. Lau also used the method of comparing examples of precise translations with faulty ones while emphasizing the fundamental importance of key terms and the inevitability of the translator's being involved in interpretation as well as translation. Ann Corley Trail limited her observations to a particular previously published translation of Shakespeare into Chinese, but she also used the technique of pointing out triumphs, failures, and inbetweens. She affirmed that it is much more difficult to render a work into a language not only linguistically unrelated but culturally unfamiliar than it is to translate into a sister language. This opinion clashed forcibly with that of George Steiner, as quoted by Lau, that "the more remote the linguistic-cultural source, the easier it is to achieve a summary penetration and a transfer of stylized, codified markers." One can hardly object to Trail's further statement, therefore, that there has been a plethora of treatises in the West on the theory of translation, but "no agreement on a single universally applicable method of translating."

Most of the papers that adhered to the announced topics of the conference provided substantive knowledge, developed new facets of recognized concepts, or illuminated major texts by bringing them into contact with other literatures. Those treating the theme of literature and milieu revealed how social forces control not only the content of many literary works but also the way in which they are disseminated. Papers on the image of China in world literature demonstrated beyond all question that

Asia has had considerably more than a negligible influence in American and European letters. In regard to intra-Asian culture, it has long been a truism that Chinese literature has been a dominant force in this geographical area, and the congress revealed new approaches toward a systematic examination of this relationship, particularly in regard to modern times.

While this conference, like the two previous ones held at Taiwan, was a large-scale venture, offering upwards of a score of papers and attracting more than two hundred participants, an East-West conference sponsored by the Chinese University of Hong Kong during the following week was limited to a small number of specially invited participants and to a total of five papers. Of these, three took up the general concept of adapting Western methods of literary criticism to Eastern texts and each of the others offered a concrete illustration of the application of a particular method.

The keynote address by Heh-hsiang Yuan, although modestly entitled "An Inquiry into Possibilities," represented a solid analysis of the major problems of East-West comparative literature, including those that have been stressed previously in this book concerning universal literature and the role of criticism. Yuan warned against two antithetical tendencies, one fostered by Western or Westernized Asian comparatists "who treat the study of Comparative Literature East-West as largely an affinity study by either imposing already established Western models on Eastern literature, or by finding in Eastern literatures types of literary expressions that superficially resemble those of the West; the other, resulting from provincial-minded indigenous native scholars who unilaterally and unequivocally rule out any possibility of comparison between the literatures of the East and the West." According to Yuan, superficial or inappropriate comparisons are the result of the failure to comprehend cultural pluralism, and the stubborn refusal to admit parallels in other literatures is a consequence of cultural chauvinism.

I fully agree with Yuan's emphasis on cultural pluralism, but instead of using the great diversity in cultural traditions as an argument against affinity studies, as he seems to do, I would use it as a reason for rejecting the commonly expressed goal of attaining a common poetics for evaluating literary and artistic

work in the two hemispheres. Taking England and Japan as examples, it is obvious that aesthetic particularities represent a
major ingredient in their cultural identities. Even within individual cultures such as the English or the Japanese, moreover,
there exists a considerable degree of aesthetic pluralism: some
writers and artists in either culture, for example, advocate balance and symmetry; others favor irregularity and asymmetry.
Aesthetic standards within single cultures, moreover, change
with the times. Much has been made of the absence of the epic—
of a long narrative in poetic form—in the Chinese tradition;
whereas many epics exist in the West. I have already noted that
some Western critics such as Edgar Allan Poe, however, argue
that the epic genre is deficient aesthetically—that the essence of
poetry is destroyed by length—and that a long poem is a contradiction in terms. Superficially Poe's structures seem to be a vindication of the Chinese tradition and as such are an argument in
favor of a common poetics, but more realistically his attitude
merely serves to illustrate the lack of aesthetic agreement in the
West.

Yuan is certainly right in objecting to studies that "impose"
established Western models on the East or that draw attention to
elements in Eastern literatures resembling those in the West in a
merely superficial manner. It is, nevertheless, possible to discern
resemblances in literary works in two cultures without seeking
to impose one culture upon the other. Indeed, the imposing of
models has nothing to do with pointing out affinities or resemblances in style, structure, mood, or idea between two works
that have no other connection. The discerning of analogies without question of influence has been widely used as an instrument
of drawing together the literatures of the West, and it may be
legitimately used in the broader context of East-West relations.
And it may be used from the perspective of the West as well as
the East—that is, in showing how Western works resemble those
in the East as well as in the reverse direction.

As an example of superficial and misleading affinities, Yuan
cited a comparison of the feeling for nature in the English poet
Wordsworth and that of the Chinese poet T'ao Yuan-ming, objecting that the comparison overlooks fundamental differences
in their conception of the manner in which a separation between

mind and body may be obtained. Yuan, nevertheless, accepted Anthony Thorlby's vindication of the principle of aesthetic awareness in recognizing not identical but merely similar elements in kindred genres. Yuan quoted approvingly, and properly so, in my opinion, the following passage from a letter by Thorlby, originally published in the *Times Literary Supplement* (25 July 1968): "There need be no factual connexion between the two examples, but the comparatist must know how to juxtapose them. If he goes far afield for his comparisons, this is not in order to prove any thesis of universal philology or historical evolution or structural aesthetics, but primarily for the pleasure of the thing, to broaden the basis of his experience, as an adventure." I have already indicated that Irving Babbitt in a classic diatribe against romanticism compared the dependence upon nature in Taoist philosophy to the primitivism of Jean Jacques Rousseau. This affirmation of similarity may be as far afield as that between Wordsworth and T'ao Yuan-ming, but it has been widely accepted in the United States and reaffirmed by Etiemble (1980, xlviii). Both Wordsworth and Rousseau are ordinarily regarded as romantic writers, but their resemblances to each other are probably much less striking than the affinities of either one to Taoist philosophy.

Professor Yuan revealed his awareness of the distrust of comparative literature manifested by some professors of the national literatures, whether Chinese and Japanese in the East, or French and German in the West. This may explain his theory that an inherent contradiction weakens the discipline. As I interpret his remarks, he found two contradictions or contrasts: one between the relative homogeneity of the "Western heritage dimension" and the tremendous diversity in the rest of the world, resulting in the relative ease of studying writings belonging to the former and the considerable problems involved in expanding studies to include the "global dimension"; the second between the need of "narrowing down the scope of our pursuit" in order to define its objectives and that of broadening its province to include all parts of the world. One cannot emphasize too strongly the contrast between the cultures of what is known as the West and what is known as the East. The West, as Yuan indicated, is more or less unified and homogeneous with its Judeo-Christian tradition in

religion and its Greco-Roman tradition in literature. The East in
the Hong Kong conference usually meant China, but in the
broadest sense it is also taken to include the cultures of the Near
East, India, Japan, and the Pacific. The global dimension must
also take into consideration the cultures of Africa.

Because of the great diversity among Asiatic nations, it is
really inaccurate or at least misleading to speak of the cultures of
the East in the sense of a single, identical phenomenon, regardless of the appropriateness of including all the nations of Europe
and the Americas as representative of the culture of the West.
Japan and China, have, nevertheless, had continuous close ties
in literature, religion, and art, which may justify attributing to
them a common culture. Conditions in the modern world,
moreover, are changing so rapidly that the cultural distinctions
between East and West may soon become mainly historical. The
Tokyo of our times, for example, probably approaches more
closely the future city of the twenty-first century than does any
contemporary metropolis of the West.

Even at present the literary contrast between East and West
resides more in linguistic differences between the various nations in each area than it does in divergent aesthetic views.
Indeed there has been a remarkable unanimity in the attitudes of
one part of the world toward the literary masterpieces of the
other; critics from the East have not argued that some Western
masterpieces have been overvalued and sought to replace others
with more resemblance to Eastern works in their place; nor have
critics from the West reacted in a similar fashion toward Eastern
works. The obvious cultural diversities between East and West
do not call for any limitation in the materials and methodologies
of comparative literature beyond those required by reason and
good sense. Instead, the emphasis should be in the other direction—that is, in considering as valid sources for investigation all
literatures, major and minor, throughout the globe. There should
be a broadening rather than a narrowing down of "the scope of
our pursuit."

Obviously there is a tremendous difference between subject
matter that can be embraced by an entire intellectual discipline
and that which a single scholar may hope to encompass. Many
Western professors who are not sympathetic to comparative lit-

erature have expressed sentiments similar to those manifested by one of Yuan's colleagues who argued that since a Chinese scholar cannot master all the writers and works of a single dynasty he has no time to devote to any other literature. The answer is to be found in selectivity. No single comparatist can deal with entire literatures any more than a single stonecutter of the Middle Ages could erect an entire cathedral. The comparatist is not an expert on every literature, and he should not be expected to have even a superficial knowledge of all literatures. Instead, the comparatist specializes in certain narrowly circumscribed areas of particular literatures. He or she has a general knowledge of the major literary works in a variety of national cultures, together with a familiarity of the various methods of investigation, but his or her individual research projects are for the most part as limited and precise as those of colleagues in single literatures. Comparative literature is a cooperative enterprise covering a vast and diverse area, and it is to be explored or conquered in narrow segments. In the days of exploration, it would have been impossible for any single European navigator to cover in a lifetime the entire geographic expanse of the two American continents, but in the twentieth century any tourist can visit by jet airplane all of their major centers of population in three or four months. One may hope for similar future progress toward universal coverage in the study of literature. Even today there can be little excuse for a professor of any national literature who does not have some acquaintance with universal literature. As Voltaire remarked in the eighteenth century about universal science, it is no longer in its entirety within the range of any individual, but true men of letters are preparing to venture into each of its different areas even if they cannot cultivate them all (*Dictionnaire philosophique*, "Gens de lettres").

Any single comparatist would be justified, if he or she wishes, in discarding "some of the less significant authors and their works" in favor of the "important literatures," in Yuan's words, but from the perspective of literary study as an academic discipline, there exist no value hierarchies for admission. If literature is defined as the communication by means of written symbols when the purpose is to provide aesthetic pleasure as well as to convey a message, then all works, both major and minor, ancient and modern, must be accepted as legitimate objects of study, and no national literature has a privileged or superior position. This does not mean, however, that one must ignore the historical record, which indeed reveals that some literatures embody centuries of rich tradition whereas others are only now in the process of emerging. Nor does it mean that one cannot affirm values or erect standards of judgment. When a biologist maintains that ants and elephants are completely equal as legitimate material for study, for example, he is not placing ants and elephants on the same level or suggesting that they have equal strength or intelligence. Nor is he maintaining that every individual biologist should devote equal attention to the two disparate species. He is merely affirming that all living organisms are the province of his intellectual discipline. The individual comparatist similarly chooses the single works or theoretical problems to which he or she wishes to give special attention, but still recognizes that the province of the discipline is universal. Yuan indeed implied assent to this principle by quoting Harry Levin's proposition that the comparatist must assume "an equal belief in the equal validity of all traditions constituting the unity of knowledge."

Yuan's special concern was to determine whether or not it is possible to arrive at a definition of "Comparative Literature East-West," and his major contribution consisted in successfully formulating a working definition, if not an absolute one. One can hardly challenge the statement that comparative literature East-West comprises "a branch of literary study which compares literary works of both the East and the West beyond the confines of national boundaries, seeking mutual understanding through exchange and comparison of ideas, denying not the uniqueness of a national tradition but giving its manifestation a new dimension and making Comparative Literature a universal medium of communication" (Deeney 1980, viii). Significantly this definition speaks of comparing individual works of the East and the West rather than comparing the two cultures. Indeed, comparative literature East-West at its best consists of treating the art of written communication with appropriate examples drawn from the two hemispheres. It is not primarily a medium of communication, but rather an analysis of forms of communication that resemble each other. Some critics have been reluctant to attri-

bute to the discipline the function of promoting mutual understanding, perhaps one of the reasons for an objection raised in
the subsequent discussion of Yuan's paper to the combining of
moral enthusiasm with scientific methodology. I agree that the
fostering of international harmony is not one of the primary
functions of literature, but, on the other hand, it cannot be denied that individuals who are acquainted with an alien culture—
even on a superficial level—show much greater receptivity toward that culture than they would otherwise. I am not, of
course, referring to political relationships since it has been em-
pirically proved that culture and politics do not necessarily go
hand in hand. Cultural similarities are powerless to prevent civil
wars, shifting alliances, and ideological splits such as the one
between capitalism and communism that at present separates
Eastern and Western Europe as well as the two governments of
China.

Because of the discreteness of culture and ideologies, I question the view that "cultural and philosophical diversities" have
given rise to the historically divergent views that have been
expressed about comparative literature, particularly those associated with the so-called French and American schools. The
first method to develop was the one that stresses influence and
reception, or *rapports de fait,* and considers comparative literature as a branch of literary history; at the time French scholars
were the most productive. Emerging subsequently was the
method that admits in addition, or rather recommends, the study
of resemblances or affinities rather than source-influence relationships and that discerns these resemblances by means of *rapprochement* or placing one passage in juxtaposition with
another. At first the major practitioners were Americans, but
eventually many Europeans followed their example. Neither
method bears the imprint of French or American culture or philosophy. At present the two methods are practiced indiscrimi-
nately by citizens of both France and the United States, as well
as of other countries in every part of the world. Scholars choose
one or the other method not according to their cultural background but according to the nature of the problem in which they
are interested. These fundamental methods have more recently
been succeeded—but not superseded—by other techniques

stressing linguistics and ignoring history. Those who pursue any of these methods are merely using available tools, not revealing cultural or philosophical conditioning. Incidentally, the method of relating literature to other disciplines such as sociology, psychology, and the arts—which Yuan considered the primary characteristic of the American school—was originally rejected by American purists, including among their number many eminent scholars. When American universities as a whole subsequently developed the interdisciplinary approach to knowledge, however, most American comparatists, including the reluctant purists, accepted this broad vision for literature as well as for the university at large.

According to Yuan, French scholars have had a tendency to subordinate the discipline of comparative literature to literary history in general and to emphasize material information over aesthetic considerations; whereas Americans have encumbered the comparative method by advocating the study of literature in its relationship to other intellectual disciplines. He was right that the positivist methodology associated with the French school has only limited application to East-West relations, but not, in my opinion, because an emphasis upon material information implies the neglect of aesthetic values, but because until recent times knowledge of direct historical connections between the two cultures was either entirely lacking or merely fragmentary. There still remain significant *rapports de fait* to be investigated. The nineteenth-century German poet Heinrich Heine, for example, reported Goethe's self-satisfction in hearing that scenes from his novel *Werther* were being depicted on porcelain in China, and Heine in turn gloated upon hearing that an edition of his own poems had been published in Japan. Yuan at first seemed to be even more intransigent toward the American school, on the grounds that its involvement of multiple disciplines renders the study of East-West relations so complex as to be impossible. He later relaxed his opposition, however, by observing that "for a Chinese scholar, the study of literature often involves the study of philosophy and art." He also accepts the axiom of the convertibility of poetry and painting, the theme of a subsequent paper by Wai-lim Yip.

Yuan's preferred method seemed to be a combination of the

French and American perspectives. He proposed that the scholar isolate a cause-and-effect relationship in one literature and investigate the cultural and philosophical elements bearing upon the relationship. He would then isolate a similar cause and effect in another literature and pursue an identical investigation of relevant cultural and philosophical elements. Finally, he would bring the two pairs together for comparison, pointing out the parallel elements. I heartily approve of the combination of history of ideas and literature in this method, but I am afraid that its other features would drastically limit the possibilities of comparison. It would not be easy to find examples in either an Eastern or a Western literature of a cause-and-effect relationship that could be paired with one in the opposing literature; the demonstration of the parallels would be cumbersome and the conclusions would probably be sociological or anthropological rather than literary. Although this method may have been used successfully in the investigation of ancient myths, to adopt it as an exclusive or even preferred method of research would almost bring comparative studies to a standstill. In my opinion, it is significant enough to isolate any extensive parallelism in theme, style, or portrayal of human condition without requiring in addition the demonstration of similar causes and effects. Yuan's example of close parallelism, Lao She's *Looking Westward to Ch'ang-an* and Gogol's *The Inspector General,* the former "almost a copy" of the latter, provided a superb model for East-West research; yet the parallelism is not based upon the causes and effects leading to the creation of either work, but upon the internal resemblances in plot and characterization. As Yuan observed, the ideological backgrounds of the two works are diametrically opposite, but they reflect social reality in an identical manner; in treating them, therefore, the critical emphasis should be generic rather than sociological. There would also seem to be a good case to be made that Lao She wrote under the direct influence of his Russian predecessor, but even so it is the thematic and narrative resemblances that are essential. The same is, of course, true about the parallels between Lao She's *City of Cats* and Jonathan Swift's *Gulliver's Travels.* Little need be said about the backgrounds of these works, for they have almost nothing in common. What counts is that both may be interpreted as dystopias, allowing for the portrayal of extensive thematic and generic parallels.

At this point a distinction needs to be made between the stylistic and the thematic elements that comprise literary genres. Style consists of mechanical or technical components such as rhyme schemes, metaphors, internal divisions, or narrative voice, most recognizable and essential in such forms as the sonnet and the haiku. Theme consists of conceptual elements such as mixing of tragedy and comedy, character development, or portrayal of reality, most recognizable and essential in such forms as the Bildungsroman or the Utopia. To be sure, there is considerable overlapping, but usually either the technical or the conceptual dominates in particular genres. Yuan seemed reluctant to admit studies that emphasize parallels in style without taking into consideration cultural differences, and he is also wary of attempts at periodization based on stylistic criteria.

It is probably impossible to devise a valid system of periodization that incorporates both Eastern and Western literatures before the twentieth century. Yuan observed, however, a concrete parallelism in the creation myths of both civilizations. Investigation of ancient mythologies might be extended to include myths and folklore of later centuries. Some fascinating parallels emerged during the conference, suggesting that the area of myth may well be a fruitful one for subsequent scholarship.

The analysis of themes is closely related to the history of ideas, a methodology that Yuan recommended as a means of discerning affinities between different cultures and the basic aspirations of man. Here again, I believe it is possible and desirable to separate the study of literary texts from the study of cultures. Authors, for example, may express ideas completely alien to the culture or climate of opinion in which they live. Our mission as literary scholars is not primarily to compare cultures (a function of anthropology), but to observe parallels in ideas, themes, and manifestations of the lyric, dramatic, and narrative modes. Yuan was closer to the mainstream of our discipline when he agreed that comparative literature "is not comparison of different national literatures by setting one against another" than when he sought new light "on the cause-effect relationship between two literatures."

In broaching the topic of criticism, Yuan seemed to disengage himself from the prevailing effort of Eastern scholars to affirm and to establish a common poetics for East and West. Certainly he warned against the dangers of misunderstanding and misrepresentation inherent in forcing Western models upon Chinese works. I heartily concur with this caveat; indeed, as I have previously said, there is no more need for a common poetics than for a common religion. Nothing approaching a critical consensus exists in the West—opposing, even antithetical theories compete with each other—and in recent years new ones have appeared and faded away with astonishing frequency. There would be no advantage in transposing this anarchy to the East. Classical Chinese criticism, moreover, as Yuan observed, comprises both intuitive and emulative branches. These are loosely parallel to a similar dichotomy in Western neoclassicism. The Confucian emulative goals of moral integrity embodied in unity of form and content have their counterparts in Aristotelian principles of unity and imitation; whereas the concept of intuitive appreciation corresponds to European eighteenth-century notions like *je ne sais quoi* and judging literary works by pointing out beauties and faults. It is not surprising, therefore, that the general discussion following Yuan's presentation developed into a debate over the relative merits of impressionistic and objective criticism in which opinion was not divided along geographic lines; some scholars from the West defended impressionistic judgments and others from the East argued for objectivity. The obvious conclusion is that neither the East nor the West has a monolithic approach to literature and that the study of East-West relations cannot be based upon a single system of criticism.

In Chinese culture the inherent relationship between literature and the fine arts is probably more clearly established than in the West. As Yuan pointed out, the study of Chinese literature traditionally involves the study of painting, calligraphy, and seal-carving. In the West, the concept of the resemblance between painting and poetry was accepted as a commonplace from classical times until the late eighteenth century, when Lessing observed an essential difference—that poetry describes consecutive action while sculpture (and by extension painting) portray special relations confined to a particular moment of time. Wai-

lim Yip, the second conference speaker, in summarizing the contrary arguments of Herder, Pound, and others, related the controversy to Chinese aesthetic theory and poetic practice. His
examples of arrested action or static description in Chinese
poetry and of the passage of time in Chinese landscape painting
are convincing arguments against the absolute application of
Lessing's theory. Similar portrayals of time may be cited in
Western art such as Picasso's canvas *Guernica*. Going beyond
these concrete illustrations, however, Yip maintained that
poetry and painting are aesthetically unified in the sense that
both transcend the physical to arouse a feeling of something
beyond or outside. In Ezra Pound's expression, the two means
of communication possess a common bond or "inter-
recognition," a type of energy or power that creates an aesthetic
state in the viewer or reader. In short, Yip argued that poetry
and the plastic arts have an identical aesthetic function. This is
saying a great deal, indeed—much too much to be defended in
the limited scope of a conference paper. Yip's theories are based
upon a particular aesthetic, that of the Pound-Eliot coterie; they
may indeed fit the poetry of this school and of many Chinese
exemplars as well, but they do not, as he admitted, apply to all
poetry, all painting, or all music in the West. His theories concern a certain type of lyric poetry, sometimes called pure poetry,
which indeed had affinities to abstract painting, but there are
many other forms of poetry, including narrative, which, as Yip
correctly affirmed, Lessing had in mind in his famous treatise.
As lyric poetry resembles abstract painting and sculpture, so
narrative and satirical forms resemble representational art. Because of Yip's emphasis on pure poetry, the discussion of his
paper turned into a debate over absolute versus relative standards in aesthetics. It is significant that the participants were
about equally divided, but again not along East-West lines. The
discussants on both sides, however, seemed to believe that some
single principle should be found to explain all poetry rather than
recognizing that there are many kinds of poetry and that each
kind has its own standards. Some is discursive, some abstract,
some concrete, and some intellectual, whether in the West or the
East. Poetry like the arts has its genres and subgenres, and although all of them may be related and provide, as Yip declared,

correspondences with the others, it does not follow that all forms work aesthetically in the same way.

One concrete example of a form of literary criticism adopted by both East and West is that which affirms, in Yuan's words, that "cultural values are the product of social and economic conditions." This view is held by Marxist critics in both East and West, although it is, of course, not universally accepted in either area. Since it is the official ideology of the People's Republic of China, however, it is quite understandable that the conference organizers should have requested Douwe Fokkema, the third speaker, to treat the Marxist theory of literature with special reference to the China mainland. Since his analysis was precise, comprehensive, and reasonably objective, it is surprising that it should have been subjected to rather harsh attacks during the discussion period, particularly on the grounds that he made insufficient distinctions between the attitudes of Soviet Russia and the China mainland and that he failed to consider Marxists who live outside the communist hegemony. Given the broad scope of his topic and his limited time, simplification was inevitable. It is true that Fokkema did not concentrate on criticism as such as it is found in the writings of Marx and Engels or in such modern spokesmen as Georg Lukács and Lucien Goldmann, but rather on the official attitudes toward literature inculcated by political states. The latter topic, however, was the one announced in Fokkema's title. The attacks to which he was subjected may have been provoked by his introduction setting forth a methodology that he claimed to belong to "the scientific study of literature." In attributing to himself the invulnerability of science, he was guilty of one of the critical attitudes that he found objectionable among the Marxists.

In his way, Fokkema was prescribing the same doctrine of a single truth and a single approach to it that flawed Yip's analysis of artistic correspondences. Although the study of literature may be made relatively precise and systematic, it can never attain the objectivity of science any more than the study of aesthetics can isolate absolute or eternal values. Fokkema's analysis, moreover, clearly showed a bias against the system he was examining, reflected in such phrases applied to Marxism as "truth should be represented in only a selective way" and "applicability will be decided by ideological and political contingency." It would be possible to take almost any other social-ideological system and unearth weaknesses similar to those discovered by Fokkema. The above phrases, for example, could certainly be applied to various sects of institutionalized Christianity or to governments dependent upon a capitalistic economy. Indeed, a book published in the United States in 1978 by Edward W. Said, *Orientalism,* comes close to making these applications. It portrays European and American scholarship devoted to the Near East or the Arab World as deliberately reflecting a will to cultural domination and repression. Fokkema was somewhat unfair to Marx and Engels, moreover, in suggesting that neither has written extensively about literary problems while citing three times their *Über Kunst und Literatur.* Marx himself through the wide range of quotations in his various works reveals himself as a connoisseur of world literature.

The final two papers brought into focus the question of structuralism, and a fiery debate ensued in the discussion period over the validity of the method. It was generally accepted that both speakers, Han-liang Chang and Ying-hsiung Chou, had presented well-organized and sophisticated examples of the method, but questions were raised concerning the value of structuralism itself. It is, of course, as useless to debate methods of criticism as it is to argue over religion. On both subjects, it is impossible to change anyone's mind. Innovators adhere to their innovations and traditionalists cling to their traditions. I would merely observe that criticism is subject to more fads or new methods than any other branch of literary study and that it is a risky business for young scholars to invest years of their formative periods acquiring a vocabulary and techniques that may be superseded before they are established in the profession. In his presentation Chang introduced four traditional stories about tigers and argued that they needed to be classified into more specific genres than merely the category of animal stories. That "incommensurate categories" exist in Chinese scholarship and that they are far from perfect instruments of taxonomy has been publicized in the West by the Argentinian prose stylist Jorge Luis Borges by means of a parody of a Chinese encyclopedia. According to his imaginary *Celestial Emporium of Benevolent*

Knowledge, "animals are divided into (a) those that belong to the Emperor, (b) embalmed ones, (c) those that are trained, (d) suckling pigs, (e) mermaids, (f) fabulous ones, (g) stray dogs, (h) those that are included in this classification, (i) those that tremble as if they were mad, (j) innumerable ones, (k) those drawn with a very fine camel's hair brush, (l) others, (m) those that have just broken a flower vase, (n) those that resemble flies from a distance" (Rabkin 1976, 5).

One can readily understand Professor Chang's desire to find more precise categories for his tiger stories, but it is perhaps not necessary for him to follow the systems of Barthes or Todorov in order to do so. Indeed Chang concluded after explaining Barthes at length that the latter's system "is not adequate enough for universal applications." He had better luck with Todorov's discriminations of the uncanny, the fantastic and the marvelous, but even here he was obliged to invent a new denominator, the fantastic-marvelous. Since Chang modestly admitted that any approach "has to run the risk of confining the description to certain features while ignoring the others," I venture to suggest that it would be possible to classify his stories by means of traditional terminology without recourse even to Todorov. All of them could very well be labeled either fable, parable, allegory or fantastic. The story of a tiger who shows gratitude for having a thorn removed is a fable, defined as a narrative in which animals represent human beings to point a moral. The story of a bride snatched by a tiger from an impending marriage and delivered to another suitor to whom she had been promised is a simple parable, defined as a narrative designed to illustrate any principle, here the moral one that promises must be kept. The story of a tiger who changes into a beautiful woman is an allegory with overtones of myth. The tiger skin represents evil or a tribal taboo. The two stories of a man changed into a tiger and then back into a man are examples of the fantastic, a category reserved for stories and themes completely devoid of moral and allegorical overtones in which events not to be explained by natural causes are accepted as plausible by the reader.

From the perspective of Chinese literature, Chang's contribution consists in establishing some order in the classification of national fiction; from the perspective of comparative literature it consists in drawing attention to motifs that exist also in the West. The story of the grateful tiger is exactly parallel to a story told by Aulus Gellius, a Roman author of the second century A.D. In this story a gladiator named Androclus is confronted in the Circus Maximus by a lion who turns in a flash from ferocious to docile. Androclus then reveals that he had previously plucked out a splinter from this same lion's paw and that they had subsequently lived and eaten together in the same cave for three years. This became the basis of a twentieth-century play, *Androcles and the Lion,* by George Bernard Shaw. The story of the tiger who turns into a beautiful woman is related to the theme of the demonic woman in Western literature, particularly to the story related by Flavius Philostratus, a quasi contemporary of Gellius, concerning a Lamia, a beautiful woman who turns into a snake. Both the tiger and the snake may be allegories for evil.

The elaborate analysis in the final paper by Ying-hsiung Chou of *hsing* as a rhetorical device had relevance merely to Chinese literature, but his additional treatment of bird motifs in a narrative poem, *Southeast Fly the Peacocks,* opened up the possibilities of comparison with the mythologies of other nations. This famous narrative has at least one major resemblance to Western literature apart from the theme of the double suicide, which was widespread in the Renaissance and taken up by Shakespeare in *Romeo and Juliet.* In the Chinese poem, Lan Chih and her husband are buried in adjoining graves from which two trees eventually grow and their branches intertwine to form a canopy. In one of the stories of Ovid's *Metamorphoses,* a married couple, Philemon and Baucis, offer hospitality to two gods, Zeus and Hermes, who reward them by turning their hut into a temple in which they serve as priests. When they die, they are buried in front of the temple and are turned into trees. The two sets of lovers are, of course, not entirely parallel; the Chinese characters commit suicide in youth and the Latin ones die from old age, but the symbol of their transformation into adjoining trees commemorates the fidelity and devotion of both couples.

The single concept that seemed to unite all of the sessions of the conference was that of the approach to truth. Wai-lim Yip argued for eternal values and aesthetic absolutes even though stressing as models literary texts that many other critics would reject. Fokkema flatly denied the existence of aesthetic absolutes, but insisted that literary criticism can attain to scientific objectivity, a position that was tacitly, if not overtly, accepted by the two advocates of structuralism, Chang and Chou. Yuan stood alone on the other side by recognizing impressionistic along with prescriptive or imitative criticism and accepting the validity of a wide number of methodological approaches to the study of literature. In my opinion, Yuan is right. I accept aesthetic relativism, with due regard to the consensus gentium, and I do not believe that the study of literature can be made scientific, although statements made about it should be precise and verifiable. Students of East-West relationships in particular should emphasize the historical, the concrete, and the specific in revealing parallels and similarities where they exist, but they should be on guard against the superficial and the irrelevant. If the goal of literary study is the expanding of knowledge and understanding, our approach must be eclectic, polysystematic, and, above all, factual.

Obviously no consensus was attained at the conference, although certain implications seemed to be generally accepted: that the study of East-West relations is a worthy enterprise, that there is no preferred manner of going about it, and that it is beset by the same difficulties that exist in the study of national literatures and by several other dificulties as well.

A fourth conference was held at Tamkang University in 1983 with sessions on critical theories, translation, thematology, and genology.

P'eng-hsiang Chen, in an ambitious attempt to survey the theory of thematology in the West and East, characterized the method as "an outgrowth of the 19th-century German mania for folklore." He consequently accorded myth and folklore center stage in the rest of his exposition. Doing so was somewhat of a departure from the third Tamkang conference, where, as we have seen, some folklorists complained that the discipline of comparative literature had almost entirely neglected their domain. It is hardly necessary to state that themes were studied historically long before the advent of any textbook of comparative literature, and in the Western tradition themes are frequently associated with the history of ideas. The alternate approach through myth and folklore may, however, be more appropriate for Eastern literatures. Several papers touched upon the concept that Chinese narrative, like Chinese poetry, is less conceptual and explicit than Western counterparts, and this may explain why the history of ideas approach is more appropriate for the West than the East. Chen's paper defined thematology as "the study of the evolution of specific themes, motifs, and especially mythical figures, dealing at the same time with different writers' treatment of a same theme or motif to voice out their preoccupations and to reflect their times." Few of the papers in the conference, however, followed this prescription. Neither ideas nor mythical figures were treated extensively.

Several of the themes actually introduced were developed from a sociological perspective. Considerable and well-deserved attention was devoted to a well-known novel in both China and the United States, *The Woman Warrior,* by a Chinese-American, Maxine Hong Kingston. This novel was analyzed both thematically and stylistically by various scholars. Amy Ling portrayed the novel as an account of the author's "anguished search for selfhood and for coherence," while developing the theme of woman as a victim and woman as a victor. The protagonist's aunt, having borne an illegitimate child and suffered the stigma attached to her situation, is driven to madness and eventually a degrading suicide through drowning in a well. She is the victim. The protagonist's mother, on the other hand, against great odds enrolls in a medical school and emerges as a licensed midwife, while serving as a role model for her daughter. The mother is the victor. Accompanying or perhaps transcending these themes of personal tragedy and victory is the sociological background of the protagonist, which reflects the struggles of ethnic Chinese in American society. Kingston's recording of the tension between her racial background and her American self was skillfully compared to similar experiences of American writers from other ethnic groups. Ling portrayed these books as part of a "large wave revitalizing contemporary literature" in reaction to the hollowness of the nouveau roman. She asserted that "life demands meaning, purpose, and affirmation."

Concentration on ethnic minorities represents a new direction in the study of American literature, parallel to the thrust of comparative studies and certainly contributing to the understanding of universal literature. A paper on cultural consciousness amid the multicultures of American society revealed that the traditional concept of the United States as a melting pot is being replaced by racial awareness and cultural autonomy. Traditional textbooks of American literature have emphasized national themes, focusing on common or shared creeds, values, and mores in order to establish the typical and the uniform as national prototypes. The current objective of placing the various ethnic American literatures in their respective cultural contexts was presented by Wayne Miller as perhaps "the key to the next literary history of the United States." Comparatists especially will not quarrel with this goal. Most Americans recognize that their best restaurants are the ethnic ones, and they should presumably welcome efforts to keep their literary production and criticism from emulating the uniformity of the fast food industry.

Escape, survival, and exile are other themes with sociological overtones introduced during the conference. Western *fin de siècle* aestheticism was revealed by Bangok Lee as the means chosen by a Korean writer of the 1930s to escape from the drabness of daily life during the Japanese occupation of his country. Survival was delineated in an analysis of two novels concerning the mass killings accompanying the dropping of the atomic bomb in Japan. In comparing John Hersey's *Hiroshima* and Masuji Ibuse's *Black Rain,* John T. Dorsey observed that "writing itself is an affirmation in an age when man's destructive capacity not only matches his worst imaginations but also threatens to exterminate the creature who imagines." Exile was treated by Yu-ch'eng Lee in connection with a Chinese poet of the fourth century, Hsieh Ling-yun. The author revealed that much of the poet's work concerns his actual contact with the landscape of the country where he was exiled—obviously nothing unusual for Chinese poetry—and that he also expressed the sorrow, grief, and loneliness resulting from the enforced absence from his native land. Unfortunately this paper completely lacked a comparatist component, which could have been supplied by reference to the parallel experience of the Latin poet Ovid, who was also exiled to a coastal town at about the same period in history.

An American scholar, Don McLeod, quoted an eminent Chinese critic now living in the United States to the effect that the seven major themes characteristic of Chinese thought and feeling are nature, time, history, leisure, nostalgia, and rapture with wine. But apart from nostalgia, which is associated with exile, none of these themes was formally treated in the conference. Another scholar added the theme of eroticism as it occurs in Chinese fiction, and David Dai analyzed this element as part of the emotion of love in the Chinese Book of Odes and the Western Song of Songs.

Most extensive treatment of a single theme was accorded by Byung-wook Moon to poetic narcissism in Korean literature, which in actuality is only superficially connected with the Narcissus theme in Greece. Regardless of the outcome of the handsome Greek's self-infatuation, scrutiny of his own image provided pleasure; whereas the examples of narcissism from Korea for the most part represent sadness. Also as Douwe Fokkema pointed out, the myth of Narcissus became the center of the universe as perceived by Western Symbolists. His love of himself is as "unnatural" in the latter-setting "as the varyingly interpreted mysterious motivations of Salomé." The classic Korean version concerns a pair of parrots. The female dies and the male is stricken with grief. The king orders a mirror to be placed in front of his cage, and the parrot, at first assuming he is seeing another of his own species, begins pecking at it. But when he realizes it is nothing but his own reflected image, he dies of grief. The other Korean examples suggest a number of other possible reactions to one's reflected image: identification (the original Narcissus situation), idealization, rejection, and even hatred. The mirror may even represent a separate world as in the fantasy of Lewis Carroll.

In a later version of the Korean parrot story, the king himself loses his wife and his courtiers suggest that he remarry. He replies that if a bereaved bird grieves for the loss of its mate, he should also respect the memory of his wife. A number of other papers treated birds or animals as symbols or representatives of human beings. K. C. Leung, analyzing three plays of the seventeenth century, two English and one Chinese, pointed out that in both Chinese and English cultures the wolf and the dog evoke cruelty, cunning ferocity, and rapine. The crane, however, occupied a privileged position in Chinese letters while almost entirely absent from those of the West. In Europe the cuckoo is celebrated for laying its eggs in the nests of other birds, and in China its cry symbolizes nostalgic longing. Both cultures employ mythical creatures, especially the dragon, the unicorn, and the phoenix. Animals are used as symbols of both perpetrators and victims of violence, but in the three plays in question animal imagery has as its main purpose the underscoring of the brutish in man.

The earlier exiled Chinese poet to whom I have already alluded, Hsieh Ling-yun, looked upon himself as "a hibernating dragon, a measuring worm." The exposition of multiethnic society in the United States revealed how early American culture has been portrayed as a snake "sloughing off its skin as it grows too large for its old one." In various modern dystopias, moreover, such as *Animal Farm* and *The City of Cats,* animals are used to portray a variety of human characteristics. A Japanese scholar, Sanehide Kodama, showed how the black American poet Richard Wright developed the English "haiku" as a genre. In one of his poems Wright humorously personified the domestic animal:

> With a twitching nose
> A dog reads a telegram
> On a wet tree trunk.

Bangok Lee also indicated that in Korean fiction of the early twentieth century a boy's angelic innocence is reduced to "the bestiality of a wolf," and a female character determines to pounce upon a man who has not returned her love and, in her words, "tear him apart with my claws, and suck his blood to my heart's content." Some participants of the conference who were oriented toward esoteric schemes of criticism have objected that themes and imagery such as the foregoing are so commonplace that they are not worthy of serious attention, but it is precisely the element of universality that makes them appropriate for discussion in an international forum. In contrast, many of the critical theories expounded under the rubric of thematology have merely historical interest, for their vogue lies already buried in the past. Even the more current systems are relevant merely to selected texts in Western national literatures alone.

A classic example of the universality of animal symbols is the collection of fables attributed to Aesop of ancient Greece. Kei-ichirō Kobori combined thematology with literary history in tracing the influence of these fables in the East, especially in Japan. A purely historical treatment should perhaps have indi-cated in addition the origins in the East of some of these fables, but this author primarily intended to illustrate the shifting inter-pretations of various symbols in successive chronological pe-riods. Before World War II, animal fables were utilized in Japan as media of moral instruction in the elementary grades, but as in other parts of the world there has been a noticeable decrease in the effort to weave ethics into the preliminary stages of educa-tion. The fable of the frog and the cow—a contrast to the legend of Narcissus—illustrates a political interpretation. A frog, envi-ous of the large size of a cow, puffed herself up to her maximum size out of envy and a spirit of rivalry and continued the effort to such an extent that she finally burst and fell over dead. The great Japanese novelist Sōseki in 1909 applied this fable to the aspira-tion of the Japanese people to rival the Western nations of his time. In Sōseki's words, "It's like the frog that tried to outdo the cow—look, Japan's belly is bursting." A related paper by an Italian scholar, Lina Unali, traced intercultural relations be-tween India and England during the nineteenth century to show how the fables in *The Arabian Nights* could be "attuned to the spirit of mercantile enterprise of the English people" in extend-ing their world-wide economic empire.

To Western readers *The Arabian Nights* represents the ulti-mate in romantic mystery and splendor, but Tarek A. Jawad revealed that from earliest times "in Arab chronicles, travel-ogues and wondertales" China has occupied a vital place always associated with wealth and exoticism. The famous fourteenth-century Moroccan traveler, Ibn Batuta, moreover, described Chinese women as "surpassing beauty." According to Jawad, the realistic description of Batuta served to explode the myths that heavily enriched the tales of wonder in the *Arabian Nights* such as Sinbad the Sailor.

One of the papers offered a vigorous criticism of the comparative method as it is commonly practiced in the area of East-West relations. According to Wilt L. Idema, affinity studies are likely to be lame or superficial, and the comparison of individual works or period styles often degenerates from lameness into "the wheelchair of modish critical jargon." This author proposes as an alternative "the comparative study of the concept of literature—whether explicitly formulated in writings on literature, or indirectly observable productions, reception, and preservation of literary works," together with "the comparative study of authors as a social group and their role in society." This, I interpret, not as a call for comparing literatures as coherent wholes, but rather for a reinvigoration of the sociology of literature. The application of this scholar's method consisted in a comparison of literary clubs or societies in two countries, Chinese *shu-hui* and Dutch *kamers rhetoriken.*

Since English was the official language of the conference, it is hardly surprising that as in the previous Tamkang gatherings most of the Western writers treated were English and American. The papers on criticism, of course, ranged over Russian, Hungarian, French, and German texts as well, but presumably these critical discourses had been studied in English translation. Since criticism has become almost an autonomous discipline, authors of these papers did not necessarily profess knowledge of the literatures represented by their favorite Western critics. The truly international flavor of the conference was communicated by papers on German influence in Korea, Arab notions of China, and relations between England and India in the nineteenth century.

The papers on genology did not devote themselves to distinguishing or describing the various literary kinds, but instead analyzed techniques of narrative or poetic expression. Jonathan Hall expounded the theory of totality in Karl Marx and its application to literature as interpreted by Lukács and other Marxist critics. Presented as a study in the history of ideas, this paper would undoubtedly be welcomed in a journal of that discipline, but it appeared anomalous in the East-West context. The theory of totality in its literary manifestation assumes that all novels are constructed on an identical principle, which is a completely erroneous assumption even in regard to European fiction, let alone that of the rest of the world, particularly China and Japan. Happily this monolithic approach was not adopted by David Wang in an analysis of the storytelling devices in Chinese fiction, which revealed parallels with a variety of narrative techniques in the West such as completely individual texts within a frame story, the magisterial narrator, direct speech, the first-person point of view, and the characterized fictive reader. A further paper by Lucien Miller involving *The Woman Warrior* treated the mixing of the fictional and autobiographical genres. As a welcome relief to the irrelevant theory in some other papers, this author gave a sparkling example of the omniscient narrator interjecting an editorial explanation by affirming that "solace is purely spiritual but it is used here as a euphemism for sex." This author analyzed among other narrative techniques various methods of obtaining visual perspective.

Matters of perspective were taken up also by Mei-shu Hwang in a paper on the voice or "I" in classical Chinese poetry, which was based on the premise of Western classical criticism *ut pictura poesis*—that is, that painting and poetry are alike. By means of visual illustrations, the author revealed that Chinese poetry for the most part represents life from a number of varying viewpoints rather than from the fixed perspective ordinarily associated with Western art and poetry. This multiple perspective may be interpreted as both a means of concentrating on a central object or as a method of creating an overall impression without attention to specific details. Y. T. Walther suggested that the highly graphic effect of some of the verse of Ezra Pound is achieved through the juxtaposition of archetypal nouns, leading to both obscurity and discontinuity.

Lucien Miller treated this element of discontinuity in a remarkably parallel exposition of the narrative style of the Chinese novel *The Golden Cangue* by Eileen Chang. This particular style is spatial form, which was characterized as a development "in modern fiction and poetry whereby techniques are used to subvert sequence, chronology and the linear flow of words," thereby creating a synchronic rather than diachronic thrust through the juxtaposition of elements.

Another general theme not apparent in the titles of particular papers was that of the self and the non-self. In connection with

The Woman Warrior, I have already alluded to the tension established by Amy Ling between the ethnicity of the protagonist and her American self. Lucien Miller pointed out in regard to the same novel that traditionally in China the self is part of the community, but there is "little consciousness of self as a unique unrepeatable phenomenon who desires to endure as an individual in memory." Yet Mei-shu Wang indicated that classical Chinese poetry has been classified into two types, that of "a world with I (self)" and the other of "a world without I (self)." Also a textbook in English on the Japanese haiku cited by Sanehide Kodama explains that the state of mind of the poet represents "conditions of *selflessness* in which things are seen without reference to profit or loss, even of some remote, spiritual kind." Byung-wook Moon described a situation in which the self before a mirror and the reflected self reject each other. The self in the mirror does not believe the self outside, and the poet has no place for his identity either inside or outside.

The dichotomy between self and non-self resembles that between the actual world and the world of dreams, a contrast that is noticed nearly always in regard to *The Dream of the Red Chamber,* and this conference was no exception. Mei-shu Wang cited the classic paradox by the author of the *Dream:*

> Truth becomes fiction when the fiction's true,
> Real becomes not real when the unreal's real.

The paper on *The Golden Cangue* quoted a passage from the latter novel in which the narrator asks, "What is real and what is false?" And the student of Korean aestheticism cited a novel that made him recollect Oscar Wilde's artistic credo that life should imitate art.

The foregoing examples of intercultural themes are for the most part original and significant. Supplementing the Western student's familiar stock of characters, situations, and attitudes, they show that it is feasible for universal literature to be studied from the practical as well as the theoretical perspective.

The following chapters are intended to provide further illustrations of pragmatic methods for tracing interactions of the East and the West.

Chapter 4. References

Deeney, John J., ed. 1980. *Chinese-Western comparative literature theory and strategy.* Hong Kong: Hong Kong Univ. Press.

Etiemble, René. 1974. *Essais de littérature (vraiment) générale.* Paris: Gallimard.

——, ed. 1980. *Philosophes taoïstes.* Paris: Gallimard.

Miner, Earl. 1958. *The Japanese tradition in British and American literature.* Princeton, N.J.: Princeton Univ. Press.

Rabkin, Eric S. 1976. *The fantastic in literature.* Princeton, N.J.: Princeton Univ. Press.

Said, Edward W. 1978. *Orientalism.* New York: Pantheon.

Part II
PRAGMATIC APPLICATIONS

5

Voltaire and the Mirage of China

THERE IS NO NEED TO PROCLAIM VOLTAIRE'S FASCINATION FOR China. This is by now an old story, which has already been expounded by many scholars. Indeed, as part of the new information presented in this chapter, I can report that at least one Sinologist began studying Voltaire before the eighteenth century had reached its end. A Russian courier, Vasilii Bratischev, who had been sent to Peking in 1756 published in the *Works of the Free Russian Assembly of the Imperial Moscow University* in 1783 an article entitled "Information about or Verification of Voltaire's Remarks on China" (Maggs 1973, 346).

There is no question that virtually all of Voltaire's material on the Middle Kingdom came from secondary sources. His knowledge was indirect, incomplete, and superficial. I do not propose, therefore, to study the origin of Voltaire's information, but rather to indicate the manner in which he applied his knowledge of China—faulty and limited as it was—to his basic philosophy and to show the relationship of his notions concerning China to other aspects of his thought. In other words, I shall try to answer the question: What was the role of China in the Voltairean philosophy?

The experts in China in the eighteenth century consisted of three major classes. To paraphrase Voltaire himself, the merchants, who had been there, talked mainly about the sharp dealing of Chinese traders; the clergy, who had also been there, complained about being persecuted by other orders; and the learned men of Paris, who had never been there, expatiated endlessly on the religion, government, economy, and origins of the Chinese people. One group of these learned men expressed a theory that Voltaire opposed—that China had been colonized by the Egyptians; a much larger group, to which Voltaire himself belonged, considered Chinese culture indigenous and heaped unlimited praise on its antiquity, wisdom, and piety. This they did primarily to expose by contrast the alleged deficiencies of the Judaic-Christian tradition as reflected in orthodox Christian doctrine and observances. A contemporary Scottish linguist and literary critic, James Beattie, gave a quite accurate appraisal of French Sinophilia: "Some of our modern philosophers affect to be great admirers of the genius, policy, and morality of the Chinese. The truth is, that Europeans know very little of that remote people; and we are apt to admire what we do not understand: and for those who, like the Chinese obstinately shut their eyes against the light of the Gospel, the French authors, now-a-days, and their imitators, are apt to cherish an extraordinary warmth of brotherly affection" (1788, 114–15).

It was written in the creed of most deists of the eighteenth-century to disparage everything Jewish as a means of attacking the foundations of Christianity. Conversely they exalted the antiquity of Chinese civilization as being far more ancient than Hebrew as a means of confounding the Old Testament account of the origin of the world. Deistical anti-Semitism was the obverse of deistical Sinophilia, and Voltaire was merely part of a trend in reflecting both attitudes, a trend that was just as English as French.

Long before Voltaire, "the most typical and most systematic single expression" of English deism, Matthew Tindal's *Christianity as Old as the Creation, or the Gospel a Republication of the Religion of Nature,* 1731, set forth the argument that God from the very beginning of creation gave man an absolutely perfect religion that "cannot admit of any alteration, or be capable of addition or diminution." The basic teachings of Christ, according to Tindal, had been anticipated by other religious leaders in many lands. Tindal pretended to place Confucius and Christ on an equal plane, but subtly insinuated the superiority of the Chinese sage. "I am," he wrote, "so far from thinking the maxims of Confucius and Jesus Christ to differ, that I think the plain and simple maxims of the former, will help to illustrate the more obscure ones of the latter, accommodated to the then way of speaking." One of the published answers to Tindal objected that "there never was a nation in the world, whose public Religion was formed upon the plan of Nature and instituted on the principles of mere Reason." Voltaire wrote in the margin of his copy opposite this passage, "the religion of Chinese government" (Torrey 1930, 171).

The mentor of Voltaire's youth, Lord Bolingbroke, wrote during the 1740s his *Fragments, or Minutes of Essays,* an extensive philosophical work that was among other things a study of comparative religion. It strongly resembles Voltaire's *Essai sur les moeurs,* which was begun at about the same time. Bolingbroke presented China as "a country, into the antiquities of which we look further back than into those of any other, and where we may find examples . . . [of] . . . the effects of natural religion, unmixed and uncorrupted, with those of artificial theology and superstition."[1] (St. John 1809, 8:49). Bolingbroke claimed, moreover, that natural religion, the deists' name for their ideological system based on reason rather than revelation, "seems to have been preserved more pure and unmixed in this country than in any other, and for a longer time from that when it was first inhabited, and government was first established." Voltaire in his *Essai sur les moeurs* spoke with the same assurance and for the same purpose. "It is evident," he declared, "that the Empire of China was formed more than four thousand years ago." "Their religion was simple, wise, august, free of all superstition and all barbarousness, when we did not even have the Teutâtes, to whom the druids sacrificed the children of our ancestors in big wicker baskets" (Introduction XVIII).

Both Bolingbroke and Voltaire specifically described the early stages of Chinese society as a kind of Golden Age. According to Bolingbroke, "this people enjoyed, under their two first imperial families, which continued eleven hundred years, all the blessings of public and private virtue, that humanity is capable of enjoying. So we must understand the descriptions of this golden age" (8:49). In reference to Confucius, Voltaire affirmed that "the happiest and most respectable age that was ever on the earth was that in which his laws were followed" (*Essai* Chap. II). The latter passage is quite out of character for Voltaire since elsewhere in his works he savagely ridicules the concept of a Golden Age itself. But it must be emphasized that it is natural religion—not primitive innocence—which both Voltaire and Bolingbroke were extolling. Both established this age of simple wisdom in order to castigate later corruption allegedly brought about by artificial religions imposed by priests. The two philosophers differed, however, in their interpretations of the consequences of this corruption. Voltaire held that only the lower classes in China fell under its sway while the upper classes preserved their traditional wisdom; whereas Bolingbroke affirmed that religion contaminated the whole country, which eventually became entirely atheistic.

Relatively late in his literary career, Voltaire published a collection of miscellaneous essays entitled *Lettres chinoises: indiennes et tartares,* 1766, in which he summarized the ostensible reasons for his admiration of China: its great antiquity, its large population, its humane and efficient government, and the sublime morality of its religion as expressed in the writings of Confucius. These are the main lines of his discussion of China from his first reference in 1722 to his last in 1778. He was impressed by these characteristics of Chinese culture partly for themselves because they represented the achievements of a great civilization and partly because they could be used as proofs or illustrations of polemical doctrines that he was advocating in his lifelong war against bigotry and superstition.

The single work of Voltaire that might seem to be pure in its devotion to China—that is, free from any ulterior propaganda or ideological aims—is his drama *L'Orphelin de la Chine,* 1755, which was inspired by an authentic Chinese tragedy, *The Orphan of the House of Chao.* Actually it is not one of Voltaire's most effusive panegyrics of Chinese civilization, and despite its dramatic form it is heavily laden with ideological overtones. Before Voltaire, the original Chinese play had been adapted in England by William Hatchett and in Italy by Metastasio, both following their model more closely than did Voltaire. As a matter of fact, Voltaire took little from the ancient Chinese tragedy except the setting and title. Entirely on his own authority, he introduced the Tartar conqueror Genghis Khan as a major character and elevated all the other personages to the high aristocracy. (Ya-Oui 1937; 141). In his preface, moreover, Voltaire did not overwhelm the Chinese with compliments as in his other works; if anything, he was unflattering—drawing attention to the failure of the Chinese to make any appreciable progress in the arts and sciences after the initial period of their ascendancy in antiquity. He even compared them to the Egyptians, who had first given lessons to the Greeks and then regressed to the stage of being incapable of following in their footsteps.

The original Chinese drama was written in the thirteenth century by Chi Chün-hsiang. Voltaire's source was a translation of 1731 by a French Jesuit, Joseph Henri Prémare, which was later included in a famous compilation by another Jesuit, Jean Baptiste Du Halde, under the title *Description géographique, historique, chronologique, politique, et physique de l'empire de la Chine et de la tartarie chinoise* (1735). Among the essential ingredients of the original Chinese work were song and music, but these were completely eliminated from Prémare's translation and from Voltaire's adaptation as well. Since Voltaire's neoclassical drama departed from both the form and the substance of his Chinese source, one would be justified in asking whether his work should really be considered as an example of the penetration of Chinese culture. Should it instead be dismissed as mere Chinoiserie? The answer is that Voltaire himself understood a great deal more about Chinese civilization than his play reveals, but that he was prevented by the prevailing taste of the times from closely following his model. "If the French were not so French," he explained, "my Chinese would have been more Chinese and Genghis more Tartar. It was necessary for me to impoverish my ideas and restrict myself in the portrayal of manners in order not to shock a frivolous nation which laughs foolishly, but thinks it is laughing gayly, at everything which is not conformable to its customs or rather to its modes" (Voltaire 1953–65, 5874). Despite these restrictions, Voltaire attempted, especially by means of staging, to give a realistic portrayal of Chinese customs. For the first time in the history of the French stage the costumes and scenery were those of the place and time of the events being depicted rather than those of eighteenth-century France. The leading lady, Mlle Clairon, for example, wore a network of golden tassels instead of the conventional hoopskirt. According to one of the younger critics, La Harpe, "this is the first time we have been shown a Chinese nation" (La Harpe 1870, 2:366). Voltaire's play was adapted for the London stage in 1759 by Arthur Murphy, and it was translated during the eighteenth century into English, Spanish, German, and Italian. There were also several French lyrical adaptations that added dancing and singing, bringing the work somewhat closer in form to its Chinese original.

Voltaire intended his *Orphelin* to carry a thesis—which was that the arts and sciences are beneficial to a nation and that they serve a salutary purpose even when that nation is conquered by hostile invaders. Rousseau in his famous *Discourse on the Sciences and the Arts,* 1750, had cited China as the example of a country rich in science and humane letters that had, nevertheless, fallen prey to the yoke of the ignorant and barbaric Tartars. Voltaire constructed his drama to illustrate a contrary principle frequently expressed elsewhere in his works—that the Chinese by dint of their superior culture had assimilated their barbarian conquerors, who had in admiration adopted the Chinese customs—a theme that I shall henceforth describe as that of the conquerors-conquered. In the preface to *L'Orphelin de la Chine,* Voltaire described his Chinese model, *The Orphan of the House of Chao,* composed during the dynasty of Genghis Khan, as "a new proof that the conquering Tartars did not change the customs of the conquered nation"; they protected all the arts established in China and adopted all the laws of the country. This was, in Voltaire's words, "a great example of the natural superiority which reason and genius provide over blind force and barbarousness." He exaggerated this theme in the play itself to such a degree that his English adapter Arthur Murphy accused him of transforming Genghis Khan without adequate preparation from a crude barbarian to "le chevalier Genghis-khan" (Voltaire 1953–65, 7559). In the last scene of the play, Genghis Khan himself proclaims the theme, "Let the conquered peoples govern the conquerors." "Que les peuples vaincus gouvernent les vainquers."

Voltaire used his preface, moreover, to vindicate the theater as a salutary social institution. It had been under attack by puritanical minds for over a century because of its alleged immorality and pernicious effect upon society. Voltaire replied to this charge in his preface by praising the Chinese, Greeks, and Romans for being the only peoples in antiquity to cultivate the drama. "Nothing," he proclaimed, "more effectively renders men sociable, moderates their behavior, or develops their reason, than congregating [in a theater] which allows them to taste together the pure pleasures of the mind."

In a letter to a Protestant minister Voltaire revealed that in the earlier stages of composing *L'Orphelin de la Chine* he had considered using it as a vehicle for expressing the philosophy of Confucius, but had hesitated to do so lest it be ridiculed by insensitive and pleasure-loving Parisians (Voltaire 1953–65; 5859). He had been encouraged by the initial success of the play, however, to revise it in this direction to such a degree that he later called it his "Chinese sermon."

The theme of the barbarous conquerors vanquished in the end by the superior civilization of the defeated nation harmonizes with another major theme in Voltaire's work, that of the superiority of a polished society to primitive existence. The *locus classicus* for Voltaire's antiprimitivism is his poem *Le Mondain,* 1736, one of the major attacks of the century on the back-to-nature movement. It is no coincidence that Voltaire should be both a vociferous defender of Chinese culture and a caustic critic of primitivism; and that the two major French Sinophobes, Rousseau and Diderot, should be at the same time ardent advocates of the values associated with primitivism.

In England, Defoe in his novel *Robinson Crusoe* had presented not only a famous portrayal of primitivism, but a savage attack on China. Indeed Defoe "throughout his career, in all his references to this country, displayed a persistent antagonism that varied from deceptive irony to downright invective" (Appleton 1951, 57). Voltaire on the contrary admired the antiquity, the politeness, the intricate social organization of China, all qualities inimical to primitivism. He argued that the compiling of records attesting the existence of a vast empire is in itself proof that the organization of China into a political body must have taken place centuries before. To reach the point of merely being able to write—let alone to write well—must have required several centuries (*Moeurs,* Introduc. XVIII).

Chinese antiquity was important for Voltaire, however, not so much for its effectiveness as an argument against primitivism as for its even greater effectiveness as a symbol to be opposed to Hebrew tradition. The portrayal of Chinese civilization as flourishing in a highly advanced stage when the Hebrew was in its infancy served to disparage the latter. The argument of Chinese antiquity even more specifically damaged the Christian tradition by disputing Old Testament chronology and thereby bringing into question biblical authority as such. The Christian Scriptures declare that the world was created in 4000 B.C. and that the Great Flood covered the earth in 2300 B.C.; yet reliable Chinese chronicles existing for four thousand years implied an anterior existence of Chinese civilization for several more centuries: these chronicles, moreover, make absolutely no reference to a universal inundation such as that described in Genesis. The latter account would then appear to be fable rather than history. Voltaire was careful to point out moreover that the Chinese chronology contained no contradictions of any kind, whereas that in the Bible was full of problems—and the various texts of the Christian Scriptures—Vulgate, Septuagint and Samaritans—offered astounding variations in chronology. Voltaire appropriately quoted the question of the Chinese emperor Cam-hi (K'ang Hsi) to the French missionaries, "Is it possible that the books in which you place your faith combat each other?" (Introduc. XVIII).

In pointing to the textual weaknesses of biblical chronology, Voltaire touched on another famous controversy in the history of ideas, one completely independent of the role of China in world culture, but nevertheless related to it. This controversy concerned the Age of the World—an attempt to discover how far in the past the earth as presently constituted came into being, what were the changes it had gone through, and whether the chronology and descriptions of the Bible are in accord with reality. The problem came to the fore as early as 1561 in the *Chronologia* of Nicephorus and Camerarius and in 1598 in the *De Emendatione Temporum* of Joseph Scaliger, and it was treated by Luther, Calvin, Bacon, Grotius and scores of others (Meyer 1951). From this background emerged La Peyrère's *Praeadamitae,* 1655, an attempt to justify the Scriptures by asserting the existence of men on earth before Adam including the Chaldeans, Egyptians, and the Chinese. Other scholars attempted to identify the first legendary emperor of China, Fo-hi (Fu Hsi) with Adam (Voltaire 1962, 1669). Geological evidence was adduced by Thomas Burnet in his *Archaeologiae Philosophicae*, 1692 [*The Sacred Theory of the Earth*] in which he ascribed the flood to natural causes and allowed for an allegorical interpretation of the Scriptures, including chronology. Leibniz in 1699 argued that if Chinese historical chronology should be accepted, the date for the beginning of the world must be pushed back (Lach 1945, 453). Voltaire, therefore, had a number of respectable authorities to draw upon in questioning the authenticity of biblical chronology, but he, of course, did so in an attempt to discredit the sacred texts, whereas most of his predecessors had sought to protect the Scriptures and preserve their sanctity.

Voltaire's contemporaries clearly recognized his intentions. The naturalist Charles Bonnet, in commenting on Voltaire's "passion for the Chinese," reported indignantly "a hundred times he has turned the Chronology of this nation against that of Moses. He pretended to show that the Chinese are anterior by six or seven hundred years to the Flood" (Voltaire 1953–65, 7336). Voltaire, ingenuously, denied the charge, as he expressed it, "that the minute philosophers give such a great antiquity to China only to discredit the Scriptures." His answer was simple, that he had taken his information from the writings of the Roman Catholic clergy.

One of the devices of the theologians to vindicate Scripture chronology was to argue that the Chinese are actually not as old as they seem, and that they are descended racially from the Egyptians who had planted a colony in China. This hypothesis had actually been first introduced by one of the Jesuit authorities on China, Kircher, in his *China Monumentis . . . Illustrata*, 1657, although Voltaire suggests that Huet was the first (*Lettres chinoises,* Lettre VII). The argument was revived in 1759 by Joseph de Guignes in his *Mémoire dans lequel on prouve que les Chinois sont une colonie égyptienne.* Voltaire immediately turned the theory into ridicule during the same year in the preface to his *Histoire de l'empire de Russie sous Pierre le Grand.*

He pointed out that the argument is based on gratuitous or very general resemblances between the two cultures and on far-fetched linguistic similarities. The same method of argument, he taunted, could be used by Russian or Chinese scholars to prove that the Parisians descended directly from the Trojans or conversely that they descended from the Greeks. It could equally be proved by the same method that the French were originally Egyptians or Arabs. In a later burlesque of the theory Voltaire indicated that he would personally prefer the Chinese, who have worshipped a single god for four thousand years, to the Egyptians, who worship cows, cats, and crocodiles (*Lettres chinoises,* Lettre VII). Approaching the concept from the biological perspective, Voltaire also argued that the great peoples of the two continents are autochthonous or indigenous. That is, like other plants and animals they originated where they are found in great numbers. In most questions of biology, Voltaire's thought was surprisingly conservative or even reactionary. He accepted the opinion of Saint Thomas, therefore, that God has produced for all eternity the races of animals and that these have never changed. As a corollary, he concluded that the features of the Chinese, their manners, language, writing, and customs have nothing to do with the ancient Egyptians (*Fragments sur l'histoire,* Article IV).

Voltaire insisted as much on the great population of China as upon the antiquity of the nation and he did it for similar reasons; the proposition, if granted, further weakens the authority of Scriptures and also represents evidence of the wisdom of Chinese government. As early as his *Lettres philosophiques,* 1734, Voltaire had drawn the parallel between national virtue and large numbers, declaring that the English people were "the most numerous, the most virtuous even and consequently the most respectable party of men."

Voltaire was skeptical, however, of the large population attributed by Bible scholars to the ancient Jews. The statistics given in the second chapter of the Book of Numbers, for example, would require that there be an average of fifty children to a family (Gray 1903, 10–15). Voltaire ridiculed the conclusions of such commentators as Pétau, Cumberland, and Whiston, who magnified the population of ancient times in order to make the

Old Testament acceptable in a literal fashion. According to Voltaire, Pétau attributed to the earth 285 years after the Flood a population one hundred times greater than that in the eighteenth century (*Dictionnaire philosophique,* "De la Chine"). Whiston calculated that the population of the earth could have been 549 billion all stemming from Adam and Eve, by the $1,482^d$ year of the world (Meyer 1951, 88). Voltaire repudiated these theological mathematics with a phrase that he used several times in his works, "one does not make children with the stroke of a pen" (*Moeurs,* Chap. I). The claims of Old Testament population were exaggerated myths, according to Voltaire, but the contemporary statistics concerning China were reliable. Roughly speaking, China then had 150 million inhabitants compared to 100 million in all of Europe. In the *Gazette littéraire de l'Europe,* 1764, Voltaire declared that "the most populated country on earth is China without their having produced either books or laws to favor population" (1953–65, 11306).

Voltaire elsewhere, however, recognized a Chinese law pertaining to population, one forbidding a man to become a priest until he had attained the age of forty (*Moeurs,* Chap. CLV). Voltaire had previously suggested in *La Voix du sage et du peuple,* 1750 that such a rule be applied in France on the grounds that celibacy is a deterrent to the increase of population.

A debate parallel to that concerning the relative population of the Jews and the Chinese was waged in the eighteenth century over the relative population of ancient and modern times. Montesquieu affirmed that the peak had been reached during the Roman Empire and Hume replied that the numbers were much greater in the eighteenth century. Pertinent to this debate and discussed as part of it, as well as independently, was the question of whether the custom of polygamy increases or decreases population. Montesquieu both in his *Lettres persanes* and *L'Esprit des lois* had argued that polygamy drastically decreases the birth rate (Lettres 114–17; Livre XIII, Chaps. 17–26). Voltaire, discussing polygamy in regard to China, argued that it cannot be considered a disadvantage since the countries in which plural wives have always been accepted, India, China and Japan, are the most populous of the universe (*Fragments sur l'histoire,* Article III). He disposed of the argument that, assuming the number of males and females to be more or less equal, if a man marries four wives, three men will be forced to do without a female companion. His answer is that because of the excess of women in the birth rate, the dangerous occupations followed by most males, and the number of men who become priests or eunuchs, there is no real danger of any men being left without a mate. Polygamy, therefore, becomes not only useful, but actually necessary to the welfare of the state.

Voltaire introduced another argument in favor of polygamy that was completely original: practically no adultery exists in the Orient, whereas the West is filled with it. From this he concluded that polygamy authorized by law is vastly superior to a general corruption authorized by custom. Even the practice of some women from the lowest levels of society in China of exposing their infants, preferring to kill them at birth rather than having them die of slow starvation at a later period, Voltaire converted into an argument in favor of polygamy: had these women been beautiful, they would have found entrance into a harem and been able to rear their children with proper parental care. In other words, concubinage is a deterrent to infanticide. It has been noticed that in an early version of the *Essai sur les moeurs,* Voltaire made a similar reference to the Chinese custom of exposing infants and that he deleted it in a later version, presumably because the custom was not compatible with the high morality that Voltaire wished to associate with the Chinese (Pomeau 1964, 308). If this is the reason for the deletion, it is somewhat surprising that he should have returned to the subject in his considerably later *Fragments sur l'histoire,* the text that we have been discussing. In the introduction to the *Essai sur les moeurs* Voltaire particularly complimented the Chinese as being the only one of the ancient peoples, including the Greeks, never to practice infant sacrifice (Sec. IX).

One of the favorite methods of the deists in attacking Christianity was to point to the institution of polygamy being not only tolerated, but even commanded in the Old Testament (Aldridge 1948). By this means they ridiculed the custom of interpreting the Scriptures literally and they indirectly condemned the Scriptures for reflecting the conditions of a barbaric society. In concluding his treatment of population in China, therefore, Voltaire alluded to the authorization given by Pope Gregory II to one of the faithful to have two wives and to the same permission extended by Luther and Melanchthon to the Landgrave of Hesse.

On the subject of the humane and efficient government in China, Voltaire wrote so extensively that only a few of his motifs may be mentioned here. One of the most important was his denial that the government was despotic. This was one of the many subjects on which Voltaire disagreed with *L'Esprit des lois,* and he drew attention in his *Essai sur les moeurs* to Montesquieu's "vague imputations" against the world's most ancient government (Chap. 1). Montesquieu did not like China (according to Etiemble because his predilections toward the English led him to accept their unfavorable accounts of Chinese behavior and because he accepted the minority opinion of the Jesuit Fouquet, who adopted antiChinese sentiments of the Dominicans against the prevailing view of his own order) and Voltaire was envious of Montesquieu's prestige. He had a double reason, therefore, for refuting Montesquieu's charge of despotism. He did so by citing the Chinese custom dating from the second century B.C. of writing down on a long table placed in the palace whatever one considered reprehensible in the government and the tradition that in the time of peace the decisions of the tribunals always have the force of law. Elsewhere in his *Essai,* Voltaire described the Chinese empire at the turn of the eighteenth century as being supervised by great tribunals, the members of which were received only after several severe examinations. The laws emanated from the emperor, but according to the constitution he was required first of all to consult the tribunals. In such an administration, in Voltaire's words, "it is impossible for the emperor to exercise an arbitrary power" (Chap. CXCV).

The debate between Montesquieu and Voltaire represented two skilled polemicists trying their wits on a subject that neither knew anything about. As Etiemble has pointed out, the two historians once drew absolutely contrary conclusions from the same evidence, the execution of two Chinese princes. Voltaire said that the Jesuits were to blame for creating dissension in the royal family; Montesquieu said that despotic tyranny was at fault (Etiemble 1956, 466).

One of the commonly presented points of evidence to indict

the Chinese government of despotism was the rite of the kow-tow, which even foreign travelers were required to perform if they wished to approach the throne. Voltaire dismissed this objection with the remark that neither this custom nor that of punishing as sacrilege the least disrespect shown to the figure of the emperor proves that the government was despotic or arbitrary (ibid.). Elsewhere he argued that to assume despotism on the basis of the kow-tow is judging by the exterior: one sees men falling prostrate and takes them for slaves (Chap. 1). Yet when his main concern was attacking the Jesuits rather than defending the Chinese, he implied that the missionaries themselves performed the ceremony and that it was degrading, consisting of the ordinary genuflection and striking the ground nine times with the forehead (*Dialogues et entretiens philosophiques,* XXIV).

Like many other writers on China, Voltaire described with admiration the ceremony to inaugurate spring plowing in which the emperor himself participated in the sowing of seeds. Voltaire in one work estimated that according to the most moderate calculations the ceremony must go back at least to the time of the Flood in Christian chronology (*Dieu et les hommes,* Chap. IV). In the article "Agriculture" in his *Dictionnaire philosophique,* he reprinted from a Jesuit source an extensive description of the ceremony and followed it by advising the sovereigns of Europe to admire and blush, but especially to imitate. In the *Essai sur les moeurs,* Voltaire observed that twice a year the emperor offered to the god of the universe the first fruits of the harvest, the very harvest that he had sown with his own hands (Introduc. XVIII).

For Voltaire the most striking evidence of the efficiency and sublimity of the Chinese government was the fact that the nation had twice been invaded by Tartars from the north and twice had assimilated the invaders to its own culture. This is the theme of the conqueror-conquered that I have discussed in connection with *l'Orphelin de la Chine.* Voltaire's interpretation of the historical events, however, is by no means the only possible one. It could be asserted to the contrary that the Tartars were strong before invading China, but they succumbed to the enervating and languid atmosphere of China and grew weak in turn. Rather than the conqueror-conquered, it would be the strong man seduced in a kind of international Sampson-Delilah story. This was the interpretation of an early-eighteenth-century foe of the Jesuits, Abbé Renaudot, who affirmed, "The Tartars without philosophy made themselves masters of this great empire in a very short time when they attacked it, and as soon as they adopted Chinese customs they found themselves as a consequence exposed to the same disgraces as their predecessors" (Guy 1963, 196). One could even take the view that the Chinese did not effectively assimilate their conquerors, but instead themselves adopted some of the worst traits of the Tartars. This would be the theme of the conquered-corrupted. Catherine the Great of Russia expressed it in a letter to Voltaire, 1771, in which she denounced the Chinese of her day for their chicanery, quibbling, and intransigence. The ancient Chinese before the Tartar invasion were a superior race, she maintained, but those of modern times demonstrate that "the conquerors have not adopted the politeness of the conquered and the latter run the risk of being influenced by the dominant mores" (Voltaire 1953–65, 16093).

Voltaire, however, consistently proclaimed the theme of salutary assimilation although admitting the possibility that the Chinese culture may have had some characteristics that worked to the disadvantage of the conquerors. In the *Essai sur les moeurs* he reported that the thirteenth-century Tartar conquerors adopted Chinese names and customs and preserved Chinese law, but after several generations, surrounded by women and priests, they surrendered to effeminacy and were overthrown in turn (Chap. CLV). In his *Lettres chinoises* he merely reported that China had been twice subjugated by the Tartars and that the "conquerors had conformed to the laws of the conquered" (Lettre V).

Voltaire joined the theme of the Tartar conquest to another motif in his Sinophilia—that of the Great Wall, reluctantly and half-heartedly adopted by Voltaire as a symbol of national greatness. In the *Essai sur les moeurs,* while admitting that the Wall had been powerless to keep out the invaders, he described it in detail as a great feat of engineering, "superior to the pyramids of Egypt by its utility as by its immensity" (Chap. 1). In other references to the Wall, he considered it either a great achievement or the contrary, according to the thesis he was trying to support. In the article on China in his *Dictionnaire philosophique* he described the Egyptian pyramids as "merely childish and useless heaps" in comparison with the Wall, which he eulogized as "this great work," possibly according it praise in order to strike a blow against the theory of China as an Egyptian colony. In his *Fragments sur l'histoire,* in which anticlerical deism is paramount, he disparaged accounts of similar constructions by the Jews and described the Great Wall as "one of the monuments which does most honor to the human spirit." He added, moreover, that it was not built out of vanity as were the pyramids (Article II). In his *Lettres chinoises,* however, he termed the Wall a work "as vain as immense, and moreover unfortunate in having seemed at first useful, since it had not been able to defend the Empire" (Lettre V). And in the article "Anciens et Modernes" in the *Dictionnaire philosophique,* Voltaire denounced the Wall as a monument to fear as the pyramids were a monument to vanity and superstition. These "useless works" required great patience but no genius, he affirmed, and they could be duplicated in modern times with the expenditure of a great deal of money. But neither the Chinese nor the Egyptians could make a statue to compare with modern ones.

Here, of course, Voltaire was allowing his partisan support of the modern position in the Battle of the Ancients and Moderns to take precedence over his Sinophilia. But this position of adherence to the moderns is not one on which he stood firm throughout his literary career. The subject is too vast for treatment here, but it may be suggested that by and large he considered the moderns as superior in the realm of science and philosophy, but the ancients unexcelled in many areas of literature and morality. In praising the Chinese for their great antiquity, and in suggesting that the era of Confucius represented an ideal age, he was, of course, entering the lists on the side of the ancients. The great English proponent of the Chinese, Sir William Temple, was also the most vigorous English advocate of the ancients. Temple believed even that ancient science could compare favorably with modern, but Voltaire unequivocally extolled scientific progress in the modern age even in his works most eulogistic of China. In his introduction to the *Essai sur les moeurs* he specifically exempted himself from treating the question of Chinese backwardness in the sciences. Admitting that in his day they were no further advanced than the French had been two centuries previously, he shifted the discussion to their excellence in morality, "the foremost of the sciences."

Voltaire at least twice raised the question of why the Chinese had made great strides in antiquity and had then suddenly stopped. In his *Essai* he suggested that nature had given the Chinese organs different from the Europeans so that they were capable of providing almost instantaneously everything necessary for their immediate needs, but were incapable of going beyond the first stages (Chap. 1). In slightly different terms, he affirmed that nature had given them a wise and upright spirit, but denied them mental strength (Chap. CLV). He alleged as further reasons their ancestor worship, which made them consider everything in the past as perfect, together with the difficulty of expressing complicated ideas in their language, especially in writing. In his *Fragments sur l'histoire* he traced this difficulty to the absence of an alphabet and predicted that unless the Chinese were to adopt one comparable to that of the Europeans they were not likely to make great progress in the sciences they had invented (Article II). In his *Lettres chinoises* he made a further effort to reconcile "their great progress in ancient times and their present ignorance" (Lettre V). Again he adduced their great respect for their ancestors, and significantly compared it to the Western respect for Aristotle, another passage in which he sided with moderns in the Ancients-Moderns controversy. Voltaire took notice of the pleasure the Chinese found in mathematics combined with their appalling lack of knowledge in the subject. The explanation he offered blamed their educational system: they spent so long in learning to read, to write, and to recite lessons in morality that they were unable to learn mathematics at an early age. After introducing the subject as an example of the inferiority of the Chinese, he turned his discussion in such a way as to remove the critical implications. It is possible, he observed, to govern the state and cultivate arts without a knowledge of mathematics. The Chinese are, therefore, on a plane with French ministers and kings.

Voltaire, in company with nearly all protagonists of China,

turned eventually in his treatment of no matter what aspect of that country to a discussion of its religion and morality and more frequently than not launched into panegyrics of Confucius, his symbol of rational morality, deism, and antique wisdom. Voltaire once spoke vaguely of his *Orphelin de la Chine* as representing "the morality of Confucius in five acts" (1953–65, 5821). Probably he had in mind such appeals to the religion of nature as the following lines, which he particularly admired:

> The marriage bed and Nature are the first of laws,
> Of bonds in men and nations the sacred cause;
> These laws from God derive; all others are our own.

Voltaire did not, however, compare Confucius to Christ, as did such enthusiasts as Christian Wolff and Matthew Tindal. For Voltaire it was enough to point out similarities to Zoroaster, Moses, and Solomon. Tempering his admiration with restraint and moderation, Voltaire praised Confucius precisely because he was a teacher and thinker rather than a priest or leader, an instructor rather than a governor of men. In the *Essai sur les moeurs,* Voltaire depicted Confucius as a wise magistrate who taught ancient laws, who pretended to be neither inspired nor a prophet, and who fabricated no new opinions or new rites. Indeed there cannot even be said to exist a religion of Confucius: he merely taught that of the emperors and tribunals— recommending virtue and preaching no mystery (Introduc. Sec. XVIII). For this reason Voltaire concluded in *Le Siècle de Louis XIV* that the cult of Confucius is not idolatrous. In a quatrain in the *Almanach des Muses,* 1771, he expressed this concept epigrammatically:

> He speaks only as a sage, never as prophet,
> But he is believed even in his own country.

Voltaire was not uniformly flattering. In a personal letter to Mme. d'Epinay, he remarked that "Confucius is a babbler who always says the same thing" (1953–65, 8136). And in a little-known passage in his *Lettres chinoises,* Voltaire repeated this opinion. "Confucius is a good preacher, so verbose that one cannot stand him" (Lettre III).

In various works, Voltaire cites some of the sayings of Confucius, but none of those that have given the Chinese sage his greatest fame. Voltaire mentions but does not stress such doctrines associated with Confucius as instituting reforms from the top of society down (a doctrine that had greatly impressed Benjamin Franklin) or rewarding virtue in the state as well as punishing vice (a principle that Swift, perhaps under the influence of Temple, had woven into *Gulliver's Travels*). Voltaire openly admitted that the disciples of Confucius consisted of emperors, mandarins, men of letters—everyone but the masses (*Moeurs,* Chap. II). This is a more palatable way of expressing what the English Bishop Burnet had said caustically and negatively, "the sect of Confucius in China . . . were atheists themselves, but left religion to the rabble" (Appleton 1951, 43).

The view that men of genius and learning were able to grasp the moral principles of deism but that the lower classes needed to be kept under the restraints of religious superstition was one that aristocratic deists such as Shaftesbury and Bolingbroke and plebeian ones such as Benjamin Franklin hesitated to express directly, but strongly suggested. Voltaire ordinarily praised the Chinese for providing religion, even absurd beliefs, for the masses. In his *Essai sur les moeurs,* he observed that the educated Chinese allowed the people to accept the superstitions of the bonzes, a word that Voltaire consistently used as equivalent to priests. The magistrates recognized that the common people could have religions different from the official one just as the nourishment of the lower classes was cruder than that of the élite. The Chinese magistrates did not, however, unlike some European deists, see any good in speaking of rewards and punishments after death. Not only did they not wish to affirm that which they did not know, but they believed that people fear a law always present and always enforced more than they fear a law that is not to be applied until the future (Introduc. XVIII). This circumstance strengthens the next of Voltaire's arguments that I shall discuss—that it makes no difference to the welfare of the state whether the people believe in god or not. Voltaire observed, moreover, that the chief Chinese superstitions exist in all countries. Confucius himself attributed the greater number of crimes among the ignorant populace than among the literate to the fact that the former were governed by the bonzes (*Essai,* Chap. II).

Throughout his discussion of China, Voltaire approved the joining of the religious and political functions of the state in a single person, the emperor, rather than having them divided as in Europe. In "Dieu et les hommes," Voltaire reported that no religious dissensions have disturbed Chinese history because the government leaves the superstitions of the lower classes undisturbed, enforcing the rule, "Believe as you wish, but do as I order you (Chap. IV). Strangely enough, in a dialogue entitled "Le Mandarin et le Jésuite," Voltaire completely repudiated the doctrine of a double standard in religion. Here the Jesuit argues that it is permissible to deceive men for their own welfare, that deception or "respectable illusions" may possibly be productive of good. The mandarin repudiates this position, however, holding firm for the teaching of plain truth on the grounds that everywhere superstition produces nothing but evil.

If the double standard existed in China and superstition were allowed for the lower classes, the question still remained, what was the religious philosophy actually professed by the literate: was it a type of rational deism or was it absolute atheism? This is the question, as many scholars have pointed out, which the Jesuit missionaries debated with their opponents in other religious orders, the Jesuits insisting that the Chinese believed in a god resembling that of Christianity and their opponents charging that they were outright atheists. On this topic Voltaire allied himself with the Jesuits and repeated most of their arguments. This was by no means a necessary position for Voltaire to take if we assume that his primary objective in celebrating the Chinese was to promote deism. Bayle and Bolingbroke, who shared this latter objective, nevertheless, both concluded unequivocally that the Chinese were atheists. Once or twice in his works Voltaire expresses almost the same opinion, for example, when he affirms that the educated classes "believe that virtue is so necessary for men and so pleasing in itself that one does not even need the knowledge of a god in order to follow it" (*Essai sur les moeurs,* Chap. II). Elsewhere Voltaire denies that it makes any difference whether the Chinese believe in God or not. He points out that according to Christian doctrine, the essential principles of religion are given to man through divine revelation. But the laws of Moses or early Judaic tradition are silent concerning many great dogmas, reserved for the diviner times of Christianity (*Lettres chinoises,* Lettre III). Voltaire does not draw the conclusion, but it is obvious: if the Jews are not to be condemned for failing to anticipate various Christian doctrines, the Chinese, who also have been deprived of revelation, are not to be condemned for being atheists. Voltaire, however, decided to take the Jesuit position when directly discussing Chinese religion, and so he portrayed the Chinese élite as following the universal religion of nature, "a religion infiltering all religions; it is a metal which allies itself with all the others and its lodes stretch throughout the earth to the four corners of the world" (*Dictionnaire philosophique,* "Théisme").

Voltaire's parallel linguistic argument to prove that the Chinese are not atheists, based on analysis of the meanings and connotations of various Chinese words representing god, is taken directly from the Jesuit fathers, whose exegesis was nothing but an apology of their stand against the Dominicans and Franciscans. As Etiemble has pointed out, Voltaire accused Father Maigrot of the Société des Missions Etrangères of not knowing a word of Chinese and settling a major dispute with ramifications in theology, politics, and history by a linguistic interpretation of two words that Voltaire also knew nothing about (1956, 473). Voltaire also alleged that another enemy of the Jesuits, Father Fouquet, who had spent twenty-five years in China, had told him personally that there were very few philosophical atheists there (*Essai* Chap. II).

Obviously arguments repeated at second hand are of minor significance in an estimate of Voltaire's thought. Much more important is an argument stemming from his own logical processes, which he used at least five different times. This consists in pointing out a fundamental contradiction in the thought of the enemies of the Jesuits in rival religious orders. All of them had rejected with horror Pierre Bayle's proposition that it is possible for a society of atheists to subsist and to exemplify high moral standards. At the same time they were staunchly maintaining that the Chinese government—the oldest in the world—was a society of atheists. According to Voltaire, it was an absurdity to uphold these contradictory propositions (*Essai sur les moeurs,* Introduc., Sec. XVIII; Chap. II; *Siècle de Louis XIV,* Chap. XXXIX; *Remarques de l'Essai sur les moeurs,* Sec. VI; *Dieu et Les Hommes,* Chap. IV). He charged the priests with a similar contradiction in accusing the Chinese of being idolators and at the same time maintaining that they were atheists (*Dictionnaire philosophique,* "De la Chine"). Parenthetically, one might observe a similar contradiction in Voltaire himself in his alternately remarking that there is no priesthood in China and praising the Chinese law that a man may not become a priest before the age of forty.

Bayle's motive in discussing the Chinese had been not only to weaken the hold of orthodox Christianity on the thought of his time, but also to inculcate the positive virtue of tolerance. One might expect this to be a major element in Voltaire's treatment of China as well—since it was one of the major themes of his work in general—but actually he associates toleration with China only in one dialogue, "L'empereur de la Chine et Frère Rigolet," one of his later works. Here he compares the various priests and bonzes who have infiltrated the country to the rats that penetrate cellars and attics; the priests are allowed a free hand because of "the spirit of tolerance, which conditions the character of all the Asiatic nations," but they are suppressed if they become a threat to the order of society. In the same work Voltaire presents a long discourse of the Chinese emperor, beginning with the declaration that toleration has always seemed to be the first bond of mankind and the first duty of the sovereign, but ending with the order expelling Christian missionaries, not for their stupid doctrines, but for their interference with the social order. "Je suis tolérant, et je vous chasse tous, parce que vous êtes intolérants." "I am tolerant, and I expel all of you because you are intolerant." Voltaire's imagined speech of the emperor is based upon essentially the same reasoning that Bayle in his treatise on toleration had proposed as appropriate for the Chinese emperor. According to Bayle, "if this emperor believed in a divinity, as it is sure that all the pagans have known one, he must by a principle of conscience expel the Christians from his state" (1713, 1:190). In another dialogue between "Le Mandarin et le Jésuite," Voltaire quotes from his Jesuit sources an actual speech in which an emperor of history poses the question to a missionary—What would you do if I were to send a troop of priests to your country to foment disobedience? This speech is one of Voltaire's primary motifs, alluded to in his works at least six times. (Also in "L'Empereur de la Chine et Frère Rigolet"; *Lettres philosophiques*, "De la Chine"; *Essai sur les moeurs*, Chap. CXCV; *Lettres chinoises*, Lettre VI; *Siècle de Louis XIV,* Chap. XXXIX.)

The best evidence that Voltaire's admiration for the Chinese was at least partially sincere and not entirely concerned with his anticlerical and antibiblical propaganda is his refutation of the widely read and highly disparaging summary of Chinese history, culture, government, and comportment in George Anson's *A Voyage Round the World in the Years 1740–1744* (London, 1748). While on the whole highly complimentary of the English admiral, Voltaire in his *Précis du siècle de Louis XIV* (Chap. 27) insisted on correcting his estimate of the Chinese as a contemptible people without honor and industry. As for industry, Voltaire affirmed, they are merely not like the Europeans. And one should judge their morality by considering the head of their government rather then the common people at a frontier outpost. Evidence of integrity comes from their having inviolably maintained treaties for 150 years. It is not right to insult the most ancient and best-governed nation of the world merely because some luckless individuals had tried to trick a party of English of one-twenty-thousandth of the booty they had stolen by force from the Spaniards.

Recognizing that much of his writing on China consisted in propaganda for his philosophical ideas, Voltaire admitted in his *Dictionnaire philosophique* that one should not be fanatical about the virtues of the Chinese, "fanatique du mérite chinois." As a kind of balance sheet, he drew up a list of their good and bad points. On the credit side, their constitution is the best in the world, the only one founded on a paternal principle, the only one in which the governor of a province would be punished for not pleasing the people, the only one that instituted a prize for virtue, and the only one that absorbed its conquerors. But on the other side, the lower classes are governed by bonzes as knavish as European priests; the merchants, like Europeans, sell at high prices to foreigners; they are two hundred years behind the times in the sciences; and they believe in a thousand ridiculous prejudices, such as talismans and judicial astrology ("De la Chine").

It appears then that the role of China in the Voltairean philosophy was primarily to bolster his private system of deism, to further his attack on religious superstition and clerical domination, and to advance his plea for toleration. Although his *Essai sur les moeurs* is justly celebrated as a pioneer work of anthropology, it can hardly be argued that his treatment of China represented a serious scholarly effort to understand oriental culture. From a broad perspective, Voltaire's fascination with China illustrates the importance in his way of thinking of what A. O. Lovejoy hs described as "uniformitarianism," the view that nature has created men essentially alike in their intellect and taste and that opinions and valuations different from the norm are to be discouraged and condemned (1948, 80–81). Another way of expressing uniformitarianism is to say, as Voltaire did in the preface to his play *L'Ecossaise,* 1760, that nature is everywhere the same. In his *Poème sur la loi naturelle,* after a passage deploring the diversification of religions throughout the world, Voltaire cited Confucius as an exception—one who had adhered steadfastly to the religion of nature. In his philosophical tale *Zadig,* Voltaire brought together practitioners of the major religions of the world including the Chinese, and concluded, "You are then all of the same opinion."

Voltaire, of course, made a distinction between physical and mental differences and between opinions based upon pure reason and those based upon custom and education. He declared that "everything which depends intimately upon human nature is alike from one end of the universe to the other; everything which may depend upon custom is different and any resemblances are due to chance" (*Essai sur les moeurs,* Chap. CXCVII). But even purely human events such as the rise and fall of empires follow a universal pattern. "The world is a vast theatre, where the same tragedy is played under different titles" (*Essai,* Chap. CLV). Like all his fellow deists, Voltaire believed in the doctrine of universal consent, that men everywhere in every period of time are able to use their reasoning power to arrive at the conviction of the existence of a single god. In his "Fragments historiques sur l'Inde," Voltaire demonstrates that the mysteries of Egypt, Thrace, Greece, Rome, and China showed that they all adored a single deity. Montesquieu, however, in his *Esprit des lois* had treated China as an example of diversity and of the relativity of human institutions (Book XIX). Voltaire also had to contend with the opinion of Bayle, the Dominicans, and a host of other commentators who maintained that the Chinese were atheists. Voltaire's portrayal of China, therefore, may be considered as an attempt to buttress his notion of the universality of the conclusions of human reason, particularly in regard to the existence of a single god. For him, China was both a symbol of rational deism and a comfortable assurance of the unity of humanity.

CHAPTER 5. REFERENCES

Aldridge, A. Owen. 1948. Polygamy and deism. *Journal of English and Germanic Philology* 48:343–60.

Appleton, William W. 1951. *A cycle of Cathay.* New York: Columbia Univ. Press.

Bayle, Pierre. 1713. *Commentaire philosophique sur ces paroles de Jésus-Christ, contrain-les d'entrer; ou Traité de la tolérance universelle.* New ed. Rotterdam.

Beattie, James. 1788. *The theory of language.* New ed. London.

Etiemble, René. 1956. De la pensée chinoise aux "philosophes" français. *Revue de littérature comparée* 30:465–78.

Gray, G. B. 1903. *Numbers* (International Critical Commentary) New York.

Guy, Basil. 1963. *The French image of China before and after Voltaire. Studies in Voltaire and the Eighteenth Century,* vol. 21. Geneva: Institut et musée Voltaire.

Lach, Donald F. 1945. Leibniz and China. *Journal of the History of Ideas* 6:436–55.

La Harpe, Jean François de. 1870. *Cours de littérature ancienne et moderne.* Paris.

Lovejoy, Arthur O. 1948. *Essays in the history of ideas.* Baltimore, Md.: Johns Hopkins Univ. Press.

Maggs, Barbara. 1973. China in the literature of eighteenth-century Russia. Ph.D. diss. University of Illinois, Urbana-Champaign.

Meyer, Heinrich. 1951. *The age of the world. A chapter in the history of enlightenment.* Allentown, Pa. Muhlenberg College.

Pomeau, René. 1964. Review of *The French image of China,* by Basil Guy. *Revue de l'histoire de la France* 64:308–10.

Rowbotham, Arnold. 1932. Voltaire Sinophile. *PMLA* 47:1050–65.

Saint John, Henry. Viscount Bolingbroke. 1809. *Works.* London.

Torrey, Norman O. 1930. *Voltaire and the English deists.* New Haven, Conn.: Yale Univ. Press.

Voltaire. 1962. *Oeuvres historiques.* Ed. René Pomeau. Pléiade ed. Paris: Gallimard.

———. 1952. *Notebooks.* Ed. Theodore Besterman. Geneva: Institut et musée Voltaire.

———. 1953–65. *Correspondence.* Ed. Theodore Besterman. Geneva: Institut et musée Voltaire. Letters are cited by number rather than by volume and page.

Ya-Oui, (Lee You). 1937. *Le théatre classique en Chine et en France.* Paris: Les Presses Modernes.

6

The Ambassadors and *The Sound of the Mountain*

IN THE HISTORY OF THE NOVEL THROUGHOUT THE WORLD there are some plots containing such fundamental or universal human elements that they would fit almost every cultural or nationality group. One such example is that of a novel projected but never realized by the modern Japanese poet Noguchi. In this story, a young Japanese marries an American girl and takes her to his country home, where his parents are absolute rulers. They cannot speak a word of English and the young wife cannot bring herself to intimacy with them. She suffers so much that she eventually runs away with a missionary, and the Japanese husband marries a more suitable wife. On the universal level this story shows that a "woman cannot live without her own society and intercourse with her own people." On the national level, it indicates that "love is not the greatest factor in Japanese life" (Noguchi 1975, 5a).

Some plots, on the other hand, depend so strongly on indigenous cultural elements that they have very little in common with other nationalities. Osamu Dazai's *The Setting Sun,* for example, even though it is filled with references to Western painting, music, and literature, portrays a purely Japanese society and characters whose psychological reactions are not to be understood in any other context. The two novels discussed in this chapter fall between these two extremes: they combine elements of psychology, history, and behavior that are uniquely confined to their own cultural traditions with other elements such as character types and human situations that are universal in their incidence and consequently in their appeal.

I am treating *The Ambassadors* by Henry James and *The Sound of the Mountain* by Yasunari Kawabata at the suggestion of my friend and colleague Masayuki Akiyama, who has already prepared an extensive comparison or confrontation of the two works. Professor Akiyama has treated them primarily from the perspective of the social structures of the family in Japan and in America and the portrayal of nature by the two novelists. I shall not neglect these aspects, but my main purpose is to consider the two novels as similar by virtue of their belonging to the genre of the psychological novel—that is, by their emphasis upon the motivations, emotions, and intellectual processes of their characters. For my analysis of *The Sound of the Mountain,* I am depending upon the English translation by Edward G. Seidensticker, and my remarks, therefore, must be considered as being limited by lack of access to the original text. Both James and Kawabata have written separate critical works concerning the art of the novel, but since Kawabata's book on the subject has not yet been translated into English, I shall not treat the aesthetic theories of either the American or the Japanese novelist. I shall merely quote part of a single sentence from an article by James on the technique of a famous French actor of his time, Benoît Coquelin. Here James affirms that the psychological novelist is like a polished actor in that he "builds up a character, in his supposedly uncanny process, by touch added to touch, line to line, illustration to illustration, and with a vision of his personage breathing steadily before him" (Fergusson 1975, 51). This is exactly the method practiced by James in *The Ambassadors* and by Kawabata in *The Sound of the Mountain.* As in most psychological novels, character is more important than plot.

The use of the psychological method is the major bond uniting the two artists since they belong to separate historical periods as well as to different national cultures. James lived between 1843 and 1916, the period of sociological realism and naturalism in American letters. His own novels are for the most part characterized by a reticent realism in which he presents a highly individualized portrayal of carefully selected segments of society. Kawabata lived a generation later, between 1899 and 1972, and he is known for blending with French naturalism native Japanese elements of impressionism. In *The Sound of the Mountain,* the influence of literary naturalism is to be seen in the direct treatment of sexual matters and the extensive use of symbolism. The many references to external nature are sometimes used for their inherent poetic qualities alone and sometimes for their symbolic suggestion of themes or moods presented in the narrative.

As with most of the novels of Henry James, there is very little physical action narrated in *The Ambassadors.* Apart from conversing at length in various social gatherings, the characters do very little else but walk, eat, and take a train, carriage, or some other conveyance. The most dramatic scene of the entire novel consists of a man and a woman in a boat being seen from the shore of a river by another man and then subsequently landing to greet him. The main question at issue throughout the novel is whether this man and woman are or have been involved in an illicit sexual relationship, but the subject is presented obliquely—there is nothing more direct than speculation as to whether their attachment is "virtuous" or an uttered query as to whether she is "that kind of woman." The protagonist of the novel is neither the man nor the woman, but the third person who observes them from the banks of the river.

The story unfolds in a deliberately leisurely fashion and depends upon varying viewpoints and upon assumptions rather than facts. The perspective, involving a great deal of relativism, is primarily, but not uniformly, that of the protagonist. He sees things one way, speculates about them, and later modifies his impressions. Other characters see the same events in a different way.

The main character is Lewis Lambert Strether, a New England widower whose life has been for the most part solitary. His two surnames represent the title of a novel by Balzac, *Louis Lambert,* which incorporates the theme of the opposition between the material world and the world of ideas (Evans 1951, 23). If reduced to the opposition between the head and the heart, this can be considered as an important theme in *The Ambassadors* and *The Sound of the Mountain* as well. *Louis Lambert* is linked ideologically to *The Ambassadors,* moreover, by means of its deliberate treatment and rejection of the philosophical doctrine of the freedom of the will. James admired Balzac greatly and regarded himself as a disciple of the school of Balzac rather than that of Flaubert, notwithstanding the contrary opinion of Sartre that I have quoted in Chapter 1. In *The Ambassadors,* by means of the comment of a minor personage, James plants the notion that *Louis Lambert* is, nevertheless, a rather bad novel.

James's character Strether has suffered the loss of his only child as well as his wife. The child was considered to be a dull boy, and Strether is sometimes afflicted remorsefully by the thought that the boy may not have been dull by nature, but only by his father's neglect. In the conventional manufacturing town where he lives, Woollett, Massachusetts, Strether's primary activity consists in editing a literary periodical named the *Review,* which is financed by a wealthy widow, Mrs. Newsome, who dominates Strether and her entire milieu. Her name and other indications suggest that she belongs to the *nouveau riche.* Strether, who is fifty-five years old, about the same age as Mrs. Newsome, is portrayed as a family friend with the hint that their relationship might someday ripen into marriage. In manner and behavior, Strether seems to belong to a preceding century, although he mellows in the European atmosphere (129). A man of great dignity and very much the ambassadorial type as suggested in the title, he has, however, throughout his life lacked money and opportunity.

As the novel opens, Strether has just landed in England on his way to Paris in order to seek out Mrs. Newsome's son Chadwick, or Chad, in order to persuade him to return to Massachusetts to take over the family business. Chad had originally gone to Paris three or four years previously in order to study French art and culture, had started out by frequenting artists, and had shown vague signs of serious application. Then all came to nothing, and Chad's dedication to art was seen as merely a device to lengthen out his residence abroad. The family in New England assumed that he had succumbed to the charms of a *femme fatale,* and Strether was despatched to bring him back. When Strether encounters Chad for the first time in Paris, he realizes that the young man has been completely "made over" by his exposure to French culture (97). All of the strategies, lines and tones that Strether had contemplated taking with him have been rendered obsolete, for thanks to his exposure to Parisian society there was now "no computing at all what the young man . . . would think or feel or say on any subject whatever" (97).

Strether assumes that Chad's amorous connection is with the daughter of a countess, Jeanne de Vionnet, a typical ingénue of romantic fiction. Towards the half-way point of the novel it becomes clear that Chad is interested, not in the daughter, but in the mother, who goes by her simple married name Mme Marie de Vionnet. The seriousness of Chad's infatuaton is underscored by a Latin proverb, *All wounded, the last killed.* Even though Jeanne is "unmistakably pretty—bright gentle shy happy wonderful" (141–42), she serves little purpose other than to set off the character of her mother and to distract the reader temporarily—that is, to lead him in a false direction. James introduces several other decoys and blind alleys like those in a detective story before allowing Strether and the reader to realize that Chad's entire concern is for the mother, the last and killing lady of the proverb. Mme de Vionnet is the incarnation of the *femme du monde.* She is slim, light, bright, and gay, and could be compared poetically "to a goddess still partly engaged in a morning cloud, or to a sea-nymph waist-high in the summer surge" (173). Like Shakespeare's Cleopatra, she is "various and multifold." A minor character goes so far as to call her "fifty women" (169). Mme de Vionnet is thirty-eight years of age, ten years older than Chad (146), but physically she appears to be just as young as her daughter (142). Her husband is still living, but they have been separated for years; with people in their social situation divorce is out of the question. When Mme de Vionnet speaks, her tones are enough "to make justice weep" (176).

In a literal sense Mrs. Newsome, Chad's mother and the widow upon whom Strether depends, is not a character in the novel at all, for she never appears as an actor. Yet she is a constant offstage influence. She initiates much of the action and is repeatedly brought into the thoughts and speeches of the other characters. Her spirit or presence is even felt thousands of miles across the ocean. A remarkable example of this power is the effect produced upon Strether when she shows her displeasure by ceasing to write to him. It seems to Strether "that he had never so lived with her as during this period of her silence; the silence was a sacred hush, a finer clearer medium, in which her idiosyncrasies showed. He walked about with her, sat with her, and dined face-to-face with her—a rare treat 'in his life,' as he could perhaps have scarce escaped phrasing it; and if he had never seen her so soundless he had never on the other hand felt her so highly, so almost austerely, herself" (215). Any number of passages point out the presence of Mrs. Newsome in spirit even when she is miles away in body (287, 305, 306, 336). Mrs. Newsome to all her family represents the ideal of womanly virtues. She is the only woman Strether has known "even at Woollett, as to whom his conviction was positive that to lie was beyond her art" (63). She represents an intimidating and oppressive force, however, and in this sense has been compared to the dead wife who haunts Ibsen's play *Rosmersholm* (Egan 1972, 115). Apart from serving as a kind of *dea ex machina,* Mrs. Newsome is a foil to Mme de Vionnet. They are different kinds of mothers, leading different ways of life. The matriarch of Woollett seems to be rigidly righteous; Mme de Vionnet, tolerant and flexible. Although never guilty of an outright lie, the latter willingly connives at deception.

The other characters in *The Ambassadors* are minor and are surprisingly few for a novel of its length. Maria Gostrey, an unmarried former schoolmate of Mme de Vionnet, appears in nearly every chapter of the novel including the first and the last, and on the surface she seems to play a major role. She serves not only as Strether's confidante, but also as a source of information about the Parisian society of which Mme de Vionnet is a part and also about Mme de Vionnet herself. But her only function is that of listener or messenger. Early in the novel the reader may get the impression that a romantic attachment could spring up between Strether and Maria Gostrey, but this is a deliberate device of the author to throw the reader off the scent.

Although the action in the novel is minimal, the plot is complicated by the absence of direct reporting. All that Strether is able at first to learn about Chad is that he is involved in a romantic attachment, but that it is a "virtuous" one. When he finally sees Chad, he is tremendously impressed by the social graces and *savoir faire* the latter has acquired. He realizes that Mme de Vionnet is in large measure personally responsible for the splendid way in which Chad has developed, and he acquires a feeling of strong admiration for her. As a result, he sympathizes with Chad's desire to remain in Paris and eventually advises him to do so, in essence thereby abandoning his mission. Mrs. Newsome in the meantime senses his change of attitude and sends her daughter and son-in-law, Mr. and Mrs. Pocock, to report on the situation and, if necessary, to take charge. Strether realizes that his own relationship to Mrs. Newsome might be expected to depend on his success in persuading Chad to return to New England, but he, nevertheless, persists in his belief in the soundness of the attachment between Chad and Mme de Vionnet even though they may never marry.

During all this time, Strether romantically believes that their relationship is platonic, but towards the end of the book while he is spending a day in the country, he encounters Chad and Mme de Vionnet together in a boat while he is sitting on the river bank. All the circumstances of their attire and the time of day indicate that Chad and his companion had been planning to stay overnight in a hotel, but all three keep up the pretense of innocence and return together to Paris. In the final pages, Chad goes off to London by himself, and we never learn whether or not he returns to New England.

The Sound of the Mountain is a much shorter novel, but it contains more episodes and its plot is more complex. Like *The Ambassadors,* most of the action is described by means of conversation, but there are many more characters as well as a larger number of dramatic confrontations, and the events are more varied. Illicit sex is a primary motif; some manifestations are merely hinted at, but others are plainly described. The protagonist, Shingo, is not merely an observer of the main sexual thread, but an actual participant. Head of a family in Kamakura, he is sixty-two years old by Japanese chronology or sixty-one by occidental. He shows many signs of aging, including lapses in memory, rapidly graying hair, bad teeth, and slight deafness. He does whatever is necessary to fulfill his domestic duties, but accuses himself of lacking affection (96). The novel balances his personal problems of aging and unfulfilled eroticism with the closely related ones of keeping his family together.

Shingo's wife, Yasuko, is one year older than her husband and a rather ugly woman. Shingo is repelled by her aged flesh, and as they lie in bed together touches her only to stop her snoring by twisting her nose (5–6). Yasuko is completely subordinate to her husband in all relationships, carrying her inferior position to such lengths that she remarks that if they were to commit suicide together she would not need to leave a note behind, her identity being merged with that of her husband.

Before her marriage to Shingo, Yasuko had a beautiful elder sister who died, leaving young children. Yasuko thereupon dedicated herself to looking after these children and her brother-in-law, turning herself into a domestic slave by seeking to take her sister's place (58). Shingo as a boy had been "strongly attached" to this sister, the reason perhaps why he married Yasuko. In her marriage she continued to make self-immolation a career (16). Shingo is unable to banish his wife's sister from his mind, even as an old man, for he continues to imagine her as she was as a young girl. His memories and fantasies condition his later relation with Yasuko and his own children.

Yasuko's sister, therefore, plays a role similar to that of Mrs. Newsome in *The Ambassadors.* She is a personality never present in the flesh, but never long absent from thought. She obviously lacks the power of initiating action, but certainly influences the behavior of Shingo and Yasuko. Shingo has "certain feelings of guilt for having continued to be drawn to the sister even after she was married," and Yasuko seems to have been ashamed of being used by her brother-in-law as a substitute for a housemaid without love or respect (59). As an old man, Shingo talks of his memories of the sister's fresh young beauty (150), and even speculates about what his children and grandchildren would be like if he had married the sister instead of Yasuko.

Shingo has only one son and one daughter, both of whom have entered into unsatisfactory marriages. Shūichi, his son, works with him in the same office. Although married to a young and beautiful girl, he has taken a mistress merely two years after his marriage and spends many evenings away from home. Shūichi treats his father almost as his equal in age, but still with appropriate respect even though in the office he is constantly called upon to serve as prompter for his father's flagging memory.

Shūichi sometimes comes home drunk and then feels guilty toward his wife.

The latter, Kikuko, is still in her early twenties but sensitive to the fact that she has still not borne children of her own (21–22). She herself was a difficult birth, and a scar left by forceps can be seen at her hair line (15). After her marriage she grew perceptibly taller and was a late-bloomer in other ways (220). Although she had been reared by her parents as the pet of her family, she sensed that her mother resented her at birth; now she feels that her husband also does not want her. Oddly enough, after Shūichi acquired his mistress, Kikuko's marital relations with him ripened (20). Shingo develops a strong affection for Kikuko; indeed, he prefers her to his own daughter, an attitude which his daughter notices (181). He even behaves in a manner that suggests his attachment is in some ways sexually motivated. He realizes an undercurrent of eroticism running through his life that is attached to Yasuko's sister on one extreme and to Kikuko on the other (105). In his dreams and fantasies, the images of the two women merge into one (131, 179).

Shingo's thirty-year-old daughter, Fusako, is even homelier than her mother and possesses no positive attributes in compensation. As a result neither her mother nor her father has strong parental feelings and she recognizes this lack of affection (123). She is no luckier with her marriage than with her parents, for her husband discards her after she has had two children.

There are at least a dozen other characters, but only three are of great significance to the action. Eiko Tanizaki is a girl who works in Shingo's office and occasionally goes dancing with him as well as with Shūichi. We are told little about her except that she has small breasts and had lost her lover during the war. Her chief function is to provide a means of communication between Shingo and Shūichi's mistress, Kinuko, a good-looking woman but older than Kikuko. Shūichi's mistress has also lost a lover during the war and has thereby become embittered. She justifies her liaison with Shūichi on the grounds that since her own lover has been taken away, life owes her a replacement.

In the first chapter of the novel, Shingo literally hears the sound of the mountain, an actual sound "like wind, far away, but with a depth like a rumbling of the earth." This murmuring is clearly interpreted as a harbinger of death. It is also linked to Yasuko's sister, who also heard the sound shortly before her own demise (20). The meaning of this and other symbols is revealed gradually, and the function of some imagery in the novel is never completely resolved. Although the action takes place in a continuous line, following normal chronology, the significance of many of the events is revealed by flashbacks and penetrations of Shingo's consciousness. These devices take up considerably more space than either direct conversation or narrative.

The action begins with Shingo's purchase on the way home from the office of three whelks. Since there are four adults in the family, the question of how these three crustacea are to be divided enables the author to explain the tensions and imbalances in the family. Shingo soon learns that his daughter wants a divorce because of the ill treatment she has been receiving from her husband. Since his son almost invariably stays in the city at the close of office hours, Shingo has already divined that Shūichi has a mistress. He questions Eiko on the subject and persuades her to show him the house where the woman lives. He walks by the house, but does not enter. At this time the thought first comes to him that Shūichi and Kikuko should leave the family residence and take a house by themselves. From this point on, Shingo is faced with the problem of whether he should actively urge this solution and thereby sacrifice the pleasure he finds in Kikuko's presence, or whether he should leave things as they are and see his son's marriage destroyed. On another day Shingo notices that a stray dog that habitually makes visits to his garden is ready to give birth to a litter of puppies. On previous occasions when this animal had produced her puppies she had returned to her home to do so, but this time she has her litter under a storeroom in Shingo's house. Since Kikuko takes great interest in the dog and her puppies, the episode illustrates her own relationship to her husband and her parents. The question is suggested but not formulated: where would she go if she were herself to give birth? Shortly after she becomes pregnant.

One day at the office, Shingo remarks that he has never climbed Mount Fuji and is reminded that he has seen only one of the "three great sights of Japan." These thoughts symbolize the emptiness of his life, the lack of fulfillment of various desires. He then dreams of being on an island with a young girl and embracing her as he would have done in his youth. As he is reflecting on the dream, one of his friends of his own age, Suzumoto, enters the office for a visit. Suzumoto leads the conversation to the subject of a mutual friend who had gone away to a resort hotel with a young woman and had there experienced what Suzumoto called a "pleasant death." This man's widow had asked Suzumoto to dispose of a set of Noh masks, and Shingo buys one that is a symbol of eternal youth. As he examines it at home, the mask seems to turn into a smiling live girl. Shingo wonders whether his dream and the illusion created by the mask mean that something drastic is to happen in his own life. On New Year's Day, Eiko pays Shingo a formal visit during the course of which she promises to ask Kinuko to give up Shūichi. During their conversation both refer to Kikuko as a child, and Shingo wonders whether the abnormal compulsion that made him marry Yasuko upon her sister's death is in any way exacerbated by the presence of Kikuko in his household.

Eiko eventually introduces Shingo to Mrs. Ikeda, a woman who lives with Kinuko, and who also feels that Shūichi should give her up. She explains Kinuko's attitude that since she lost her husband in the war she has a right to another man even though he may be married to someone else. Mrs. Ikeda suddenly suggests that matters might be satisfactorily resolved if Shūichi and his wife could live apart from Shingo. Once again Shingo is faced with making the decision that will affect the welfare of others as well as himself. The evil of the present situation is revealed on another day when Shūichi comes home drunk, calls for Kikuko, and again reveals profound feelings of guilt.

The next section of the novel is dominated by the theme of abortion. Shingo first of all imagines in a dream a young girl having such an operation and at the same time sees the words from a novel "And she has become a holy child forever." He associates the dream with Yasuko's beautiful sister, with an article on abortions he had read in the newspaper (130–31), and with Kikuko. The latter soon after receives a letter from a school friend who has had an abortion and visits her in the hospital. On the way there she takes the same train as Shingo, who asks her whether she would not prefer to live with Shūichi away from the family. He does not introduce the subject of Shūichi's mistress, but wonders whether the knowledge of her existence may not have made Kikuko pregnant. Kikuko protests that she does not like the idea of moving away (139), and in a later episode she proposes to stay with Shingo even though she were to be divorced from her husband (160). One day Kikuko goes by herself to Tokyo and returns to the house complaining of a headache. Shingo then learns from Shūichi that she has terminated her pregnancy, and he is furious. Later two pines in a grove that he passes on the train to and from work no longer seem like pines, but are "entangled with the abortion"; they "somehow looked dirty" (185). Shingo even imagines the aborted baby as Yasuko's older sister reborn.

Shingo's interest in Kikuko becomes so apparent in the household that both his wife and his daughter taunt him for it. Kikuko leaves home for a visit with her parents, and while she is away Shingo has a rendezvous with her in a public garden, unknown to his wife and his son. In the presence of other couples, he feels somewhat guilty and continues to keep the meeting secret. The garden, however, has a rejuvenating effect upon him. Shingo next learns from Eiko that the money to pay for Kikuko's abortion had come from Kinuko, who had given it to Shūichi. Eiko believes that this is wrong, and she is sorry for Kikuko even though she realizes that Shūichi had given the money to his mistress in the first place. Eiko urges Shingo to make Shūichi consent to a separation; she obviously means a separation from his mistress, but Shingo, almost against his will, recognizes that the phrasing could mean as well his own separation from Kikuko. At this point, Shingo realizes that both he and his son are "caught in the same filthy slough."

Kikuko returns to the family, bringing presents for all its members, including an electric razor, representing the "sound of renewal." The razor leads Shingo to dream of various kinds of beards and of touching the young, but unresponsive breasts of a young girl. Upon waking, he wonders whether the dim figure in the dream may have been an incarnation of Kikuko or a substitute for her. Shortly after his dream, Shingo recalls seeing a picture by a nineteenth-century artist of "a single crow at the tip of a leafless tree" waiting for the dawn. Shingo takes this as a symbol of loneliness, for he also has been waiting for the dawn. Kikuko had protested against her loneliness by means of her abortion and returning to her family, but afterwards her relations with her husband became more tender and sensual. Shingo and Kikuko are thus united by loneliness.

Briefly the emphasis shifts to the other woman in the household, Shingo's daughter, Fusako. They learn from the newspaper that her estranged husband has attempted suicide in a pact with another woman, who had succeeded in ending her life. Fusako reacts with more anger than sorrow and condemns Shingo for not being upset at her plight. Despite uncertainty as to whether or not the husband is actually dead, his attempted suicide adds to Shingo's burden. He feels partly responsible for the death of Kikuko's baby and for that of the woman who had joined with his son-in-law, for if he had made more of an effort to make his daughter's marriage successful this woman would have been spared.

The next devastating news is that Shūichi's mistress Kinuko has become pregnant, a further insult to the wife, Kikuko. Shingo feels the "scent of ugly decay." He realizes that if Kinuko's baby should be born, it would be his own grandchild. Shingo decides to take action at last even though he realizes that the responsibility is Shūichi's and it is not the place of the father to interfere. He is not clear, however, about his motivations. Is he impelled by the urge to solve his son's problems or by anger at the insult offered to Kikuko? Whatever his reasons, Shingo finally takes the bold step of going to Kinuko's house. At first Kinuko insists that she is separated from Shūichi, but Shingo refuses to be put off and insists upon discussing the expected child. Kinuko then reveals that Shūichi had assaulted her physically in an attempt to persuade her to terminate her pregnancy; Kinuko even suggests that the child may not be Shūichi's, but Shingo is not convinced. He departs, leaving her a check, which she accepts. Later Shingo remembers talking to a man dying of cancer about procuring him poison in order to make his death easier. He wonders whether his interfering in the personal affirs of Shūichi is analogous to the administering of poison.

At this point, Shingo has taken a half-way step in coming to terms with his problem. He has recognized his involvement in the welfare of his son, but has still not taken the final measures necessary for resolving the situation. Shortly afterwards when Shūichi and Shingo are riding on a train, they are seated opposite to a man and a girl who resemble each other so closely that Shingo assumes they are father and daughter. As they get off at different stations, however, it is discovered that they are actually complete strangers. Shūichi then comments that it is quite appropriate for an old man and a young girl to be together. Shingo, musing on the complexity of human relationships, wonders whether the couple could actually be father and daughter without realizing it, the girl, for example, being illegitimate. Such a situation could very well arise in the future for Shūichi, but the latter reacts with great indifference to the suggestion.

In the last chapter, Shingo is seated in the garden, and Yasuko reads him an item from a newspaper about a man in Buffalo, New York, who had had his ear cut off in an automobile accident and had it replaced by a doctor. She suggests that the same process could be applied to a husband and wife. Shingo then quietly tells Kikuko that she and her husband should move away to a separate establishment. Shūichi had apparently told her previously that she should be a "free agent." Kikuko seems uncertain as to whether this freedom is desirable or not, and we are left without any indication of what will take place in the future. At dinner that evening, Kikuko distributes three trout to the seven people who are seated at the table, the three fish serving as parallels to the three whelks of the opening chapter. Shingo and his wife share one; Kikuko and Shūichi another, and Fusako and her children the third. The only suggestion of what will happen in the future is that Fusako will take up an independent life with her children.

At first glance these two novels seem to have very little in common. Indeed the differences are so striking that it is necessary to make note of them before proceeding to indicate parallels and resemblances. The structure of *The Ambassadors* is dramatic, tightly organized, and concentrated. James's novels in general have been termed "described dramas," and *The Ambassadors* in particular draws upon the standard techniques of the stage. It embodies a primary, central action; a series of situations to illuminate the action; the creation of suspense; and dialogue as a method of development. The action rises to a climax and then descends in a dénouement. Strether in the novel itself even describes his involvement in the situation as watching the play from an orchestra pit (320). A minor character, however, more properly calls him "the hero of the drama" (298). Considerable dramatic suspense is engendered by the question of whether or not Chad will return to New England. Early in the play, Maria Gostrey affirms that he will not and Strether maintains that he will. From that moment on the reader is anxious to find out what happens.

The Sound of the Mountain, however, has no single story line and no element of suspense. The outcome of the various domestic crises is kept subordinate to Shingo's day-by-day reactions and to the poetic images that accompany them. Although Kawabata's novel has fewer words than James's, it follows an epic rather than a dramatic structure. To be sure, it has a protagonist and a principal action, but it embraces at the same time a large number of characters and several subplots. The action does not ascend gradually to a crisis, but is portrayed by flashbacks and interconnected episodes. The emphasis is on the interior reactions of the protagonist rather than on external events.

Both *The Ambassadors* and *The Sound of the Mountain* are psychological studies of personal relations, but they utilize vastly different materials. James retains for the most part the perspective of the nineteenth-century drawing room in probing social amenities and proprieties. Kawabata, however, embraces topics of life and death, including biological processes and the ravages of war. *The Ambassadors* treats a series of themes, including determinism and the illusion of freedom, the value of enjoying life to the full, and the perennial Jamesian situation of an American in relation to a European context, the clash or interplay of two opposing cultures. *The Sound of the Mountain* also reflects determinism and a hedonistic approach toward life, but it concerns the author's own national milieu and treats the alien culture of the West only in regard to the manner in which it penetrates the Japanese environment. James deals in *The Ambassadors,* as in almost all of his works, exclusively with the upper classes. Although Strether may not be a man of wealth, his intellect, education, and breeding (emphasized by his occupation as editor of a literary review) equip him with the requisites for entering the most respectable levels of society, even in London or Paris. *The Sound of the Mountain,* however, is middle or perhaps upper-middle class in all of its manifestations. Shingo is an employee in an office, not an entrepreneur; he once kept a maid, but she has long since departed. He rides the subway and does some of the shopping for the family table. His son and daughter-in-law have a rudimentary knowledge of French, and Shingo himself is acquainted with the plastic arts, but otherwise few signs of leisure class amenities are apparent in his milieu. Japanese critics, on the other hand, assume that he is president of his company. He is at any rate a high-echelon executive, working beyond the usual retirement age of fifty-five. He has his own office and his own office girl, Eiko; and he entertains at company expense at a geisha house. In almost every chapter of *The Sound of the Mountain,* echoes of Japanese cultural life and of the past influence the behavior of Shingo. Strether, however, like most of his countrymen, is a creature of the present or even the future and rarely turns a backward glance.

Although James belongs to the nineteenth-century literary movement known as realism that dedicated itself to the faithful representation of contemporary society, he is one of the leading members of a subclass of authors known as reticent realists. That is, he denied that his mission was to portray all aspects of contemporary reality, but only those that appealed to his own aesthetic sensibilities. As we have seen, he chose to portray the upper or higher-middle class. He was equally as fastidious in his style and language as in his choice of subject matter. James not only does not call a spade a spade, but he does not even call it a garden implement. In *The Ambassadors* he explains that the commercial enterprise of Mrs. Newsome in New England is devoted to manufacturing, but he never explains what object it is that her factory produces. He describes the product as "a small, trivial, rather ridiculous object of the commonest domestic use" (40). Whether referring to thumb tacks or safety pins, James's language in this passage may be interpreted as either facetious or euphemistic. There is absolutely no physical violence of any kind in *The Ambassadors;* it contains only one veiled allusion to the *demimonde,* and the sexual indiscretion on which the plot is based is described in the most indirect and delicate language. The difference between the two authors in the portrayal of sex cannot be explained entirely on the basis of the increased permissiveness of the twentieth century. Kawabata, in contrast to James's reticence, adopts a style and a perspective resembling European naturalism. *The Sound of the Mountain* describes in forthright language the physical state of puppies before and after being born, nose-bleeds, automobile accidents, homosexuality, prostitution, drugs, suicide, abortion, barrenness, and old men going on trips with young girls. There is a great paradox in that Kawabata conceives of nature in terms of delicate flowers, the humming of insects and the sounds of birds; yet he treats human beings in terms of infidelity, abortion, and suicide. Although there is no brutality in his style, there is a tremendous contrast between his poetic imagery and his commonplace—and sometimes sordid—subject matter. Like Zola, he combines in epic sweep the crudeness of everyday life with poetic vision.

An important element of Kawabata's style is symbolism. Not only the title, *The Sound of the Mountain,* but nearly every chapter heading seems to have a cryptic meaning. Kawabata also uses the dreams of Shingo as an important means of portraying his personality, and these dreams are in themselves often symbolic. Both dreams and mundane events are interpreted as harbingers of catastrophes or major changes. James by contrast is completely realistic. The use of symbols is common to many realist and naturalist authors, and *The Ambassadors* also utilizes this technique, but there are absolutely no dreams, no mystical visions of nature, and no premonitions of coming events. The only concession to the occult or supernatural appears in the statement that Strether had always "been subject to sudden gusts of fancy . . .—odd starts of the historic sense, suppositions and divinations with no warrant but their intensity" (360). Although Strether may occasionally enter a world of fanciful dreaming, this is a world of daydreams, not those induced by sleep. Because of its indirect style, *The Ambassadors* cannot be considered objective in the sense of a scientific textbook, but it portrays reality in the manner of an impressionistic painting.

Turning at last to the resemblances between the novels of

James and Kawabata, I should like to quote the comments of a critic in a Canadian periodical concerning Kawabata's method and achievement. This critic finds thematic resemblances in Shingo's "renunciation of a late affection which seems to promise compensation for a lifetime of emotional sterility" and Strether's practicing "the ethic of self-denial to affect a position of perfect moral integrity" (Goody 1970, 219–20). This critic regards Kawabata as "in his own way a genuine practitioner of the Jamesian novel of moral consciousness" in his "concentration on the single viewpoint of a sensitive register of experience; in his presentation of that figure's bewilderment and sense of isolation from the thoughts and feelings of others, who remain separated from him as if by 'the curtain of life itself'; and, most important, in his intimation of both personal and historical violence lurking behind a formal and highly stylized social exterior." Apart from the reference to personal violence, which plays no part in *The Ambassadors,* this is an admirable statement concerning the two novels.

A careful look at plot, theme, and character in both works shows substantial resemblances, but nevertheless definite shades of difference. The action of *The Ambassadors* consists in Strether's mission to persuade Chad to abandon his romantic attachment in France and return to New England. The plot turns on Strether's debate between determinism and the illusion of freedom and his antipuritanical resolution that one should live to the fullest. The action of *The Sound of the Mountain* consists in Shingo's efforts to keep his family circle intact amid the social disruptions of modern times. Determinism does not figure in the plot as such, but the illusion of freedom besets Shingo's household in the final chapter. Shingo also comes to realize that a life without fulfillment is a wasted one. In both novels the family unit is important, but the family circles themselves have little resemblance and the forces prevailing against them have practically nothing in common. The theme of *The Ambassadors* is the clash of two cultures or more precisely the contrast between puritan constraints and French relaxation. The theme of *The Sound of the Mountain* is that of aging upon human behavior. That which is a primary theme in one novel is also a minor theme in the other. That is, the element of the two cultures appears in *The*

Sound of the Mountain (Shingo's fascination with a vacuum cleaner and an electric razor); and the element of aging appears in *The Ambassadors* (Strether's temporary rejuvenation and then lapsing back into the approach to old age). Both novels feature substantial character development of the protagonist. In *The Ambassadors* Strether's outlook upon life becomes more humane and tolerant as a result of the exposure to a foreign culture. In *The Sound of the Mountain,* Shingo becomes reconciled to the disappointments of life through his decision to place the welfare of his children over his own comfort. The ostensible action in *The Ambassadors* concerns, in James's own words, Strether's attempt to persuade Chad to "separate from a wretched woman" (36), but the true action is the testing of Strether's character. In *The Sound of the Mountain,* Shingo is also engaged in persuading a young man to "separate from a wretched woman," but the true action consists in his personal struggle to "separate" from his daughter-in-law. In the English translation, "separate" is the word actually used (195). The ostensible theme of *The Sound of the Mountain* is stated in Shingo's question, "Do parents have to be responsible forever for their children's marriages?" (61). The real theme is the one stated previously, the effect of aging.

The most important parallel between the novels in technique consists in the point of view assumed by the author. Both novels have an omniscient third-person narrator who sees all events through the eye and mind of the protagonist, Shingo in one and Strether in the other. James very rarely intrudes to interpolate a comment from the author himself; Kawabata never does. Both James and Kawabata report the thoughts and fantasies of their protagonists; Kawabata, unlike James, includes dreams. With Kawabata, the point of view is consistently and completely that of the protagonist. He never penetrates the thoughts of subordinate characters. James rarely does so, but he frequently reflects their psychological reactions. Kawabata avails himself of flashbacks. James for the most part follows a straight chronological narrative in which he only occasionally introduces retrospective passages of the reminiscences and recollections of his protagonist.

The period of time covered in the two novels corresponds to

the dramatic concentration of James and the broader sweep of Kawabata. *The Ambassadors* runs from late spring to late autumn, exactly the period of time required for the conventional trip of an American tourist traveling by boat from one continent to the other. Instead of the Aristotelian unity of twenty-four hours, James restricts himself to a long Parisian summer. *The Sound of the Mountain* begins early in August with the approach of autumn, continues throughout the entire year, and comes to a close in the second autumn. It covers the entire cycle of the seasons, corresponding to the life and death of a human being, but since it goes into a second autumn it seems to be entering a second life cycle. This is parallel to the description of Shingo at the outset of the novel as a man entering "his second cycle of sixty years."

James describes the structure of another of his novels, *The Awkward Age,* as a series of single "social occasions," each of which in "the history and intercourse of the characters concerned . . . would bring out to the full the latent color of the scene in question and cause it to illustrate, to the last drop," its bearing on the major theme of the novel. This is essentially the structure of *The Ambassadors* and *The Sound of the Mountain* as well, both of which present a series of "social occasions" that develop the theme and enrich the characterization. It has been said that in the typical Jamesian novel, there is no climax but rather a series of climaxes (Grover 1973, 155). This is partially true of both novels under consideration. Their social occasions are fragmentary and are not joined together in a continuous line. In both novels nuances of plot and characterization are conveyed primarily by conversation. Kawabata, although relying heavily on symbolism and imagery to create the atmosphere of his successive scenes, portrays dialogue in a highly realistic manner, incorporating short sentences and a colloquial, everyday vocabulary. The language of James's dialogue is, to the contrary, cryptic, indirect, and stylized. Rather than a realistic exchange between two people, James seems to portray a series of monologues in which two people are present.

James is famous for the technique of having one character begin a sentence that remains incomplete until finished by another character (Richards 1972, 227). When Strether is probing Jim Pocock to learn Mrs. Newsome's most recent attitude, for example, he asks whether she has "given way." Pocock repeats "given way," with a questioning tone. Strether continues, "Under the strain, I mean, of hope deferred, of disappointment repeated and thereby intensified." Pocock takes this up: "Oh is she prostrate, you mean" (240). A parallel is found when Shingo asks Kikuko whether Shūichi has been to see her. She answers: "Yes. But if you hadn't called . . ." Shingo answers mentally, "It would have been difficult for her to go back?"

Key passages in both novels illustrate a similar technique of having one character make a remark that is interpreted in a different sense by a second character. In *The Ambassadors* soon after Strether arrives in Paris and discovers the liaison between Chad and Mme de Vionnet, he is assured by one of Chad's male friends that "it's a virtuous attachment," meaning merely that they arc bound to each other by a sense of mutual obligation (117). Strether takes the adjective "virtuous" to mean, however, that there is no overt sex involved. In *The Sound of the Mountain,* Eiko makes the tearful request to Shingo, "Have them separate." She means Shūichi and his mistress, but Shingo also interprets the remark as referring to Shūichi and Kikuko, and he is ashamed for following this interpretation (195).

I have already remarked that the ostensible focus of *The Ambassadors* is on Chad; that is, the reader is led to believe that he will be required to make a decision of paramount significance about his future, but at the end of the work the reader realizes that Strether himself is the real object of scrutiny. In the same way, the focus of *The Sound of the Mountain* is not, as it seems, on the solution of Kikuko's marital problems, but on Shingo's personal adjustment to the inescapable fact that his daughter-in-law has a stronger hold upon his affections than his own daughter has. Both novels come to an end without a genuine resolution of the main problem; in other words, they are open-ended without a final conclusion. After all of Strether's diplomatic manoeuvering, we do not know at the end whether Chad returns to America; and we do not know whether Shingo after all his vacillating will finally separate from his son and daughter-in-law.

James in his earlier novels distrusted symbols in fiction on the grounds that they prevailed against the rigorous realism that he attempted to instil in his work. Under the influence of the Norwegian dramatist Ibsen, however, he recognized that "symbolism and realism were not necessarily in conflict, that the former could be employed to heighten the latter," and he scattered symbols liberally throughout *The Ambassadors*. Kawabata uses symbolism even more extensively; indeed it is inseparable from his style in *The Sound of the Mountain*. As we have already indicated, the title of the work itself, together with the title of nearly every chapter, is laden with symbolic meaning. I shall have more to say about the symbols in James than those in Kawabata since they are less obvious in the American author and, therefore, more in need of interpretation.

By an extraordinary coincidence, both authors use a piece of fabric to highlight characterization and atmosphere; James, a red one, Kawabata, a white. Soon after Strether arrives in Paris, he invites Maria Gostrey to dinner at his hotel (34). "Her dress was "cut down" or décolleté "in respect to shoulders and bosom," and she "wore round her throat a broad red velvet band with an antique jewel . . . attached to it in front." Red is the color of sensuality. Maria's attire immediately makes Strether think of Mrs. Newsome in contrast, who attends the opera in a black high-necked silk dress that makes her look like Queen Elizabeth. Maria's ribbon is "the key to a comparison of two societies," the puritanical one of New England and the cosmopolitan one of Paris (Grover 1973, 154). In *The Sound of the Mountain*, one evening Shingo asks Eiko to go dancing with him. She replies that she would be delighted, but not this particular evening and not in the dress she is wearing. She has on a navy blue skirt, a white blouse, and a white ribbon in her hair, which makes her blouse look all the whiter (50). White is the color of purity, and Eiko is wearing the conventional uniform of a schoolgirl. "When she was so dressed, the smallness of her breasts did not matter." The white ribbon also highlights the difference in age between Shingo and Eiko. Maria and Eiko have similar functions in the two novels respectively. Maria is an old school friend of Mme de Vionnet and is, therefore, assigned the role of bringing Strether into meaningful contact with the rather imposing beauty. Eiko, who is familiar with Shūichi's mistress and later works in the same establishment with her, is assigned the role of pointing her out to Shingo.

One of James's favorite symbols is that of water. Michael Egan has shown how in one of his plays, *The Reprobate,* the verbal image and symbol of water coalesce strikingly with the action (1973, 53–54). The same symbol carries through *The Ambassadors.* Mme de Vionnet is said to live "over the river," which literally means on the left bank of the Seine in Paris as opposed to the right, but symbolically means that she belongs to a social milieu different from Strether's (153). Strether invites Mme de Vionnet to a luncheon in a restaurant on the banks of the river, and during the course of the meal he watches the barges going to and fro. "In the matter of letting himself go, of diving deep" in his conversation about her liaison with Chad, he feels that he has "touched bottom" (192). Somewhat later, after he has succumbed to the charms of Mme de Vionnet, he feels that she has "pulled him into her boat" (254). The image is repeated a few pages later (267). In an interview with young Mamie Pocock, Strether fancies that he is momentarily "stranded with her on a far shore, during an ominous calm, in a quaint community of shipwreck" (281). The *locus classicus* for the water image, however, is Strether's famous encounter with Chad and Mme de Vionnet in their boat on the river. The imagery of "the stream or river of life, is drawn together with the action at the novel's central moment" (Egan, 141). Finally, at the end of the novel, Strether finds himself "well in port, the outer sea behind him," and it is "only a matter of getting ashore" (372).

There is no parallel single image running through *The Sound of the Mountain,* but there is a whole series of symbols foreshadowing the approach of death. In the opening pages of the novel Shingo tries to remember the maid who used to live with the family, but all he can remember is her manner of pronouncing a single word according to a provincial dialect: "He felt that a life was being lost." His lapse of memory symbolizes the transience of human life, not only his own aging, but everybody's. In addition to hearing the sound of the mountain, he dreams of being served by a dead man (30), he forgets details concerning a man whose funeral he attends (60), he pours tea into an ashtray instead of a cup (79), and he temporarily loses the facility of knotting his tie (256).

Other symbols may be noted in both novels. The amorphous product manufactured by Mrs. Newsome's factory seems to represent the traditional decorum of her way of life. When Strether offers to name it for Maria Gostrey in the final pages of the novel, she has no desire to know, for she has done with the products of Woollet (390). Strether is represented by the *Review,* which he edits. The apartment of Chad and the drawing room of Mme de Vionnet portray the character of each respectively, although Chad's may give a deceptive impression, probably having been furnished for him by Mme de Vionnet (64, 162). *The Sound of the Mountain* opens with Shingo buying three whelks for the family dinner and closes with the purchase of three trout. The three whelks are intended for a family of four adults, and thus symbolize the absence of Shūichi at mealtime and the consequent disturbed relations. The three trout at the end are distributed equally to the three units of the family: Shingo and his wife; Shūichi and his wife; and Fusako and her children. This distribution symbolizes a harmonious balance. In other passages, sun flowers have phallic connotations (26), and unseasonal buds on a ghinko tree signify Shingo's erotic stirrings (54).

In both novels, gardens serve a dual purpose as symbols and settings for the action. We notice in both James and Kawabata "the assimilation of the natural world into the human, and particularly the social and aesthetic, or the social as it also embodies aesthetic ideals and standards" (Grover 1973, 197, 156). For Strether, an "ordered English garden, in the freshness of the day," is delightful, particularly "the deep smoothness of the turf and the clean curves of paths" (26). Order, neatness, and stability are the qualities here represented. Elsewhere in the novel, however, James caustically describes the formal gardens of the Tuileries in Paris as "something that presented nature as a white-capped master chef" (53). Taken together, the two novels bring to mind the complex subject of the relations between Japanese gardens and formal French ones, but neither work maintains a consistent attitude toward the primacy of nature or of art. When Shingo visits an informal English garden in Tokyo in the company of Kikuko, the wide, tree-scattered lawn with couples lying down and strolling casually about symbolizes the liberation of the youth of the land (191). For Shingo, the landscape may contain beauty and order, but human nature signifies ugliness and contrariness. In regard to Kikuko's abortion, he muses that "even when natural weather is good, human weather is bad" (185). Both James and Kawabata, however, recognize that manners and morals are changing in their societies in a direction away from convention and rigorous observances. Strether observes that even Woollett "accommodates itself to the spirit of the age and the increasing mildness of manners" (49) and Kawabata consistently emphasizes the moral decline in postwar society.

The nature-art antithesis is significant for both novelists, but more pronounced in *The Ambassadors* than in *The Sound of the Mountain*. Indeed, Strether toward the end of the former novel is said to be moving "as in a gallery, from clever canvas to clever canvas" (360). Prior to the boat passage in which Strether glimpses Chad and Mme de Vionnet in their pastoral setting, Strether had left Paris with the deliberate intention of viewing the panorama of "French ruralism, with its cool special green, into which he had hitherto looked only through the little oblong window of the picture frame" (341). James proceeds to describe the natural setting in terms of a painting by an actual nineteenth-century French artist, Emile C. Lambinet. Strether had presumably had an opportunity to purchase the painting at a Tremont Street Gallery in Boston, but had not given in to his impulse. As he views the landscape, he sees it as though it were enclosed in an oblong gilt frame: "the poplars and willows, the reeds and river—a river of which he didn't know, and didn't want to know the name—fell into a composition, full of felicity, within them; the sky was silver and turquoise and varnish; the village on the left was white and the church on the right was grey; it was all there, in short—it was what he wanted: it was Tremont Street, it was France, it was Lambinet" (342). When he sees the boat approaching on the river, he has no trouble fitting it into the idyllic landscape of a pictorial perspective in the style of Lambinet or Monet. "What he saw was exactly the right thing—a boat advancing round the bend and containing a man who held the paddles and a lady, at the stern, with a pink parasol. It was suddenly as if these figures, or something like them, had been wanting in the picture, had been wanting more or less all day, and had now drifted into sight, with the slow current on purpose to fill up the measure" (348–49). This scene, which at first was "exactly the right thing," suddenly turns into exactly the wrong thing as the faces become distinguishable and Strether recognizes Chad and Mme de Vionnet and the compromising nature of their relationship. Reality had suddenly corrupted the vision of art, even though man rather than nature had served as the agency of corruption. The moral manifestations jar upon the aesthetic feelings and upset Strether's enjoyment of the scene. The comment of Shingo that I have already quoted is certainly applicable here: "even when natural weather is good, human weather is bad" (185).

Pictorial and plastic works are also used by Kawabata to stress the resemblances between nature and art. Some are perhaps without significance, as, for example, an erotic print by Harunobu, which Shingo is reminded of by the smallness of Eiko's breasts (39), or the reference to a recently deceased woman painter, who had specialized in portraying old-style beauties (44). Others carry profound symbolic meanings, as, for example, the Noh masks that Shingo considers purchasing. They represent the cycle of life and death not only in a general sense, but in specific references as well. Yasuko considers them as images of death; Shingo as images of life. Yasuko, who is blind to their aesthetic value, compares them to "heads from the chopping block" and says they give her the creeps (87). Shingo also thinks of heads separated from the body, but is not repelled by the image. Some enormous sunflowers he admires, remind him of the heads of famous people. He then dreams of having his own head detached and laundered while asleep (26–27). When a storm knocks down the sunflowers, however, and they remind him of severed heads, he does not like to look at them (57). Unlike his wife, Shingo sees lifelike qualities in the Noh masks, one of which seems to be so much like a fresh young girl that he almost kisses it (88). Shingo also associates the realistic qualities of the mask with those of a painter from the same historical period in which they were made. He had glanced at an ink sketch of a puppy by Sōtatsu and had thought it stylized and artificial, but when seeing a real puppy later, he was amazed to see the artistic puppy reproduced in life (91). His association of the artist and the mask-maker as belonging to the same period reinforces the idea of life as opposed to death in both artifacts.

Kawabata takes particular pains to emphasize that the Noh

masks are not forgeries (86), in contradistinction to a framed inscription that Shingo had bought earlier and that was not authentic (154). It purported to be a Ryōkan and set forth the message "In the heavens, a high wind."

Kawabata uses another combination of art and nature to treat the cycle of life and death. In the chapter entitled "The Kite's House," he describes a kite that is dancing on the roof of Shingo's dwelling and thus shares possession with Shingo and his family. Shingo wonders whether it is the same kite that comes each year, or rather a new generation every time taking the place of the old. Whichever it is, Shingo has a comforting sense of permanence. In a later chapter, Kawabata describes a painting by Kazan Watanabe of a single crow at the tip of a leafless tree (208). The crow, "high in a naked tree, bearing up under strong wind and rain," is the epitome of desolation. All that Shingo knows about Watanabe is that he had been poor and had committed suicide, elements that seem to be translated into the picture of the crow. Shingo contemplates the relationship of the kite and the crow to his own situation, one representing life, the other death.

I have already observed that the major link in structure between the two novels consists in the narrative point of view, which represents that of the protagonist. The novels are similar also in the characterization of these protagonists. Applying a term drawn from Aristotelean dramatic criticism, one may say that both Strether and Shingo are "flawed" in being deprived of some essential ingredient in the make-up of a well-adjusted human being. Strether's flaw may be summarized by the phrase "social passiveness." He has never asserted himself forcefully throughout his life, but has acquiesced in all the external events that have affected him, including the death of a wife and son. He has fallen into a subordinate relationship with Mrs. Newsome and is consistently led by other people, rather than taking an independent course or attempting to influence others around him. Shingo's weakness is more psychological than social, stemming originally from his youthful infatuation with Yasuko's sister. As a result he has fallen into an unsatisfying and unhappy marriage, and he clutters his life with a series of unfulfilled sexual fantasies.

Both novels emphasize questions of youth and age, particularly apparent or psychological rejuvenation, and actual aging. Throughout *The Sound of the Mountain,* Shingo receives vicarious pleasure in his relationship with his daughter-in-law as she reminds him of his youthful infatuation with Yasuko's sister. One might argue that Strether likewise receives a vicarious thrill in his relationship with Mme de Vionnet by imagining himself in the role of Chad. Strether actually admits, "I'm making up late for what I didn't have early. I cultivate my little benefit in my own little way. . . . It's my surrender, it's my tribute, to youth" (217). He also admits that "men of my age . . . and especially the least likely ones—have been noted as liable to strange outbreaks, belated uncanny clutches at the unusual, the ideal." This recognition of regret at the passing of opportunities for legitimate pleasure may perhaps suggest that Strether and Mme de Vionnet would become lovers were Chad to step out of the picture, but such a dénouement would be impossible, not only because of Strether's ingrained puritanism, but because of his conviction that his awakening is too late.

Since the novels project the viewpoint of their protagonists, Strether and Shingo are usually considered sympathetically by critics, and readers tend to look at the world from their perspective. Although Strether and Shingo are protagonists, they are not heroes and both possess major faults. Indeed, neither novel can be interpreted as a conflict between forces of good and evil, for neither work has villains or heroes. All of the characters have inherent shortcomings, and all mean well. None is any better or any worse than the other. This is true for Strether and Shingo, who can be interpreted either sympathetically or the reverse. For example, one critic has described Strether as "timid, self-centered, ungenerous, over-diplomatic, untrustworthy, and on many occasions untrusting," a man whose personal inadequacies are so serious that they would "involve him in defeat and humiliation anywhere in the world" (Richards 1972, 224, 226). One could very well make a case that Shingo is equally timid, self-centered, overdiplomatic, and untrusting, although he seems to have more of a generous disposition than the contrary. While Strether tries to avoid a too-close contact and involvement with life, he resembles Shingo in his sensitivity, thoughtfulness, and conscientiousness in social responsibilities.

Strether's dependence upon Mrs. Newsome detracts from his dignity, and Shingo reveals similar failings in the shabby treatment of his daughter and in enlisting his secretary Eiko to negotiate with his son's mistress. Both men manipulate other people in order to obtain their own ends.

Various indications reveal that neither character has succeeded in distinguishing himself in his society or in fulfilling himself in his personal life. Strether has done nothing notable at home except to have his name on the green cover of the review that he edits, and this has been thanks to the financial support of Mrs. Newsome. Shingo has grown old without climbing Mount Fuji and he has seen only one of the "three great sights of Japan" (79). Both men have been deprived or deficient in their emotional lives. Shingo has superficially enjoyed richer family relationships than Strether because of the presence of his son and daughter and grandchildren, but the necessity of continual dreaming and fantasizing reveals the emptiness or sterility of his relationships. Shingo attempts to decide whether his life has been a success, and at first he believes so merely because his food has a little of the taste it used to have before the war. Then he considers his life ordinary and mediocre and affirms that if a parent's success depends on the outcome of his children's marriages, then he has not done very well (100). Later he considers that happiness may be merely a matter of the fleeting instant (236).

Despite their shortcomings Strether and Shingo are men of principle, and both reveal signs of true nobility in their final adjustment to the crisis that each faces. As I have already indicated, Strether is willing to sacrifice his chances of marrying Mrs. Newsome and the considerable financial and social advantages that such a marriage would bring with it in order that Chad may continue to enjoy the cultural and intellectual amenities of life in Europe. Shingo likewise gives up the pleasure he finds in his daughter-in-law's company in order that she may find a more solid and compatible marriage relationship. It is perhaps too much of an exaggeration to claim that either Strether or Shingo acts in a sacrificial or self-abnegating manner, but each man certainly makes a decision in which the welfare of another person is preferred over his own narrow self-interest. In both

novels, moreover, the preferred person is younger than the protagonist. Through the assumption of a unity of interests with the
younger person, Strether and Shingo compensate vicariously for
the limitations of their own pasts—that is, the failure to obtain
the fullest measure from life. James specifically states that
Strether "held together" or established his own identity "by
bringing down his personal life to a function all subsidiary" to
that of the younger person (319). Strether realizes that "there
were some things that had to come in time if they were to come
at all. If they didn't come in time they were lost for ever" (137).
In an outpouring of recognition of his condition of unfulfillment,
Strether concludes that most of one's actions are predetermined
by circumstances despite the illusion of freedom and that to be a
puritan is not to be free. He laments that he is too old to take
advantage of his self-awareness and exhorts a younger man not
to miss the best things of life. Although *The Sound of the Mountain* has nothing to do with Puritanism, it also suggests that
freedom is an illusion. Shingo's disillusionment is even more
pronounced than Strether's and he equally illustrates the principle that if certain things do not come at the appropriate time in
an individual's life span, they will not come at all.

Obviously it is character rather than plot that brings the two
novels together, even though the two story-lines also resemble
each other—both protagonists in James's words, set out to rescue a young man whom "a wicked woman has got hold of" (36).
This mission, however, represents nothing more than the bare
bones in either novel. The chief concern of both authors is in the
development of the protagonist. Both Strether and Shingo are
given a final opportunity for positive action by means of an
awakened concern for the welfare of other people. Largely because of Shingo, we are able to see the conflicting forces inherent in Strether's role as a father figure, and because of Strether
we realize that Shingo's problems with the aging process contain
philosophical as well as biological components. *The Ambassadors* and *The Sound of the Mountain* are novels reflecting the
aesthetic values of two very different cultures and portraying
special segments of two very different societies, but they are
united by the careful delineation of universal psychological conditions or situations. In technique, the common tie consists of

delicacy of treatment; in philosophy, the notions of determinism and the illusory nature of human freedom.

CHAPTER 6. REFERENCES

Egan, Michael. 1972. *Henry James: The Ibsen years.* London: Vision Press.

Evans, Henri. 1951. *Louis Lambert et la philosophie de Balzac.* Paris: J. Corti.

Fergusson, Francis. 1975. *Literary landmarks.* New Brunswick, N.J.: Rutgers Univ. Press.

Goody, Ila. 1970. Review of Kawabata's *Sound of the Mountain. The Canadian Forum* 50:219–20.

Grover, Philip. 1973. *Henry James and the French novel.* New York: Barnes and Noble.

James, Henry. 1973. *The Ambassadors* (1903). Baltimore, Md.: Penguin Books.

Kawabata, Yasunari. 1971. *The Sound of the Mountain* (1954). Translated by Edward G. Seidensticker. Tokyo: Charles E. Tuttle Co.

Noguchi, Yone. 1975. *Collected English Letters.* Ed. Ikuko Atsumi. Tokyo: Yone Noguchi Society.

Richards, Bernard. 1972. *The Ambassadors* and *The Sacred Fount,* the artist manqué. In *The Air of Reality, New Essays on Henry James,* ed. John Allen Goode. London: Methuen & Co.

7

The Cat, the Butterfly, and the Shadow in the Pond: *The Temple of the Golden Pavilion* in the Context of Western Literature

ONE OF THE WELL-KNOWN CLICHÉS IN WESTERN JOURNALISM IS that truth is stranger than fiction. This observation might well be applied to an actual historical episode in which a young man deliberately destroyed by fire a religious edifice that was centuries old and a symbol of his nation's cultural tradition. Nearly every literate Japanese would assume that I am referring to an ancient Zen temple in the city of Kyoto that was burned to the ground in 1950, the subject of the novel *The Temple of the Golden Pavilion* by Yukio Mishima. I am indeed referring to this event, but also to a parallel conflagration that took place many centuries earlier in ancient Greece. One such event is strange; two are stranger still. Neither event would seem believable if it had appeared in a work of fiction without historical basis.

Erostratus, a native of Ephesus in Greece, set fire to the temple of Artemis in that city, a cultural landmark that had taken several generations to build. The fire took place in 356 B.C. on the same night on which Alexander the Great was born, a circumstance that led an ancient wit to remark that the destruction of the temple had been possible only because the goddess Artemis had been away attending the birth of Alexander. A later wit, Plutarch, remarked that this attempt at humor was frigid enough to have extinguished the fire. Erostratus when captured and put to torture confessed that his motivation for setting the fire was to achieve eternal fame, and as a result the city fathers of Ephesus passed a decree forbidding his name to be mentioned henceforth. The effort to consign his memory to oblivion failed, however, and Erostratus is still known throughout the West for his spectacular antisocial deed. His exploit was a precursor to that which took place in Kyoto in the present century. Even though the motivations of the two pyromaniacs may have been different, the deeds themselves were parallel: both were destructive, antisocial, and defiant. Other historical events have undoubtedly had similar motivations. It has been suggested, for example, that Nero, the Roman emperor, famous for fiddling while his city burned, himself ordered the destruction of Rome in order to perpetuate his fame (Lida 1952, 298).

In the previous chapter on James and Kawabata, I drew parallels between two separate literary works and used resemblances in one to aid in understanding the other. I noted similarities, whether in structure, style, symbolism, characterization, or theme, and accorded equal attention to each of the two works. In the discussion of *The Temple of the Golden Pavilion* I abandon this binary approach in favor of the treatment of several works from the West that have a partial bearing on Mishima's novel, just as the act of Erostratus is relevant to the act of the destroyer of the Zen temple. I emphasize the theme of beauty in its relationship to destruction and some of the ways in which this theme has been treated in Western literature.

The urge to tear down is in a sense present in all human beings, and the attempt to abolish what we hate is usually considered a normal impulse when confined within moderate limits; it is regarded as unwholesome only when carried to unusual lengths or when accompanied by extreme methods. The effort to destroy what we love is usually condemned in all of its manifestations as a perversion of human nature. Both love and hate motivate the protagonist of *The Temple of the Golden Pavilion,* a victim of the compulsion to demolish both material and spiritual objects.

The following pages will reveal resemblances between this

Japanese novel and a French work of short fiction that treats hate and an American work that treats love. This process shows that many elements seeming to be uniquely and typically Japanese are actually universal attributes of society and human nature. Burning down a temple in real life is only one of several elements in the novel that are to be found in both East and West.

Although the action of the French work treating hate takes place in the twentieth century and reflects the philosophical system of its author, Jean-Paul Sartre, the title of the work, "Erostrate" (in English, "Erostratus"), refers to the young man who burned down the temple at Ephesus. The title of the American work treating love, "The Artist of the Beautiful," suggests creation rather than destruction, and both concepts are present in the story. Although its author, Nathaniel Hawthorne, is usually associated with the analysis of the puritan mind and the portrayal of morbid personalities, the symbolism of "The Artist of the Beautiful" is bright and optimistic.

Since I am here concerned only with the aspects of *The Temple of the Golden Pavilion* that are relevant to Western literature, a complete plot summary is not necessary. It is sufficient to indicate the main and subsidiary actions, the psychological explication, and the themes. In my analysis, I must, of course, depend on the authenticity of the English translation by Ivan Morris.

The main action consists in the actual burning of the temple. Early in the novel the deed is foreshadowed when the protagonist, a student preparing for the priesthood, reads newspaper headlines speculating on whether Kyoto is to undergo air raids during the war. At this time the idea that the Golden Temple was destined to turn into ashes takes root within him and the temple increases in tragic beauty (42). Toward the end of the novel, the protagonist introduces a list of the historical structures that had succumbed to fire between the thirteenth and sixteenth centuries. Here he exhibits a fund of historical knowledge, the acquisition of which is nowhere explained. The protagonist's own love-hate relationship to the Golden Temple and other objects of unusual beauty is symbolized by his action when still a boy of defacing a young officer's ornamental sword with several ugly cuts from a rusty knife (9). The future destruction of the temple in the sense of annihilating an object that is loved and respected is foreshadowed when one of the protagonist's fellow students quotes a Zen exhortation: "When ye meet the Buddha, kill the Buddha! . . . When ye meet your father and mother, kill your father and mother! . . . Only thus will ye attain deliverance. Only thus will ye escape the trammels of material things and become free" (142, 149). The protagonist recalls these words at the moment when he is faltering in his purpose of burning the temple, and his recollection of them immediately propels him out of his lethargy and enables him to perform the deed (258).

Among the several subsidiary actions, there are three in particular that are significant in regard to Western literature. First of these concerns a young girl, Uiko, who has been apprehended while taking food to her lover, a deserter from the army. For a time she adamantly refuses to reveal her lover's whereabouts, but suddenly decides to betray him to the authorities. The protagonist, then merely a boy, witnesses the scene of her betrayal and is profoundly moved. He is "intoxicated by the pellucid beauty" of her treachery (17). This scene establishes the protagonist's perverseness and delicately suggests the peculiar combination of sadism and rejection of humanity that will eventually lead to his final act.

The next subsidiary action concerns the narrative by the protagonist's fellow student, Kashiwagi, of his own sexual problem and its solution. Kashiwagi and the protagonist have in common an obvious physical deformity: the protagonist stutters and Kashiwagi has two clubfeet. Both at first are sexually impotent as a result of their deficiencies, but Kashiwagi leads the way in overcoming his psychological inadequacy. He explains that when a young and attractive girl had offered him her "dazzling beautiful body," he had been completely impotent, but sometime later a widow in her sixties succeeded in arousing his desire and afforded him complete physical satisfaction. Kashiwagi reveals that this woman's ugliness and age managed to release him from his inhibitions; he came to understand that the conviction that he could never be loved was the basic state of his existence (103). In his words, "I realized that the problem lay not in trying to shorten the distance between myself and the object, but in maintaining this distance so that the object might remain an object" (102).

The third subsidiary action concerns a woman whom the protagonist had seen for the first time during the war. He spies upon her as she receives her lover, a young army officer. In the course of their rendezvous she serves the officer a cup of tea, takes out one of her breasts, and rubs it with both hands until it produces the warm milk for his cup. This scene makes an indelible impression on the protagonist. Some time later he learns that the girl had shortly before had a stillborn infant, a circumstance that led her lover to remark that if they could not have her child, he would like to taste the milk from her breast. A month later he was killed in the war (115). The scene between the girl and the army officer is reminiscent of a theme in universal folklore, the drinking by an adult of milk from a woman's breast. In a famous Chinese folk tale, a family group, consisting of husband, wife, the husband's mother, and an infant, is faced with acute poverty. Since they cannot afford milk to cure the old woman's illness, the couple decides that the mother-in-law should receive her daughter-in-law's milk and the infant be sacrificed. While digging a grave to bury the baby alive, they encounter a chest filled with money, a heavenly reward for their filial devotion. (Lou 1970, 15) Latin literature describes an elderly man, Cimon, who had been cast into prison for political reasons and condemned to death by starvation, but his faithful daughter Pero kept him alive by secretly nourishing him with milk from her own breast during regular visits. A variant of the theme appears in the last chapter of John Steinbeck's *The Grapes of Wrath*. In this twentieth-century American novel, an entire family has been reduced to the level of starvation. An old man who will certainly die unless he receives nourishment lies frightened and exhausted in a corner, and a young girl who has just suffered a miscarriage quietly settles down beside him, bares her breast, and forces him to accept her milk. Western literature has many other variants.

In *The Temple of the Golden Pavilion,* the girl with the stillborn child becomes Kashiwagi's mistress after she has matured into womanhood. He exploits her not only by using her body, but also by learning from her the art of flower arrangement.

Kashiwagi one evening invites her to his room in the presence of the protagonist. After being there some time she compliments Kashiwagi on a flower arrangement that he has installed in a conspicuous place. Kashiwagi uses this occasion to reply that since he has now learned all that the woman can teach him, he no longer needs her for any purpose and their relationship is at an end (147). The woman thereupon wrathfully disorders and destroys the carefully wrought arrangement. Kashiwagi then seizes her by the hair and calmly slaps her across the face. As she runs out of the room, Kashiwagi commands the protagonist to run after her and under the pretense of offering consolation to obtain her for his own pleasure (148). This he does, and the woman eventually takes him to her house. He confesses that he had previously observed the ceremony with her officer lover, and she offers to make the same gesture for him. She then exposes one of her breasts and he stares at it in a fascinated manner; it first seems to be only a material object but then assumes in his imagination the beauty and radiance of the Golden Temple. He is unable to perform sexually and the woman dismisses him scornfully (153).

All of the preceding episodes account in some measure for the protagonist's final act of pyromania, but there are a number of additional explanations offered. At the age of thirteen the protagonist witnesses an act in which his mother openly discredits his father. All three were sleeping on a mat under a common mosquito net, along with a man from outside the immediate family circle, who is a distant relative of the mother. The protagonist is awakened by the sound of this relative making love to his mother, and his eyes are then covered by his father's hands to conceal the disgrace (155). In Western literature, it is a common motif for a boy to suffer psychological damage by witnessing his parents engaged in sexual activity. A recent example of a boy seeing his mother in the arms of a man other than his father may be found in a novel *Lucy Crown* by Irwin Shaw, 1956. Here a boy of thirteen comes upon his mother sleeping with her tutor, who is twenty years of age. He reports the incident to his father and, as the latter predicts, eventually develops a hatred for both his parents. Mishima offers a further refinement and extension by having the boy and the father jointly witness the mother engaged in adultery. In later life Mishima's protagonist feels guilty when he masturbates; he has visions of the breasts of the girl who betrayed her soldier lover and at the same time imagines that he himself has turned into a small, revolting insect (70). His resulting impotence manifests itself on several occasions. His first trial is with a girl whom Kashiwagi provides for him. At the moment when he tries to arouse his lust, recollections of his major physical defect, his stuttering, appear before him, and these are followed by images of the Golden Temple (125). It appears to him that the girl has been rejected by the temple and his own efforts at adjustment toward life are likewise rejected. His second sexual failure occurs with the woman who offers him her breast. He succeeds in manifesting his virility during a subsequent visit to a brothel but only after he realizes that the vision of fire stimulates his carnal lust (220). He determines to lose his virginity as a preparatory step to burning down the temple and considers the two events as interlocked, one consequent to the other.

A second major cause of the protagonist's arson is a growing self-knowledge of his physical imperfection. His stuttering represents both the source and the symbol of his inadequacies. He regards speech as the key to the door between inner consciousness and the outside world, and the defect of stuttering makes this key difficult to manipulate (5). In other words, he is kept by his handicap from normal adjustment to the external world. Just before the committing of his unpardonable deed, moreover, the protagonist wonders whether it may not have been the concept of beauty itself that had given rise to his stuttering (217). Although one of the protagonist's friends believes that he is obsessed with the temple because it reminds him of his father, who was also a priest, the protagonist fully recognizes that his attachment to it is "entirely rooted" in his own ugliness (39).

A final reason for the protagonist's action is his aversion to mediocrity in human attainments, an aversion that he feels even in regard to old men (184). He has a keen sense of his own mediocrity, which gnaws and rankles upon him. He describes his situation just prior to setting fire to the temple: "No one had paid any attention to me during the past twenty years and under present conditions this was bound to continue. Under present conditions I was still a person of no importance" (239). This is exactly the attitude that led Erostratus of ancient Greece to destroy the Temple of Ephesus. He also was "a person of no importance" and he committed his infamous act to acquire fame and celebrity.

Some of the subthemes of the novel embrace philosophical concepts of dualism. As a boy, the protagonist had access to the real Golden Temple in photographs or in textbooks, but it was the image of the building as described by his father that made the greater impression (4). In other words, the imaginary dominated the real. Later when the protagonist saw the actual building for the first time, he was fascinated by the shadow it cast on an adjoining pond (24). He discovered that for him the shadow or image of the temple is more beautiful than the temple itself.

Another aspect of this duality is involved in Kashiwagi's method of overcoming his sexual impotency. He places a distance between himself and the person with whom he is involved—that is, the object. He realizes that sexual desire or what most people call infatuation is made up for the most part of dream and fantasy; that the beauty and attractiveness that seem to be in the object are actually in the mind of the beholder. Reality lies in a cold assessment of both the individual and the object; desire is merely an apparition. That which is ordinarily known as romantic love is the "effort to join reality with the apparition" (102). Kashiwagi is able to lose his virginity through a double dualism, by separating imagination from reality and by separating himself from the object.

The protagonist similarly uses the logic of Zen philosophy to establish a more fundamental duality between being and not being. He explains that "the essence of Zen is the absence of all particularities, and the real power to see consists in the knowledge that one's own heart possesses neither form nor feature." It is the mission of the true Zen believer to realize this concept of formlessness in order to merge into absolute existence, but the protagonist is unable to obtain a sense of solidarity with being or even to have "any feeling of solidarity with nothingness" (130). Even though he is unable to attain a state of oneness with absolute existence, he achieves a related identification with the Golden Temple. The absolute, positive temple envelops him, and he asks, "Did I possess the temple or was I possessed by it?" (131). A more correct manner of description, he affirms, would be to say that "a strange balance had come into being," a balance that would allow the Golden Temple to be him and him to be the Golden Temple. From this experience he proceeds to the intuition that when the temple should be destroyed, he would be destroyed with it (132). Because of this identification of the temple with existence and beauty and its destruction with nonexistence, the protagonist develops an obsession for both beauty and nonexistence. During one of his many daydreams, the protagonist participates in his imagination in a ceremony at the Golden Temple in which a Superior is installed, taking the place of a previous one who has died. The protagonist imagines that he is the one in the ceremony to utter the name of the new Superior and rather than pronouncing the individual's name, he starts to stutter "Beauty," but it is the word "Nihility" that comes out (164). A final dualism concerns the human personality. In a dialogue with one of his teachers, the protagonist observes that he was one personality that he envisages himself and another that other people have attributed to him. He is perturbed whether to act in conformity with his own conception of his self or to act according to the pattern expected by other people (246).

A theme closely resembling the preoccupation of the Russian novelist Dostoevski with the dark side of human character is Mishima's evocation of the atmosphere of gloom. The protagonist's deliberate defacing of a schoolmate's sword teaches him that he was "not qualified to enter life through its bright surface" (123). The clubfooted Kashiwagi, moreover, reveals the "dark by-way" along which he could "reach life from the back." In one of his earliest outings with Kashiwagi, "the entire day was colored by the gloom, the irritability, the uneasiness, the nihilism that belong to youth" (114). The only wholesome or normal individual in the protagonist's immediate circle is a school friend who is suddenly taken away by death. This was the one and only thread that still connected the protagonist with "the bright world of daylight."

Throughout the novel the protagonist comes face-to-face with evil; indeed on one occasion he contrives a situation to prove to himself that evil exists and that he has embraced it in his real life.

He had committed an action in the past that he knows is reprehensible, but he feels that by confessing it to his superior he would be relieved of guilt. The act of confession itself would be trivial, but the deliberate decision to keep his guilt to himself would be a matter of great significance. While still debating whether or not to confess, he conceives that he is "experimenting with the single problem: 'Is evil possible' " (88). Persisting in his silence, he realizes that he has embraced evil. The protagonist restates the problem of evil in regard to his later failure to achieve adequate sexual arousal because of the persistent image of the Golden Temple in his consciousness. He wonders why the temple seems to be protecting him or separating him from life without being asked to do so. "It may be," he muses, "that the temple is saving me from falling into hell. But by so doing, the Golden Temple is making me even more evil than those people who actually do fall into hell, it is making me into 'the man who knows more about hell than anyone' " (153).

A closely related theme is that which is known in French literature as gratuitous action—an action that does not belong to the normal chain of cause and effect, but is spontaneous, without reason or logic, and completely unmotivated. Although the notion of gratuitous action is ordinarily associated with Gide, the best known example is that of the protagonist in Camus' novel *L'Etranger,* who was a French inhabitant of North Africa. One day, seeing by chance an Arab on a lonely beach, a man who is a complete stranger, the protagonist kills him with a revolver. In *The Temple of the Golden Pavilion,* the protagonist actually contemplates his deed in advance, but tries to persuade himself that it is based on impulse. First of all, he deliberately seeks to establish that his action is the result of his extensive reading of novels and philosophy, none of which have any relationship to Zen thought. He does not wish to mention the names of these writers and philosophers, but the reader realizes that they might well have included Dostoevski, Sartre, and Camus. In his words, "I am aware of the influence that they had on me and also of the fact that it was they who inspired me to the deed that I committed; yet I like to believe that the deed itself was my own original creation; in particular, I do not want this deed to be explained away as having been actuated by some established philosophy" (135). In a later chapter he discusses one of his actions preparatory to the burning of the building, a temporary flight from his duties at the temple. "When I thought about it later," he writes, "I realized that this flight of mine, which seemed so sudden, had in fact been preceded by considerable reflection and hesitation. I preferred, however, to believe that I had been driven by some abrupt impulse" (171). When the notion of actually burning down the Golden Temple comes to the protagonist, he associates it with events in the past, but nevertheless ascribes it to the impulse of the moment (191). He is "seized by the notion, as though . . . struck by light." Yet that idea which had never previously entered his mind "began to grow in strength and size as soon as it was born." The protagonist, "far from containing the idea" is himself wrapped up in it. In a sense, the notion is more powerful than his own will.

As I have already shown, the protagonist becomes infatuated with the Golden Temple as a mere boy as a result of his father's conviction that it is the most beautiful thing on earth. Its mystic and fabulous qualities become indelibly engraved on the protagonist's own heart (4). When he eventually sees the building itself, its shadow seems to him more beautiful than the actual structure (24). In other words, he is possessed by his imagination. After the protagonist makes the acquaintance of Kashiwagi, the latter explains this uncanny power of beauty in an impromptu sermon or exposition of a Zen problem. "Although beauty may give itself to everyone," he declares, "it does not actually belong to anybody" (144). Kashiwagi is not the spokesman for either Mishima or the protagonist, but he gives a convincing explanation of how an obsession with beauty may cause the destruction of the object that incarnates it. His exposition is based on the parable of an ancient priest who settles the fate of a kitten that has been a bone of contention between two groups of monks. Seizing it, he says to the priests, "If any of you can say a word, this kitten shall be saved; if you can not, it shall be killed." Nobody speaks and the kitten is killed. Later that evening, the priest relates the happening to his chief disciple, who "immediately removed his shoes, put them on his head, and left the room." The priest then remarks that if the disciple had been present earlier in the day, the kitten's life would have been spared (65). Kashiwagi draws a parallel between beauty and the aching of a decayed tooth; both are dependent upon material objects, but, nevertheless, separate from them. When the bad tooth is extracted by the dentist, the pain is gone, but one cannot say that it resides in the dead object that the tooth has now become (144). To have killed the kitten, therefore, was like extracting a painful tooth, like gouging out beauty. In this sense, even though the kitten was dead, its beauty may have been alive, and the disciple, understanding this solution but satirizing it, placed his shoes on his head. The protagonist's final action in burning down the temple may in this light be interpreted as an effort to probe to the depths of its beauty.

Kashiwagi, true to his perverse character, later in the narrative gives a completely different interpretation of the parable of the kitten. This time he maintains that the disciple intended to suggest that "beauty is a thing which must sleep and which, in sleeping, must be protected by knowledge." But knowledge in this sense belongs not to any individual, but to all humanity or the general condition of human existence. This leads Kashiwagi to the conclusion that beauty is merely illusion, and the marriage of this illusion of beauty on one side and knowledge on the other gives rise to art (217). The protagonist on hearing this explanation then admits that beautiful things are now his "most deadly enemies." Previous to this, as I have already mentioned, he had himself suggested that beauty and nihility are identical (164). Finally, at the instant just before committing the building to the fire, the protagonist's entire conception of beauty, the power of memory combined with the vision of the moment, associates beauty with nothingness. He realizes that each part depends for its perfection upon the other parts with which it blends, and that the beauty is, therefore, not completed in any single part. "The adumbration of beauty contained in one detail was linked with the subsequent adumbration of beauty, and so it was that the various adumbrations of a beauty *which did not exist* had become the underlying motif of the Golden Temple. Such adumbrations were signs of nothingness. Nothingness was the very structure of this beauty" (255).

The concept that excessive obsession with an object may lead to one's destroying the object itself was expressed in the nineteenth century by the English poet Oscar Wilde.

> Yet each man kills the thing he loves,
>   By each let this be heard,
> Some do it with a bitter look,
>   Some with a flattering word,
> The coward does it with a kiss,
>   The brave man with a sword!
>   (*The Ballad of Reading Gaol*, 1.7)

The related theme of infatuation with beauty causing the power of the imaginary to prevail over the real constitutes the basis of Hawthorne's "The Artist of the Beautiful." Although the subject matter of the story seems to blend science fiction with the fantastic, the plot and characters of the work are entirely symbolic. The artist depicted in the story has two great passions in his life, a dedication to the beautiful in art and a love for a childhood sweetheart, Annie, who is wooed in turn by a blacksmith. Early in life he experiences a "love of the beautiful, such as might have made him a poet, a painter or a sculptor, and which was as completely refined from all utilitarian coarseness as it could have been in either of the fine arts." Painfully aware of the contrast between brute strength and spiritual beauty, he aspires "to put the very spirit of beauty into form and give it motion." The artist is obsessed by butterflies, which in Western literature frequently symbolize the soul but in Hawthorne's story represent the idea of beauty. Going through alternate periods of lassitude and inspiration, the artist takes to excessive drinking, but is redeemed by the sight of a particularly beautiful butterfly, which flies in through the open window. The girl Annie has in the meantime married the blacksmith and given birth to a child. The artist one day visits the family, taking with him as a wedding gift a beautiful and elaborate mechanical butterfly of his own design and manufacture. The butterfly is actually able to flutter its wings and fly around the room, and the assembled watchers cannot tell whether it is alive or a "wondrous mechanism."

The artist explains that in the secret of this butterfly and in its beauty, "which is not merely outward, but deep as its whole system—is represented the intellect, the imagination, the sensibility, the soul of an Artist of the Beautiful." He had not as yet adequately realized, however, that "the reward of all performance must be sought within itself, or sought in vain."

When the butterfly is touched by Annie's skeptical father, it seems to fade and droop, but it is reinvigorated by the nearness of the innocent child because of the "spiritual essence it has imbibed." At the end of the story, as the butterfly soars toward the ceiling of the room and down again, the little child grasps it in flight and compresses it into a myriad of fragments in his hand. The artist is not at all perturbed. "He looked placidly at what seemed the ruin of his life's labor, and which was yet no ruin. He had caught a far better butterfly than this. When the artist rose high enough to achieve the beautiful, the symbol by which he made it perceptible to mortal senses became of little value in his eyes while his spirit possessed itself in the enjoyment of the reality." For him, as for the protagonist of *The Golden Pavilion,* beauty and nothingness were equivalent.

The action in Hawthorne's story is, of course, not parallel to that of Mishima's novel. It is not the man obsessed with beauty who destroys the material object; the destruction is carried out by a third person. Yet the theme of the two works is identical— that spiritual beauty transcends material beauty—or as Mishima expresses it, that the shadow of the temple is more beautiful than the temple itself.

This is a somewhat idealistic or ethereal motion strangely contrasting with the sordid and pessimistic light in which Mishima portrays human nature. The English translator of *The Temple of the Golden Pavilion* remarks that the work "has around it an aura of Dostoevskian violence and passion" and that one finds within it "many reminders of Dostoevski's involved and tortuous struggle with ageless questions." Nearly every informed Western reader would have a similar reaction. There is no question that Mishima's novel is related to the Russian nineteenth-century master of fiction through the latter's concept of the Underground Man. The latter is the model or prototype of what has come to be known in twentieth-century Western fiction as the antihero, a designation that perfectly fits the protagonist of

Mishima's novel. According to the Underground Man, "reason . . . is an excellent thing, there is no disputing that, but reason is only reason and can only satisfy man's rational faculty, while will is a manifestation of all life, that is, of all human life including reason as well as all impulses" (Dostoevski 1960, 25). As a more attractive alternative to reason, the Underground Man offers behavior motivated by one's whimsical or even foolish will. "One's own free unfettered choice, one's own fancy, however wild it may be, one's own fancy worked up at times to frenzy— why that is that very 'most advantageous advantage' which we have overlooked." Action based on this impulse, no matter how harmful or painful it may be to the one who carried it out, still offers the greatest attraction to that person. According to the Underground Man, "it preserves for us what is most precious and most important—that is, our personality, our individuality." It is not hard to fit Mishima's protagonist into this mold.

Even before Dostoevski and Gide, the American poet and author of fantastic literature, Edgar Allan Poe, developed the concept of gratuitous behavior directed toward destroying an innocent object. Poe describes this behavior as deriving from an innate spirit of perverseness that all men possess. His particular example is that of a man who kills a household pet, the black cat, in a story of that name. According to the narrator of this work,

perverseness is one of the primitive impulses of the human heart—one of the indivisible primary faculties, or sentiments, which give direction to the character of Man. Who has not a hundred times, found himself committing a vile or a stupid action, for no other reason than because he should *not*? Have we not a perpetual inclination, in the teeth of our best judgment, to violate that which is *Law*, merely because we understand it to be such? This spirit of perverseness, I say, came to my final overthrow. It was this unfathomable longing of the soul *to vex itself*—to offer violence to its own nature—to do wrong for the wrong's sake only—that urged me to continue and finally to consummate the injury I had inflicted upon the unoffending brute. One morning, in cold blood, I slipped a noose about its neck and hung it to the limbs of the tree;— hung it with the tears streaming from my eyes, and with the bitterest remorse at my heart;—hung it *because* I knew that it had loved me, and *because* I felt it had given me no reason of offence; hung it *because* I knew that in so doing I was committing a sin—a deadly sin that would so jeopardize my immortal soul as to place it—if such a thing were possible—even beyond the reach of the infinite mercy of the Most Merciful and Most Terrible God.

One cannot help seeing here not only a foreshadowing of Dostoevski's Underground Man, but also a parallel to the Zen parable of killing the kitten. Poe's narrator is impelled to kill the black cat by some of the same forces that lead Mishima's to destroy the temple.

In Sartre's related short story "Erostratus," the title character illustrates the extreme individualism of the Underground Man and serves at the same time as a vehicle for portraying aspects of the author's philosophical system of existentialism. Erostratus, we remember, is the name of the man who in ancient Greece burned down the Temple of Artemis. Sartre's short story does not concern this episode, but instead a twentieth-century parallel to it. The event portrayed is not the burning of a building, but the shooting of a random victim. The protagonist, however, hears the story of Erostratus and is fascinated by it. He observes that nobody knows the name of the man who built the temple, but to this day the name of Erostratus is preserved. Sartre clearly intends his protagonist to serve as an Erostratus of the present, a modern example of a twisted individual seeking to affirm his existence. Sartre's story is quite short, but it, nevertheless, illustrates a number of aspects of the author's philosophy. As I analyze the story, I shall point out some parallels with Sartre's formal expression of his philosophical system in an extensive theoretical work entitled *Being and Nothingness.* At the same time I shall indicate resemblances to *The Temple of the Golden Pavilion.* In so doing, I shall not be suggesting that Mishima is an exponent of French existentialism or even that he was necessarily aware of Sartre or his system. I shall merely be giving examples of the universality of literature. Both "Erostratus" and *The Temple of the Golden Pavilion* are psychological studies of the forces that lead a mediocre personality to carry out a perverse and utterly irrational crime.

The crimes in both works represent high degrees of criminality; two protagonists plan to commit suicide in order to frustrate the justice of society. Yet both Sartre and Mishima adopt the literary device of having the protagonist tell his story and explore his inner thoughts in the first person. This in itself is a remarkable resemblance, for it is highly improbable that in real life a man guilty of a crime of this magnitude would write down his thoughts and continue his narrative to include the perpetration of the deed itself and its immediate aftermath. A French critic has made a distinction between "good" criminals, who have no fundamental intention of doing harm to others (characters such as Erostratus), and evil ones, who have no feeling for others at all and who enjoy their acts of cruelty. According to this dichotomy, the evil criminal must be described through the objectivity of third person narrative, but the first-person style is more appropriate to the "good" one "because he alone may speak of his experiences, no one else being susceptible of penetrating sufficiently into the plotting which has led him into the inhuman" (Magny 1945, 124). This reasoning is not very convincing since it is not necessary for an author to adopt the first-person perspective to enter into the mind of his protagonist. In *The Sound of the Mountain,* for example, even the protagonist's dreams are effectively described in the third person. The decision of both Mishima and Sartre to use the first-person perspective should be regarded, therefore, not as a logical consequence growing out of similar subject matter, but rather as a stylistic coincidence.

There exists in Western literature a long tradition of first-person narrative by criminals. It was customary in the eighteenth century for condemned prisoners to make a speech on the gallows just before being executed, and many of these speeches—or fanciful ones like them—were published in periodicals or in pamphlet form. In Western literature, moreover, the desire for confession is an observed human trait. Poe's story "The Black Cat," for example, is narrated entirely in the first person.

A related resemblance in form is that neither author refers to his protagonist by name, but keeps up a deliberate anonymity. The name of Mishima's protagonist is known since he was, of course, a person in real life; the name of Sartre's protagonist appears only once—as the signature to a letter that he sends to a large number of eminent French authors, announcing his intended crime. In both works, the narrator refers to other characters by name but to himself only by a pronoun.

"Erostratus" begins with the protagonist looking down from a seventh-floor balcony upon pedestrians in the street below. By means of this downward perspective, he acquires a superiority over other men that he realizes is only a superiority of position, but is, nevertheless, satisfying. He affirms that in life moral superiorities must be propped up by material symbols "or else they'll tumble." In his formal philosophy, which is a type of phenomenology, Sartre recognizes that one of the fundamental problems of the philosopher is to demonstrate the existence of other beings that are thinking substances of the same essence as oneself. Quite apart from this traditional problem, Sartre presents the Other as "the indispensable mediator" between oneself and one's reflective self. One becomes ashamed of one's being as it appears to the Other (Sartre 1965, 222). For this reason a hostility develops between the individual and the Other, a hostility symbolized in "Erostratus" by the act of looking down upon other people from the balcony. A similar attitude is reflected by Kashiwagi as he separates himself from his sexual partner (102). He rids himself of his shame in relating to the Other at the same moment that he releases himself from love, which is replaced by pure physical desire (98). His success in emancipating himself from shame and love, which leads in turn to his overcoming sexual impotence, is closely related to Sartre's explanation of sadism, "to seize and to make use of the Other not only as the Other-as-object but as a pure incarnated transcendence" in which emphasis is placed on the incarnated Other as a mere instrument (399). The protagonist of *The Temple of the Golden Pavilion* also experiences sadistic pleasure when he tramples upon a prostitute's stomach at the command of an American army officer. Even though he had been forced to commit this deed in order to induce a miscarriage, he fully admits that it was not compulsion that had made him enjoy the feeling of the girl's stomach and the sound of her suffering, a sensation that seemed to pass "like some mysterious lightning" from the girl's body into his own (85). He was unable to "forget the sweetness of that moment."

The protagonist of "Erostratus" obviously derives satisfaction from considering people as ants, which he is unable to do when he finds himself on the same level as they are. He remembers having once seen a dead man on the street. "He had fallen on his face. They turned him over, he was bleeding. I saw his open eyes and his cockeyed look and all the blood. I said to myself, 'It's nothing, it's no more touching than wet paint. They painted his nose red, that's all.'" This same impression of emptiness or artificiality of a corpse is portrayed by the protagonist of *The Temple of the Golden Pavilion* as he describes his reaction to seeing his deceased father. "A dead man's face falls to an infinite depth beneath the surface which the face possessed when it was alive, leaving nothing for the survivors to see but the frame of a mask; it falls so deep, indeed, that it can never be pulled back to the surface. A dead man's face can tell us better than anything else in this world how far removed we are from the true existence of physical substance, how impossible it is for us to lay hands on the way in which this substance exists" (32).

Even before contemplating a crime, the protagonist of "Erostratus" buys a revolver and discovers that its mere possession makes everything seem better for him (83). In his words, "You feel strong when you assiduously carry on your person something that can explode and make a noise. I took it every Sunday, I simply put it in my pants pocket and then went out for a walk— generally along the boulevards." The protagonist of *The Temple of the Golden Pavilion* has similar sensations when he buys a knife preparatory to his deed—although it is suicide rather than terrorizing other people that motivates his purchase. In his words, "I took the pocketknife out of its case and licked the blade. The steel immediately clouded over and the clear coolness against my tongue was followed by a remote suggestion of sweetness. The sweetness was faintly reflected on my tongue from within the thin steel, from within the unattainable essence of the steel. . . . Happily I imagined the day when my flesh would be intoxicated by a great outburst of that sweetness" (240).

The protagonist of "Erostratus" abruptly admits, "I never had intercourse with a woman" (84). He explains that he customarily frequents prostitutes, but instead of using them to consummate the sexual act, he requires them to undress and after watching them, masturbates. He describes in detail one of these sessions in which he forces a prostitute to strip and walk back and forth in front of him. He explains: "Nothing annoys women more than walking when they're naked. They don't have the habit of putting their heels down flat. The whore arched her back and let her arms hang. I was in heaven." Sartre in *Being and Nothingness* calls behavior such as this sadistical pleasure, as distinguished from what is called the obscene, which he defines as "a species of Being-for-Others which belongs to the genus of the ungraceful" (400). According to Sartre, "The obscene appears when the body adopts postures which entirely strip it of its acts and which reveal the inertia of its flesh. The sight of a naked body from behind is not obscene. But certain involuntary waddlings of the rump are obscene. This is because then it is only the legs which are acting for the walker, and the rump is like an isolated cushion which is carried by the legs and the balancing of which is a pure obedience to the laws of weight" (401). As I have already observed, the protagonist of *The Temple* also relies upon masturbation until just before committing his crime, and he is finally able to carry out normal sexual relations at a visit to a brothel. There his behavior is not overtly sadistic because of his diffidence. His experience represents, nevertheless, an effort to demonstrate his own identity and to separate himself from the Other. He examines his partner's body, he explains, "because the act of looking was a proof that I existed" (227).

When the protagonist of "Erostratus" leaves the prostitute, she is dumbfounded at his extraordinary behavior, and he thinks to himself, "That's what I want. To surprise them all" (89). Before fully realizing that his brooding will eventually lead him to commit murder with his revolver, he imagines himself shooting various victims and actually prepares his friends for the deed. This he calls arranging his publicity (90). His character is revealed most fully in a conversation with his fellow workers that establishes the parallel between himself and his Greek prototype. When his colleagues express admiration of the American flyer Lindbergh, the protagonist confesses that he likes black heroes—that is, "black as in Black Magic" (91). One of his companions then observes that an appropriate hero would be Erostratus: "He wanted to become famous and he couldn't find any-

thing better to do than to burn down the temple of Ephesus."
Since nobody knows the name of the builder of the temple, the
protagonist concludes that Erostratus, with his enduring fame,
"didn't figure things out too badly." He finds inspiration in the
story. Erostratus "had been dead for more than two thousand
years and his act was still shining like a black diamond."

Sartre's protagonist, like Mishima's, is a victim of hate. Sartre
explains in *Being and Nothingness* that "hate is a black feeling,
that is, a feeling which aims at the suppression of an Other and
which qua project is consciously projected against the disap-
proval of others" (411). It makes no difference whether the expression of hate entails the destruction of another human being
or an inanimate object such as a temple; the act represents not
only the release of pent-up resentments, but also the assertion of
one's own existence. "Hate knows only the Other-as-object and
attaches itself to this object. It wishes to destroy this object in
order by the same stroke to overcome the transcendence which
haunts it" (411). Sartre's protagonist boasts that he does not love
his fellow men, that he loves them so little that he intends to kill
six of them the next day, and that he is quite calm in making his
plans (94–95). The burning of the Golden Pavilion is equally an
action based upon careful calculation. Although the protagonist
wants to believe that he has "been driven by some abrupt impulse," he admits that his action has been "preceded by considerable reflection and hesitation" (171).

From the moment that each protagonist determines to commit
his crime to the moment of its execution, the parallels between
the two narratives are numerous and close. Both men lose interest in their everyday careers; one stops attending classes at the
university; the other goes for weeks at a time without reporting
to his office and is finally dismissed. Both narrators specify exact
dates; the French, 27 October as the crucial day when he starts
to commit his crime; the Japanese, 1 July 1950. One takes three
further days for consummation; the other, merely two. Both
narrators deliberately use up all their money. The protagonist of
"Erostratus" begins to live more expensively, particularly in
consuming food. He has hot meals sent up to his room from a
neighboring restaurant until nearly all his money has been exhausted. He eats a final meal at a restaurant and then throws his

remaining few coins in the gutter. The protagonist of the *Golden Pavilion* is given a large sum of money to pay his fees at the university, but he determines to spend it instead. Hunger also plays an important role in both novels. The protagonist of "Erostratus" stays in his room for three days without eating, and as a result he has disordered erotic dreams. Throughout the last day, hunger comes and goes in waves, and toward the evening it strikes with great intensity. The protagonist of *The Golden Pavilion* makes special preparations to allay his hunger on the day of the crime, buying a bag of sweets, which, he says, he acquired because of uneasiness. He speculates at length on the relationship between himself and his supply of sugar: "I knew that however my spirit might be enlivened, my stomach and my intestines—those dull, stolid organs lodged within my body—would insist on having their own way and would start dreaming some banal dream of everyday life" (242).

The protagonist of "Erostratus" loads his revolver with six cartridges, planning to kill six people, but after killing one victim, he loses his nerve and takes refuge in the lavatory of a café. He contemplates committing suicide with a remaining cartridge, but lacks the courage to do so. He throws away the revolver and opens the door. The protagonist of *The Temple of the Golden Pavilion* runs from the scene of his crime, takes out a bottle of arsenic and a knife that he had provided for his suicide, and then throws them down a ravine. He wants to live. Both characters lack the resolution to cast themselves free from the world their philosophies pretend to despise.

Some of Mishima's critics have accused him of exalting fascist ideals in his fiction; whereas Sartre is known as one of the fiercest literary opponents of fascist ideology. Indeed, one of his best-known short stories, "L'enfance d'un chef," concerns the manner in which a young man with character weaknesses similar to those of the neo-Erostratus develops an anti-Semitic bourgeois mentality. Many resemblances may be traced between the two misfits, one inept and ineffectual, the other blustering and domineering. Political overtones are unmistakable in Sartre because his portrayal points to a parttern of social behavior, to a type rather than an individual. Mishima, to the contrary, seems to be describing a unique personality. Whatever Mishima's personal attitude may have been toward such aspects of fascism as a strong military or absolute state control, it is hard to see any reflection of a political philosophy in *The Temple of the Golden Pavilion.* Mishima's protagonist, far from representing the potentiality for the evil use of power, has more in common with disenchanted American teenagers like Holden Caulfield in J. B. Salinger's *Catcher in the Rye.* The connection is more than literary. In December 1980, a twenty-five-year-old disciple of the Pop singer John Lennon, who identified himself with his idol, shot and killed Lennon outside the latter's New York City apartment. On the preceding night, the killer had checked into an expensive hotel and consumed a big meal. After the shooting, the police found on his person a paperback copy of *Catcher in the Rye* (*Time* Magazine, 22 December 1980, 19). This copy contained the slayer's handwritten words: "This is my statement." Like Mishima's protagonist, this young man, unable to adjust to ordinary society, asserted his misproportioned individuality by destroying the one element of that society that he valued beyond all others.

From the perspectives of history and society, *The Temple of the Golden Pavilion* seems to have almost no materials relevant to Western culture, with the exception of a few-allusions to past events taking place during the Second World War. In execution as well, the work is uniquely Japanese, primarily in its delineation of Zen philosophy as a guide to life and in its delicacy of style. Its main character is a young man studying to be a Buddhist priest, its principal symbol is an ancient Buddhist Temple, and its ostensibly philosophical passages are taken from Buddhist writings. At the same time, the main action of the novel— the burning down of an important edifice as an act of defiance or self-assertion—could take place almost anywhere in the world. The significance of the work for universal literature comes partly from its subject matter, but mainly from aesthetic themes, primarily that an obsession with beauty when perverted may lead to the destruction of the objective manifestation of beauty; and that in the aesthetic realm, the imaginary prevails over the real. The burning of the actual temple and the slaying of John Lennon show that in life, as well as in literature, the infatuation with an object may lead to its destruction.

CHAPTER 7. REFERENCES

Dostoevski, Feodor. 1960. *Notes from underground.* Translated by Ralph E. Matlaw. New York: Dutton.

Lida de Malkiel, Maria Rosa. 1952. *La idea de la fama en la edad media Castellana.* Mexico: Fondo de Cultura Económica.

Lou, Tsu-k'uang, ed. 1970. *Folklore and folkliterature.* Peking: Peking Univ. Press.

Magny, Claude-Edmonde. 1945. *Les Sandales d'Empédocle.* Neuchatel: Baconnière.

Mishima, Yukio. 1959. *The Temple of the Golden Pavilion.* Translated by Ivan Morris. Tokyo: Charles E. Tuttle Co.

Sartre, Jean-Paul. 1965. *Being and nothingness: An essay in phenomenological ontology.* Translated by Hazel E. Barnes. New York: Citadel Press.

———. 1939. Erostrate. In *Le Mur.* Paris: Gallimard.

Afterword

I HAVE PRESENTED THE FOREGOING EXAMPLES OF WORKS IN Western literature compared with others in the East for methodology, not content. I do not suggest that Eastern scholars necessarily should be acquainted with the writings of Voltaire, James, and Sartre, nor that Western scholars base their studies of Eastern literature on the novels of Kawabata and Mishima. Hundreds of other works from both hemispheres have already been translated into the languages of the other, and the principle of polysystematic criticism offers the adventurous scholar ample scope for exercise of his individual powers of perception and analysis. In the East, the study of selected Western masterpieces has been for many years an essential part of undergraduate education. American universities stress the theory of comparative literature, but provide few opportunities for pursuing East-West studies. Adequate materials exist, however, for the expansion of courses in culture and civilization to include the literatures of the East. Because of the need for using translations—even by scholars who know one language from the other hemisphere—the neophyte and the established professional are almost upon an equal footing. The early years of the next century will perhaps see the emergence of new generations of experts able to dispense with translations and to deal with a multiplicity of languages and literary texts in the original.

But Western recognition of the literary richness of China and Japan, both traditional and modern, cannot await the development of general linguistic competence. Comparative study in the West must embrace non-Western materials, and exclusively Eurocentrism must be exposed as an intellectual dead end.

Index

All names are given in the Western style except those of well-known Chinese personalities such as Li Po and Mao Tse-tung.